Bad News for Labour

'The essays in this book provide evidence and arguments that are deeply troubling for all concerned, and demand careful attention.'

Peter Golding, Emeritus Professor, Northumbria University

'At last! Here is a book that rigorously examines the facts behind the allegations of antisemitism in the Labour Party. The reality is more shocking, and more surprising, than the headlines in the press would have you believe. Here is the evidence – read it. Then learn the lessons suggested here.'

Ken Loach

'What the careful research reported in this book reveals is a successful disinformation campaign. Anyone who cares for facts needs to read it.'

Colin Leys, Honorary Professor at Goldsmiths University of London

'Reading this timely book convinces me that the media campaign against antisemitism in the Labour Party is similar to the media onslaught on the "loony left" in the 1980s. Both campaigns connected to some disturbing truths: and both inflated and weaponised these truths for political purposes.'

Professor James Curran, Goldsmiths, University of London

'This compelling, thoughtful text is essential reading for everyone on the left wanting to confront antisemitism. It provides a benchmark for future research and strategy when tackling this explosive issue of our time.'

Lynne Segal, Birkbeck University of London

Bad News for Labour

Antisemitism, the Party and Public Belief

Greg Philo, Mike Berry, Justin Schlosberg,
Antony Lerman and David Miller

First published 2019 by Pluto Press
345 Archway Road, London N6 5AA

www.plutobooks.com

British Library Cataloguing in Publication Data
A catalogue record for this book is available from the British Library

ISBN 978 0 7453 4065 4 Hardback
ISBN 978 0 7453 4066 1 Paperback
ISBN 978 1 7868 0571 3 PDF eBook
ISBN 978 1 7868 0573 7 Kindle eBook
ISBN 978 1 7868 0572 0 EPUB eBook

This book is printed on paper suitable for recycling and made from fully managed and sustained forest sources. Logging, pulping and manufacturing processes are expected to conform to the environmental standards of the country of origin.

Typeset by Stanford DTP Services, Northampton, England

Simultaneously printed in the United Kingdom and United States of America

Contents

Acknowledgements

We would like first to thank Yajun Deng for her tireless work in researching and also preparing the manuscript for this book. Thanks also to Louise Jones for her help and patience and to Annie McKeachan for providing cakes and other important research facilities. Thanks also to all those who helped set up and who took part in our focus groups. We interviewed many people, most of whom we have not named and we would like to thank them all for their time and the thoughtful responses which they gave. Thanks also to David Castle at Pluto Press and to Harry Mason at Survation. Very many people have helped us along the way with advice and support. As always, thanks to you all.

Preface

To say that the issue of antisemitism in the Labour Party has received a great deal of national attention hardly does justice to the sheer volume of coverage in press, television and social media. A search of national newspapers for coverage that mentioned Corbyn, Labour and antisemitism between 15 June 2015 and 31 March 2019 shows five and a half thousand articles. We have included a timeline at the end of this book to help follow this extraordinary panoply of events and news output. In trying to explain the issues involved, we have interviewed a large number of people who offered different perspectives on what occurred. Not everyone we approached was available to comment and where that was so, we used secondary sources to ensure that we featured a wide range of opinion.

One purpose of our work here is to examine the possible impacts of the volume of media coverage on public beliefs about the Labour Party. In pursuing this, we commissioned a national poll and used focus groups to examine the processes by which people make judgements and have formed opinions. The results showed that on average people believed that a third of Labour Party members had been reported for antisemitism. A key research question for us was to examine how it could be that so many people came to believe this when the actual figure was far less than 1 per cent. In the first chapter, we examine the conditions under which people accepted or rejected what they were seeing and hearing in the media, as well as the sources of information which they used in forming their beliefs.

As a left wing political party, it is at the core of Labour's mission that it must be anti-racist. In that sense, one case of antisemitism is too many. But the huge disparity between public perception and the actual number of reported cases must make this one of the worst public relations disasters that has been recorded. It raises the question of why the Party was so unable to deal with the issue. Part of the reason for this is the extraordinary divisions which existed within it following the election of Jeremy Corbyn as leader in 2015. From these divisions, different accounts emerged about the nature and the extent of antisemitism within the movement. In Chapter 2, we examine this range of arguments as well as the suggestion that they were linked to the internal politics of the Party and to conflicts over attitudes and policy towards Israel. There was debate over what was acceptable criticism of that country and whether any attempt to 'delegitimise' it would be antisemitic. Alternatively, it was argued that a movement such as Boycott, Divestment and Sanctions was simply a legitimate political strategy against what some saw as a racist state.

In Chapter 3, we examine what might have been done to resolve the crisis, and why it took the Party so long to develop a coherent and planned response. We look at the conflicts which developed between the leadership, members of the Parliamentary Party and Labour's own bureaucracy. Another important dimension is the role of the media and we look at how the story was sometimes distorted. In Chapter 4, Justin Schlosberg presents a content analysis of media coverage showing a catalogue of reporting failures. This was particularly so in relation to the adoption by the Labour Party in 2018 of the working definition of antisemitism offered by the International Holocaust Remembrance Alliance.

In Chapter 5, Antony Lerman offers a detailed commentary on both the IHRA definition of antisemitism and the claims that the Labour Party is institutionally antisemitic. He examines these two areas of the criticism levelled at Labour for its handling of the perceived problem of antisemitism. In the first, he shows how the IHRA definition of antisemitism was widely condemned for not being fit for purpose. He asks whether its adoption has helped the Party deal with the issue of antisemitism, or has it made Jews more vulnerable to antisemitism. The second is charges levelled against Labour for 'institutional antisemitism'. In effect, this is the accusation, currently being investigated by the Equality and Human Rights Commission, that is, that Jews in the Party, and the Jewish community generally, face serious discrimination as a result of Labour's dealings with them. Can such a charge against a complex organism like the Labour Party be credible? Both issues have the potential to create more difficulties for Labour going forward, with the second perhaps more serious since legal sanctions may be imposed. What might be done to mitigate further damage?

One of the issues in contemporary public arguments is how antisemitism is defined and the types of complaints that have been made to the Party over descriptions of Israel. This relates centrally to the interpretation of the IHRA definition of antisemitism. In Chapter 6, David Miller describes the course of one of these complaints to which he was subject, the processes and thinking behind it and why it was eventually dismissed. In the final chapter, we look at contemporary developments in racism and the struggle against it. From our own knowledge of communications and policy, we offer suggestions on a way forward for Labour as a key progressive force and we point to the need for unity against all forms of racism in the times that lie ahead.

1
Believe It or Not

Greg Philo and Mike Berry

We began this work by interviewing a small number of people for a pilot study. We wanted to get a sense of possible impacts of media on public beliefs about antisemitism in the Labour Party. This was in March 2019 and we knew that figures had just been published on cases that had been investigated. These related to about 0.1 per cent of the membership, but over the previous three years, there had been extensive media coverage of the issue and many allegations of antisemitism in the Party. A search of eight national newspapers shows that from 15 June 2015 to 31 March 2019, there had been 5497 stories on the subject of Corbyn, antisemitism and the Labour Party.[1] The issue was also extensively featured on television and in new and social media. These headlines give a sense of the accusations that were being made:

Labour Party Is Anti-Semitic And Racist
(LBC, 18 February 2019)

Jeremy Corbyn, the anti-racist who turned Labour into the party of anti-Semitism
(*Sun*, 18 July 2018)

1. This was based on a Nexis search using the search string [Corbyn or Labour party and antisemitism or anti-semitism]. The sampled newspapers were the *Telegraph, Guardian, Independent, The Times, Daily Mail, Express, Mirror* and *Sun*.

> **Chuka Umunna condemns 'nasty, bullying and racist' Labour Party**
> (*Evening Standard*, 19 March 2019)
>
> **Scottish Jewish leader blasts Labour as racist party**
> (*The Scotsman*, 28 February 2019)
>
> **Corbyn has brought anti-Semitism 'into the MAINSTREAM'**
> (*Express*, 19 April 2019)
>
> **No wonder Corbyn's Labour is riddled with anti-Semites**
> (*Mail Online*, 3 September 2018)

Labour should not have any racism within it. But the headlines give the impression of a party 'riddled' with antisemitism. This contrasts with the actual number of reported cases. So we asked our pilot interviewees this question:

What percentage of Labour Party members do you think have had complaints made about them for antisemitism?

The results surprised us since the answers ranged from 25–40 per cent of members. The interviewees also gave clear reasons for their judgements which mostly focus on the very high level of media coverage, which they assumed meant that many people were involved. As these interviewees put it:

> I heard so much about it – there is an awful lot of these folk. It was things I have been reading or seeing on the news. (Middle class, female, retired, estimated 40 per cent, 1 March 2019)

> I thought it because of this furore and upheaval and all this publicity in the media. (Middle class, female, retired, estimated 25 per cent, 2 March 2019)

The second of these also believed that there would be levels of prejudice latent in the population as a whole 'whatever their politics were'. Another interviewee pointed to the financial cost of what she assumed were very extensive investigations and therefore judged it would involve about a third of the members:

> You would think that with all the hoo-hah and the money spent on investigating it, that it would be about that (a third). (Low income, female, self-employed, estimated 30 per cent, 6 March 2019)

Given these early results, we thought we should test the question further with a national poll. This was undertaken by Survation in March 2019. They put two questions to 1009 people online. The first was to establish whether respondents knew about the issue:

Have you seen or heard anything about accusations of anti-semitism (hostility to or prejudice against Jewish people) made against members of the Labour Party?

Of the total, 62 per cent indicated that they had, and this group answered the second question:

From what you have seen or heard, what percentage of Labour Party members do you think have had complaints of anti-semitism made against them?

The result of this was that, on average, they believed that 34 per cent of Labour Party members had had complaints for antisemitism made against them. Just 14 per cent of the sample believed that the number who had been complained about was below 10 per cent. The data on how estimations broke down by age, gender and voting in the 2017 General Election can be seen in Table 1.1.

As can be seen from the table, there are variations in how widespread different social groups think antisemitism is within the Labour Party. Women see it as a greater problem than men, as do younger people in comparison to those over 45. It is also seen as a more significant problem by Conservative voters than by those who support Labour, the Liberal Democrats and the SNP – though the results for the Liberal Democrats and SNP should be treated with caution because the subsamples from which the data was drawn had very small numbers. However, while it is possible to point to demographic variations within the poll, these are very minor in comparison to the differences between the estimates and the actual number of people being reported for antisemitism within Labour.

We then decided to examine these beliefs in more detail using focus groups. The purpose was to analyse how people decided on a figure. What were the conditions under which they thought it was higher or lower? Did they accept media accounts or did they use other sources of information, such as personal experience, to criticise what they have seen or heard? We conducted four focus groups in April and May 2019.

1. **Glasgow focus group**, 5 April 2019
    - Seven members (all female)
    - Age range: 64–80
    - Political allegiance: Conservative (3), SNP (3), Liberal Democrat (1)
    - Newspaper consumption: *Herald* (3), *Telegraph* (1), *The Sunday Times* (1), *Daily Mail* (1), The *i* (1), *Guardian* (1), *The National* (1), *Huffington Post* (1)

Table 1.1 Estimates of the percentage of Labour Party members who have been accused of antisemitism by gender, age and 2017 voting behaviour

	Total	*Male*	*Female*	*18–34*	*35–44*	*45–54*	*55–64*	*65+*	*CON*	*LAB*	*LD*	*SNP*
0–9%	14	16	12	10	16	13	15	17	10	20	26	14
10–19%	11	12	10	7	10	11	13	13	11	15	–	12
20–29%	13	14	12	20	9	10	15	11	16	14	11	–
30–39%	8	6	10	9	11	7	6	7	6	9	3	–
40–49%	5	4	5	6	4	6	3	4	7	2	3	2
50–59%	6	5	8	4	7	10	5	6	6	8	7	–
60–69%	4	3	6	7	8	2	2	3	5	4	2	–
70–79%	4	4	5	7	7	3	3	4	6	4	2	–
80–89%	3	3	4	6	5	4	1	0	3	2	–	5
90–99%	2	3	2	5	4	–	1	1	1	4	2	–
100%	0	0	0	1	1	1	–	–	0	1	–	–
Don't know (%)	29	32	27	19	18	35	38	35	29	18	46	68
Mean	34	30.6	37.5	41.6	39.9	32.4	25.7	28.5	36.4	30.8	25.3	21.9

- Estimates of percentage of Labour members accused of antisemitism: 30 per cent or less, 15 per cent, 5 per cent, 4 per cent, 3 per cent, 2 per cent, 0.1 per cent.

2. **Coventry focus group**, 22 April 2019
    - Four members (two male and two female)
    - Age range 67–81
    - Political allegiance: Labour (3), Conservative (1)
    - Newspaper consumption: *Daily Mail* (1), *Coventry Evening News* (1), *Daily and Sunday Telegraph* (1)
    - Estimates of percentage of Labour members accused of antisemitism: 10 per cent, 5 per cent, 5 per cent, 0.2 per cent.

3. **Newport focus group**, 21 May 2019
    - Four members (three female and one male)
    - Age range 32–58 (two female and two male)
    - Political allegiance: Conservative (1), Liberal Democrat (1), UKIP (1), Non-voter (1)
    - Newspaper consumption: *Daily Mail* (1), *Sun* (1), *Telegraph* (1)
    - Estimates of percentage of Labour members accused of antisemitism: 40 per cent, 20 per cent, 20 per cent, 5 per cent.

4. **Cardiff focus group**, 24 May 2019
    - Four members
    - Age range 38–75
    - Political allegiance: Conservative (1), Labour (1), Liberal Democrat (1), Plaid Cymru (1)
    - Newspaper consumption: *The Sunday Times* (2), *Guardian* (2), *The Times* (1), *Telegraph* (1)
    - Estimates of percentage of Labour members accused of antisemitism: 30 per cent, 20 per cent, 20 per cent, 15–20 per cent.

The focus group meetings began with a series of brief questions about beliefs to which people gave written answers and these were then discussed over a period of an hour. We also gathered basic data on occupation, gender, age, media use and voting intention. The initial questions asked were:

1. From what you have seen and heard, what percentage of Labour Party members have had complaints of antisemitism made against them?
2. What made you think that, how did you arrive at that percentage whatever it was?
3. What sources of information would you use to inform your opinion? Which would you trust the most?
4. Do you think the public argument over antisemitism has damaged the Labour Party?
5. Do you think it might affect how people vote?

We grouped the answers to these and the subsequent discussions into three key areas:

1. Reasons for higher estimates and influences on decisions made about these.
2. Reasons to doubt the story and give lower estimates.
3. Beliefs about impacts of the story on perception of the Party and voting.

1. Reasons for higher estimates

The media and the extensive coverage that the story has received featured very prominently in the reasons that were given. This related both to the volume of coverage and the persistence of the theme in reporting. As one member of the Cardiff focus group put it: 'it's because of the coverage isn't it? It's constant' and another participant replied 'it's had a really high profile'. Even amongst people who claimed to never read a newspaper and declared themselves completely uninterested in the subject it was clear that the story had cut through because of its sustained prominence in newspaper headlines. One participant who had given an estimate of 20 per cent of Labour members explained the source of his belief in this way:

> Headlines I see. I work in Tesco's. As I walk into the shopping mall I read the headlines every day … Most of my perception was based on – as I say I didn't read newspapers – my perception was based on the number of headlines and how long it was in the papers. [participant 4 nods in agreement] (Newport group, 21 May 2019)

As well as headlines, photographic evidence was also significant. One participant said that part of the reason he thought antisemitism was a problem in the Labour Party was that 'Corbyn came in with his Hezbollah lot ... that's when it started ... it went on he [Corbyn] never checked it then and it grew and grew'. When then asked why he believed Corbyn was 'with Hezbollah' he replied:

> There are photographs of him in Libya, one of the terrorist funerals laying a wreath or it was at one of the gravesides and there's photographs of him with the IRA and there's his Hezbollah friends ... those photos they've not been photoshopped. (Coventry group, 22 April 2019)

It was also clear that some of the televised testimony of those directly experiencing racism had a strong impact on beliefs about the prevalence of antisemitism. One participant argued the person they trusted most on the issue was:

> someone who has suffered it like Margaret Hodge, she's been on the television saying I was told, this, this, this and this and making a song and dance about it. Is she lying I doubt it very much ... why is she on the television because she's suffered antisemitism. (Coventry group, 22 April 2019)

The heavy coverage given to Margaret Hodge was also seen as important by a member of another focus group who cited it as a factor influencing her estimate (30 per cent) of complaints of antisemitism against Labour members:

> I heard a lot of interviews with Margaret Hodge and she said there's a lot more of this than is coming out ... she was so alarmed and concerned and she was quite vocal about it on the news and she was interviewed a number of times. (Cardiff group, 24 May 2019)

The media seem to have an impact even where people did not want to believe the story – for example, by disliking the idea that such a thing could exist. This interviewee, for instance, wanted to believe that antisemitism had been put behind us because of its terrible history:

> I am surprised at the level of publicity that antisemitism has at the moment. I never thought it would rear its ugly head again, but it has. I was very unsure when I wrote it. [The idea came] because of the amount of media coverage. I don't know why I said 15 per cent, because you never actually see people speaking about it in the media, it's just written about in a general way – you know you never get any figures.

The interviewee cited the *Daily Mail* as the source of her information and specifically named Jeremy Corbyn for the problem:

> There is a lot of publicity about antisemitism just now, and sadly a lot of it is directed at the leader of the Labour Party, Jeremy Corbyn. And I have got to come right out to say it – I cannot think of any way he could ever run our country because of his associations with Hamas, Hezbollah and the antisemitic rumours that are about him, whether they're true or not. This is why I put it high, at 15 per cent, because this man has a tremendous following.

She had remembered the report of the laying of a wreath by Jeremy Corbyn. The story is explained in the words of the paper, in one of its sub-headlines:

> **Daily Mail obtained photograph of Labour leader holding wreath near graves of terror leaders linked to the 1972 massacre**
> (*Mail Online*, 5 April 2019)

The massacre referred to was of the Israeli athletes at the 1972 Munich Olympics. Corbyn insisted he was there to honour those killed in another attack in 1985 by Israel on the PLO in Tunis. But a version of the *Daily Mail* account had stuck with the interviewee:

> I believe that he is antisemitic – if he can associate with the people that he has associated with, if he can hold up a wreath to the bombers who, ahh, I can't remember who they bombed, if he can do all that and be all that, he could be antisemitic. (Glasgow group, 5 April 2019)

The group made the point that to reject this view of Corbyn required a very strong denial. Corbyn had a long record of anti-racism and had in fact apologised in August 2018 for 'the hurt that has been caused to many Jewish people' (*Guardian*, 6 August 2018). This had been done in a video message on social media, and was featured in mainstream media but it had passed over the heads of most in the group:

> Speaker 1: And there's been no strong denial. If he stood up and said I'm not antisemitic.
> Speaker 2: Uh-uh!
> Speaker 3: Good point, yes, yes, yes, he never apologised!
> Speaker 4: I think he has.
> Speaker 2: I don't think he has to the people he's supposed to have offended.
> Speaker 3: I don't think he has. (Glasgow group, 5 April 2019)

This belief that Corbyn had failed to take a strong stand against antisemitism also came across strongly in another group where one group member went even further and argued that the leader's lack of 'clarity' served to 'encourage' antisemites in the party:

> Speaker 1: ... he never stamped it down until quite recently with sort of fairly weasel words about it by almost reluctantly I think rejecting the complaint made ... he wasn't strong enough to stand up for being prosemitic. His weakness and lack of clarity in counteracting this.
> Speaker 2: And because of that I think because he has taken that approach I think he is encouraging more people to maybe be antisemitic because if the leader is not giving clarity on where they stand then they're going to be influenced on the negative aren't they which is on the antisemitic.

> Speaker 1: ... He's still being accused because he hasn't stood up and said look - well I think recently I have heard him say – but for a very long, long time he seemed to be very much on the fence about this in my opinion. (Cardiff group, 24 May 2019)

This was perceived by some as being part of a broader failure to provide strong rebuttals to damaging claims about the Party which could mean that attacks were seen as having merit. When questioned as to whether participants had heard anyone in the Labour Party challenge the narrative that antisemitism was widespread, the response of participants in one group was:

> Speaker 1: Nobody in the party actually said no did they? Nobody in the party actually said no this is not true. You know the Labour party?
> Speaker 2: I haven't heard that.
> Speaker 1: I haven't heard that thing anybody there denying it so there must be something there. (Newport group, 21 May 2019)

When the question was put to another group, again nobody could recall Labour sources denying the narrative. In fact, what the participants recalled was Labour 'people' arguing that antisemitism was widespread:

> Moderator: Have you heard anyone in the Labour party actually say you know this is not a widespread problem and challenge that narrative?
> Speaker 1: No.
> Speaker 2: No.
> Speaker 3: No I don't think anyone in the Labour party. I think the people in the Labour party say the opposite.

> Speaker 4: I think they're reinforcing it.
> Speaker 3: Watson is it? Confirmed that it exists.
> Speaker 1: A number of people in the party. (Cardiff group, 24 May 2019)

This does underline the necessity of message discipline and strong, alternative public relations, together with consistent rebuttal and a powerful rejection of false information and distorted claims. Without this, Labour's response can appear feeble or non-existent.

The issue of a lack of clarity in messaging also came up in relation to what actually constituted antisemitism and how it should be separated from criticism of Israel. One participant felt that the Labour Party should be more vocal on where that line should be drawn so as to avoid confusion and false accusations of antisemitism:

> There's confusion here there's confusion in the message that's being delivered by the Labour party in so far as they haven't clarified that I think some of the antisemitism that I might guess might be anti-Israel. I don't know nobody has told us that. Could you clarify that? Be more specific about that so the argument, the conversation is not with Jewish people whereby they can say very honestly we're absolutely not against Jewish people the Jews in this country ... this is a totally separate issue. (Cardiff group, 24 May 2019)

2. Reasons for lower estimates and to doubt the story

Amplification

Some in the groups began with high estimates and then revised them downwards as they thought about the issue. One in the Glasgow group began with 30 per cent and then said 'or less' and then said 'maybe less than 10 per cent'. The reason was that she began to think of the interests that might be promoting the story. She was a Conservative voter and read the *Telegraph* and *The Sunday Times*, but commented that the story had been 'blown up by the media and the Conservatives'. Another participant made a similar point:

> The media have kept the story going – more and more stories are freshened up. The Tories keep trying to update it. (Glasgow group, 5 April 2019)

In another group a participant talked about antisemitism being used as a 'political football' to 'smear' the Labour Party because it had become more 'left wing': 'I also think it's [antisemitism] being used to smear other parties because we never used to hear about it did we?' (Coventry group, 22 April 2019). However, the belief that accusations of antisemitism were being amplified for political ends could also correspond with high estimates of the number reported. One participant said the issue was being 'pushed' and was 'overblown' and is 'not a big issue it's people basically talking trash about each other ... the fact that it was in the papers for so long and was so pronounced leads me to believe that there was an agenda at play' (Newport group, 21 May 2019). Yet the same person gave an estimate that 20 per cent of Labour members had been accused of antisemitism. In another group, a participant who had estimated 15–20 per cent of members had been accused of antisemitism commented that

> When this first surfaced in the news I thought something was being quite overblown because I thought it was a kind of conspiracy against Corbyn [participant 3 nods head in agreement] and some sort of thing Tory media dreamed up because they were kind of getting worried with Corbyn's

popularity … I remember thinking that early on. (Cardiff group, 24 May 2019)

Experience and knowledge of the Labour Party

Some in Glasgow pointed to the history of the Party to contest the story:

> Speaker 1: It's been manipulated, political, it's blown out of proportion.
> Speaker 2: I think it has too, because both Milibands are of Jewish descent and others. I find I don't believe the way the media report it, that there is a high level of antisemitism within the Labour Party. I wouldn't agree.
> Moderator: You think it's just a bit unlikely.
> Speaker 2: Well I think so.
> Speaker 3: But what about all the publicity about it? (Glasgow group, 5 April 2019)

One participant in Glasgow pointed to members that she had known:

> It's such overkill – so much that you begin to think, 'Oh come on. I just think of people I have known in my life, I can't imagine any of them would have that attitude.' (Glasgow group, 5 April 2019)

In another group, a participant had no personal experience of the Labour Party or its members but felt that the 'traditional values' that she associated with the Party made her not want to believe it was a substantial problem even though she personally had given a high estimate:

> It's hard to think given what Labour did stand for historically that they would have so many people with those views in that party ... I said 20 per cent but really I wouldn't want to believe that's true because it feels so disjointed from what Labour stands for. (Cardiff group, 24 May 2019)

Use of logic

Use of logic was another reason for criticising the suggestion that a very high percentage of members would have been reported. One participant noted that the standards of evidence would have to be high, commenting that:

> It is probably a very small number – to report someone would require cast iron evidence. (Glasgow group, 5 April 2019)

The quality of reported evidence was not always 'cast iron'. People were reported who are not in fact Party members. This applied for example to around 80 per cent of the cases referred by Margaret Hodge. But the people in the group made no reference to any such difficulties.

The estimates from some members of the focus groups, such as in Glasgow, were relatively low at 2, 3, 4, and 5 per cent. But these still greatly overestimated the actual numbers; 5 per cent would be one in 20 members, a figure of over 22,000 people. One group member spotted the problem with high estimates. As soon as she was asked about the percentage of members, she exclaimed, 'But that's millions of them!' The figure which she gave was 0.1 per cent. She did not attribute this to any source, but said simply that it was 'an educated guess'. This does point to the extraordinary absence in news accounts of the basic information that would be required for audiences to understand and make a judgement on the story, for example, the number of Labour Party members and how this relates to claims that are being made.

An important point, which these discussions illustrate, is that the lower estimates that are given emerge from resources within the group. That is, they come from prior beliefs about the media, personal experience or processes of logic. None of the people in the Glasgow group, for example, made any reference to statements by the Labour Party or counter information that had been issued to correct media accounts and the amplification that had taken place. As was said, as far as they were concerned, 'there were no figures'.

One other logical deduction was made by three people who suggested that because there was antisemitism in the society, it would also exist in Labour. One, for example, pointed to comments made by friends who were not in the Party: 'It might just come out and I'd be surprised the person would say that. That's a general thing whatever their politics are' (6 April 2019).

3. Damage to Labour Party and voting

Overall, there was a strong belief that the issue had damaged the Party. We can see this in each of the groups. None of the Glasgow group voted Labour – they were split mostly between SNP and Conservative. All but one thought that the antisemitism issue had damaged the Party, noting for example that:

> One of the reasons people left in disgust was because of antisemitism. (Glasgow group, 5 April 2019)

Another commented that:

> It's damaged it dramatically and it's been in all the headlines. And lots of people are not like us, they don't look behind

> the headlines. It keeps coming up time and time again. (Glasgow group, 5 April 2019)

But then it was noted in the group that even a critical person would still be affected:

> I think it can, you read it and you think, 'Oh Gosh – there is so much'. It does influence you a wee bit. (Glasgow group, 5 April 2019)

On voting intentions, all but one again thought it would affect Labour negatively. One of our earlier interviewees in the pilot work, a Labour voter, had also commented that in the period of an election:

> People will look back at them over a number of years and think, 'do I want them? Are they worthy of me trusting them?' (Middle class, female, retired, estimated 25 per cent, 2 March 2019)

In the Coventry focus group where three out of four participants were traditional Labour voters, only one person believed that it hadn't significantly damaged Labour and only because she thought that a lot of people were quite tribal: 'a lot of people vote Labour because they've always voted Labour and they don't think about anything else'. The other three participants were very clear that it had damaged the party and were concerned that if Corbyn 'got away with antisemitism' then he might try and introduce very radical policies. In this respect, the antisemitism issue became linked in people's minds with other perceptions of Labour and its relationship to Muslims and migrants.

> Speaker 1: Well if they get away with the antisemitism ... surely a few years down the road they'll bring something else in whatever it is.
> Speaker 2: They'll bring in Sharia law bit by bit.
> Speaker 1: Shari law yes. It could be anything.
> Speaker 3: Oh god no I hope not.
> Speaker 1: No I disagree with that.
> Speaker 2: They said that in Germany in the '30s when they started burning books.
> Speaker 3: Oh my God.
> Speaker 2: And when a country starts burning books the next thing they start burning is people. (Coventry group, 22 April 2019)

The moderator then asked whether Jeremy Corbyn would bring in Sharia law and two people in the group thought he would. The other two people in the group didn't think he would. However, this wasn't because they believed he wouldn't try but rather because they thought that the LGBT community was now so well established it would mobilise to stop it. Nobody in the group made reference to Labour or Jeremy Corbyn's long history of support for LGBT issues which appeared to have completely passed people by.

All four people in the Newport group were convinced that the row had damaged the Labour Party – and Jeremy Corbyn personally. All four also believed that it would affect how people voted, though one participant suggested that it would mainly impact less partisan voters:

> A lot of swing voters pick based on image and mud sticks to put it politely and I think it was just a smear campaign so I think it will – could – possibly affect the number of votes they get though but I don't think it will be as pronounced as some people believe it will be because I don't think the issue

> matters to that many people but if people are throwing shit at the Labour party it will be at the back of some people's minds who are on the fence.

The Cardiff group were absolutely unanimous that the accusations of antisemitism had damaged the party. However, people were more divided on how significantly it would impact on voting behaviour. One participant said that it 'had definitely offended people' but the 'whole situation was so fixated on Brexit anything else has got lost now'. Another argued that it was 'not central' to most voters so wasn't sure it would affect 'a large number of people'. However, the other two members of the group believed it had been more damaging. One commented:

> [It] will effect a significant minority ... will be scared off by this association with antisemitism … because every day there just seems to be something in the media about Labour and antisemitism, some new uproar or something. It seems an everyday thing.

The other participant suggested that what was happening would worry people because they would see parallels with what happened during the Second World War:

> Speaker 1: 'I think it's a case of people worrying people who've had to flee Germany and there's so much worry in communities in this country that we're going back, that we're raking up all that anti-jew feeling again. You know I watch programmes where people who did manage to escape, elderly are being interviewed and being told it's in the past and they're saying it's not in the past.

> Moderator: So you've heard. I just want to make sure I'm on the right page here – that in a sense what's going on in the Labour party has echoes of other dark periods of history?
> Speaker 1: Yes.
> Speaker 2: Yes.
> Speaker 3: It's probably triggered it.
> Speaker 1: Exactly.
> Speaker 3: Triggered experiences and memories.
> Moderator: Do you think those are realistic fears?
> Speaker 1: Well I feel yes because it's crossed my mind well this is like almost, well it is as you say triggering fear again that there is this anti feeling towards Jewish communities and antisemitism ... There were rallies in London of the Jewish community. They were actually rallying weren't they so they're obviously feeling threatened. I feel from what I've read and heard that the Jewish communities are feeling threatened.

This does illustrate the extraordinary power of media images, the accounts that were given and the impact of these on public belief. This does raise the question of what Labour's response to these should have been.

Labour's response

The Labour Party would agree that one case of antisemitism is too many, and there was a problem, but there is still the question of how the media coverage and statements made by public figures could have generated such a huge disparity between the number of cases and public belief about them. An additional question is what could the Labour Party have done to offer a better and more informed account. Put another way, how could its public relations have gone so wrong?

The Labour Party is committed to anti-racism and should always in principle pursue it, but it is also the case that in any large organisation, individuals within it can exhibit unacceptable behaviour. In the same way, a hospital is committed to the safety of its patients, but still sometimes things go wrong. When this happens, there needs to be a clear explanation of exactly what has occurred, and what is being done to resolve the problem or make sure that it does not recur. This is the essence of 'good' public relations. The same principles apply for a medical accident or for finding unacceptable behaviour in a political party.

The essential principles are:

1. Acknowledge what has happened is wrong and completely unacceptable for your organisation.
2. Limit exaggerated claims of what has happened. Be as precise as possible, give details of clear and accurate information.
3. Show how all the resources of your organisation are being used to put the situation right and to prevent it happening again.
4. Defend the integrity of your organisation as a whole and its membership. Show that your intentions and the ethos of your organisation are fundamentally good.
5. Establish all of this as a key narrative and do not change your story.

The question is, why were these basic principles not followed in the Labour Party to the point that it occasioned such an extraordinary public relations disaster. What were the political arguments, institutional divisions and policy decisions that made this crisis so intractable? We look at these in the next two chapters.

2
Divisions and Competing Accounts

Greg Philo and Mike Berry

To understand how this crisis developed, we need first to look at the extraordinary range of arguments and divisions which developed both inside and outside the Labour Party. The Labour leadership was navigating through a complex series of conflicts as different groups and fractional interests asserted their own accounts of what was occurring and what needed to be done. The main areas of these were: first, the argument that there was a serious and widespread problem of antisemitism within the Labour Party; second, that the issue was being used to attack the left leadership, and specifically Jeremy Corbyn, as part of the internal politics of the Party; third, that the issue was linked to the defence of Israel and attempts to change political policy in relation to that state.

On the first argument, Ruth Smeeth MP was quoted in September 2016 as saying:

> I've never seen anti-Semitism in Labour on this scale. There were one or two incidents before and the reason why they were so shocking is that there were only one or two. Now the sheer volume of it has made it normal. (Edwards, 2016)

Anthony Silkoff of the Board of Deputies of British Jews commented that:

> Make no mistake, this is not just about individual incidents ... This is about a culture of victim blaming and racism-denial which is now endemic at every level of the Labour left ... The default position among the Labour left, who now form the majority of the party, is that Jews are devious, privileged, conspirators, not a minority deserving of a liberation campaign, like any other BAME group. (Anthony Silkoff, Twitter post, 29 March 2018)

There was in fact evidence that antisemitism existed and it was therefore the responsibility of the Party to acknowledge this and deal with it. The argument really focused on the nature and scale of what was occurring. We spoke with 15 Labour activists who between them had experience of multiple constituencies, Labour meetings and conferences. This was not a random sample. They were selected on the basis that they would be likely to have seen any unacceptable behaviour because of the extensive range of their experience. Our intention was to assess the types of activity that might have been encountered. Most said they had seen nothing in Party circles. But four pointed to examples of antisemitism. One activist who had administered Red Labour gave his view that at local level, instances were sporadic, resulting mostly from ignorance. Online, he argued, it was different:

> Online is much worse. I see antisemitism from people who identify as Labour left often enough to have reported at least a dozen people a year – and I don't report unless it's open and shut and they refuse to engage in discussion. (24 February 2019)

Another activist who had been a staff member in Corbyn's first election campaign also notes the prevalence of antisemitism online and also pointed to the issue in his own CLP.

He refers to a member who 'subscribed to various conspiracy theories that had a tendency to quickly descend into Jew bashing – the Rothschilds, Mossad did 9/11 and all the Jews were warned to stay out of the twin towers on the day etc.' (16 March 2019).

He believes that such views had gained a foothold in antiwar and global solidarity movements:

> In my view this kind of stuff has had a foothold in the movement for years now, mostly as a result of the way the antiwar and other global solidarity movements were contaminated by the appeal of 9/11 truthers and (far right conspiracy theorists) and it's symptomatic of the massive political education shaped hole the left has had for years. (16 March 2019)

But again, the main issue for him is online:

> The frequency with which I now see antisemitism online from people purporting to be on the left is a genuine cause of concern. Admittedly, much of it is undoubtedly a reaction to the way this has been weaponised to bash Corbyn, is almost always to do with Israel and the vast majority of it is down to naivety as opposed to any conscious hostility towards Jews, but it's concerning nonetheless. (16 March 2019)

Another activist who had been Party secretary for a CLP described what was effectively entryism by an antisemite who then 'groomed' new members culminating in the setting up of an antisemitic sub-group within the local party. She comments on how this developed from 2016:

> We had an influx of about 100 Corbyn supporters – nothing apparently wrong with that as I had voted for him, but they had no idea of party rules, and you know Labour has them, and for a while meetings were suspended. Well (they thought) that was a conspiracy of course, and they formed their own group and that's where it started.

She describes how this group set up a website, putting up its own material:

> At one stage they were posting 4–5 posts a day, all about Israel, Palestine, blood libel, Rothschild, conspiracy etc etc. I was appalled.

One post from it listed a number of historical events which Jews are supposed to have done including 'getting the USA into WW1 and getting Britain to invade and occupy Palestine on their behalf in 1917' and 'financing and tormenting the Bolshevik revolution' and 'later slaughtering millions of Russian Christians'. The post culminated in outright Holocaust denial with a claim of 'the deliberate, systematic faking of WW2 atrocities to "justify" their theft and rape of Palestine and win billions in "reparations" from Germany'.

This was too much for some of the group's members who then left it. Not surprisingly, there was intense controversy in the CLP as a whole over the period, and some senior members wanted it to be suspended – but this did not happen and the main instigator left. The Party secretary who gave this account also noted the increase in online activity in 2016:

> Those arguments appeared 'en masse' about a year or 6 months after my experience in the summer of 2016. Those arguments suddenly came out of the pro-Corbyn FB

> [Facebook] pages, and there clearly was someone or some people stoking that. (16 February 2019)

Another activist who was in the Palestine Solidarity Campaign had seen one case of a person who had supported the views of Gilad Atzmon and was expelled from the local PSC branch and also reported to the CLP. She commented on the effect of the antisemitism argument in the Party and on activism over Palestine:

> There certainly isn't (any antisemitism) now. Everyone is terribly conscious of it. On Palestine, on BDS (Boycott, Divestment, Sanctions movement) that's the thing, that's being hit hardest. Activists are being silenced. (25 April 2019)

Other members who we interviewed have said that in their constituencies they had seen no antisemitism, but they had outside of the Party. This interviewee, for example, has stood twice as a parliamentary candidate and had experience of multiple constituencies:

> I have never, ever heard any antisemitic comments, arguments or statements made. Nor have I heard comments about Jewish bankers being responsible for the crash, Jewish malign influence, Jewish capitalists and the like. Anti bankers, anti-capitalist comments yes, lots of those but not any associating these issues with Jewishness which might be interpreted as antisemitic. I am completely at a loss to understand what this antisemitism row is all about. It doesn't make sense to me. I quite often hear antisemitic comments and jokes outside the party but I really cannot say I have heard anything within it. (20 March 2019)

Another with a long history of being an MSP echoed this saying that he had seen nothing in 'Party circles', but had outside of them. One other interviewee, a very experienced Labour activist and organiser commented:

> The only antisemitism I've ever witnessed was at a Stop The War Coalition conference a couple of years ago when someone started ranting about the Rothschild rubbish. I doubt whether he even knew what the name Rothschild meant. There was also a loony woman ranting about Jews (in relation to Palestine). She was asked to leave. I don't think either of them were Labour Party. (21 February 2019)

This view contrasts with the assertion of Margaret Hodge and others that antisemitism is widespread and her view that under Corbyn, antisemitism 'has been given permission to come into the mainstream and like a cancer, is infecting and growing through the Party'. These words appeared in a *Guardian* article on 8 March 2019 with the headline 'Just close them down: Margaret Hodge on antisemitism in Labour's branches' (Mason, 2019a). This was immediately followed by a letter to the *Guardian* (which it did not publish) from 205 Jewish women disputing the claim. It noted that: 'Hodge provides no evidence of such horrific wrongdoing by Corbyn, nor throughout the 'mainstream' party. Her own submissions to the Labour Party certainly don't do the job' (Gelblum, 2019).

A major issue for some interviewees was online abuse, but it is difficult to ascertain how many of the people engaged in this are actually Party members or are from the extreme right, or are even fake. Research by Asa Winstanly (2019) showed a network of Twitter accounts using a series of fake names and profile photos which were then used to post antisemitic material presented as being by Labour supporters. As he writes:

> All 10 accounts present themselves as belonging to Labour Party supporters, activists or even staffers. Reverse Google Image searches confirm that seven of the 10 profile images are stolen photos – the other three are likely screen grabs from videos. Six of the 10 profiles present as ostensibly Muslim – it is these profiles that have posted some of the most disturbing anti-Semitism, including direct calls for violence against Jews.

The next sets of arguments related to the view that the level of antisemitism in the Party was exaggerated and the persistent focus on it was part of an attack on the left leadership and particularly Jeremy Corbyn. This was either because of decisions in the Party over his leadership or was part of an attempt to defend Israel. Avi Shlaim notes that Corbyn is the first leader of a political party to give unqualified support to Palestinian rights and also oppose the sale of arms to Israel. The attacks, he argues, 'originated with what might loosely be termed "the Israel Lobby"'. He points to the well-known al Jazeera programme, titled *The Lobby*, which documented:

> covert operations by the Israeli embassy and improper interference at every level of British politics ... The most shocking revelation is that Shai Masot, a senior political officer at the Israeli embassy, set up a number of political organisations in the UK that operated as though entirely independent. He was also secretly caught on camera plotting to 'take down' MPs he regarded as hostile to Israel. (Shlaim, 2017)

This does not prove any specific involvement in the Labour antisemitism issue but the hostility to Corbyn is well documented. *The Times of Israel*, for example, carried an interview with Ruth Smeeth MP accusing Corbyn of lacking the political will to root out antisemitism and illustrated the story with a picture of the rolling billboard campaign organised by Jonathan Hoffman in 2018. The billboards on the side of the lorry read: 'Institutional antisemitism in Corbyn's Labour' (Philpot, 2019).

Within the Party, there were deep splits. Some, such as the Jewish Labour Movement, asserted that the problem was extensive and were very critical of Corbyn's leadership. The smaller Jewish Voice for Labour was supportive of Corbyn. It did not deny the evidence of antisemitism, but argued that 'some of the Labour leadership's critics have been cynically exploiting and exaggerating the incidents of antisemitism that do occur' (Manson and Levane, 2018).

Avi Shlaim also makes the point that the controversy over antisemitism was intrinsically tied to the internal politics of the Labour Party:

> In truth, the crisis in the Labour Party was not primarily about anti-Semitism. It was part of a broader effort by a group of disgruntled Blairites and their allies outside the party to overthrow Jeremy Corbyn and to reverse his progressive policies. In short, the crisis was manufactured to serve the ends of a right-wing faction within the Labour Party as well as those of the Israel lobby. (Shlaim, 2017)

The divisions over the issue were a recipe for the most bitter conflict. On one side, there was a body of Party members and some MPs of the left who supported the Palestinians and their view that Israel is a racist state, taking their land and water and enforcing an illegitimate military occupation. They were more likely to believe that antisemitism has been exaggerated and 'weaponised' to attack the left leadership of the Party. The other side included many Labour MPs who are negative towards Corbyn's leadership as well as people who asserted that there was a serious antisemitism problem and that Israel was being attacked unfairly on grounds that were antisemitic. There were views between these, for example, a left figure such as Jon Lansman, founder of Momentum, could also make statements on antisemitism being 'widespread'.

The divisions are well illustrated by the respective positions and histories of the leader Jeremy Corbyn and the deputy leader Tom Watson. Corbyn was a prominent patron of the Palestine Solidarity Campaign. His vigorous support for the Palestinians was widely questioned in Israel and also at home. In June 2018, he was criticised on the question of the right of return for Palestinians by Joan Ryan MP who was then chair of Labour Friends of Israel. She took issue with him on remarks he had made about making 'the Palestinian right to return a reality'. *PoliticsHome* reported that 'Jeremy Corbyn has clashed once again with Labour Friends of Israel'. The headline is:

> **Jeremy Corbyn criticised by Labour group for demanding Palestinian 'right to return'**

Joan Ryan is said to have written to him saying:

> 'The claim of an intergenerational Palestinian right of return ... would effectively turn Israel into a Palestinian state and destroy the Jewish people's right to self-determination.'
>
> Ms Ryan also said the demand was supported by Hamas, who do not believe in Israel's right to exist. (Schofield, 2018)

In Israel, his association with the Palestine Solidarity Campaign was seen as particularly challenging. The newspaper *Ha'aretz* had this headline:

> **Jeremy Corbyn Is Patron of Blacklisted pro-BDS Group Whose Senior Members Will Be Barred From Israel**
> U.K. Labour Party leader was also once chairman of the Palestine Solidarity Campaign, one of Britain's most active pro-Palestinian groups (*Ha'aretz*, 7 January 2018)

In the UK, Jonathan Arkush, who was president of the Board of Deputies of British Jews, made comments on anti-Israel discourse which he linked to Jeremy Corbyn. Arkush had originally been interviewed in the *Telegraph* and was later quoted in the *Jewish Chronicle* as saying, 'Delegitimising the state of Israel is antisemitic' and '[Mr Corbyn] was a chairman of Stop the War, which is responsible for some of the worst anti-Israel discourse'. He made the point that: 'If he shares the prevalent discourse about Israel, then that view is unquestionably antisemitic.' Rhea Wolfson of the Labour National Executive Committee (NEC) challenged him on this in a subsequent article accusing him of conflating 'antisemitism with criticisms of the Israeli government'. The *Jewish Chronicle* notes:

> In response to her article Mr Arkush said that his original comments were 'carefully referencing the views of PSC and Stop the War on Israel, and Corbyn's support for those groups'. (*Jewish Chronicle*, 1 June 2018)

In another episode, Corbyn had also drawn criticism for celebrating Passover with Jewdas, a radical left wing Orthodox Jewish group. On this, the *Sun* reported that:

> THE Labour leader is under fire after marking Passover with a group that has called for Israel's destruction – in the midst of a raging antisemitism row in his party.

It describes Jewdas as 'a secretive organisation':

> On their website, the secretive organisation describes itself as a group of 'radical Jewish voices'.
>
> According to The Jewish Chronicle, Jewdas is a 'Jewish diaspora group, known for its far-left anti-Zionism'. (*Sun*, 3 April 2018)

The *Sun* also quotes the views of MPs John Woodcock and Angela Smith:

> Labour MP John Woodcock called his leader's actions 'irresponsible and dangerous', while Angela Smith MP tweeted: 'Corbyn's attendance at the Jewdas seder reads as a blatant dismissal of the case made for tackling anti-Semitism in Labour'. #EnoughisEnough
> (*Sun*, 3 April 2018)

The *Guardian* gives a different view of Jewdas noting that:

> The group has itself campaigned against antisemitism within anti-Zionist and far-right movements, publishing a 2014 guide to how activists could criticise Israel without being antisemitic and marching against a neo-Nazi group. (*Guardian*, 3 April 2018a)

In another story, there had been questions asked about a fundraising dinner for Corbyn's 2015 leadership campaign. It had been organised by the Friends of Al-Aqsa. As the *Observer* reported: 'Labour leader urged to explain £10,000 raised for his 2015 campaign at dinner organised by Palestinian group' (*Observer*, 6 August 2016). According to the *Observer*, the gift had not been declared. Donations and loans to MPs are recorded in the parliamentary register of interests. They can be used in election expenses and also for areas linked to MPs' work, such as research on policy, travel or constituency business. In this case, one other donation of £2000 from the dinner had been registered. On the amount of £10,000, the Corbyn team replied that the wrong name had been put on the cheque and the bank had rejected it, so it had not been registered. John Woodcock commented on the 'revelations' that:

> These revelations raise incredibly serious questions about the probity of the campaign's finances and the relationship between Mr Corbyn and this organisation. We need Mr Corbyn to give full and frank explanations. (*Observer*, 6 August 2016)

While Corbyn was associated very much with the Palestinian cause, Tom Watson by comparison was seen as being close to that of Israel. He was also a leading proponent of the view that antisemitism was a major problem and was not being properly addressed in the Party. The *Jewish Chronicle* gave a headline to his views in an account of a Labour Friends of Israel event:

> **Tom Watson: I am proud to defend Israel and we have moral obligation to rid Labour of antisemitism**
> (*Jewish Chronicle*, 26 September 2018)

Watson had also received donations and support which were criticised. As the BBC reported: 'Some critics have accused him of taking money from the "Israel lobby"' (BBC News Online, 6 August 2018).

Alistair Sloan writes of how Watson had received £4500 in kind from Labour Friends of Israel and other funding. He notes how Watson was guest of honour at an LFI dinner and thanked his supporters. Sloan then argues that there is nothing conspiratorial in this:

> This may seem like something lifted from a conspiracy theory; it isn't. This is merely how politics works; a confluence of personal beliefs, commercial interests, geopolitical concerns and money, with foreign countries involved on occasion. (Sloan, 2017)

He compares it with the influence that trade unions are able to assert in the Labour Party – as in the funding they provide and donations given to MPs for their constituency work. The left critics would be unlikely to accept that comparison, but Sloan makes the point that the support which many Jewish people in Britain give to Israel comes from their history and family experiences of the Holocaust, not because they are taking orders from the Israeli embassy in London.

The final area for discussion here is how the divisions within the Party over Israel were linked to the definition of antisemitism.

Israel and the argument on the nature of antisemitism

For many who supported Israel, the focus on it by the left was itself a manifestation of antisemitism. Robert Winston, for example, is asked on a BBC news programme if the adoption by the Labour Party of the International Holocaust Remembrance Alliance (IHRA) definition of antisemitism in 2018 has now brought the issue to a satisfactory conclusion. He replies that it has not:

> I am really sorry to say this as a member of the Labour party but I regret that it has not come to a satisfactory conclusion and I hate saying that and the reason why I say that is that it constantly singles out one country Israel and it ignores all the things that are going on in countries where there are not democracies where people are treated far worse, where there is genuine apartheid. (BBC Radio 4, PM, 30 October 2018)

The argument is that there is too much emphasis on Israel, as other countries have a bad or worse human rights record. But the critics of Israel would argue that this is posing the issue the wrong way round. The question is not why they are so obsessed with what is said about Israel. It is rather why Israel and its supporters devote so many resources to promoting and defending the country and how effective is this in excluding critical voices, such as those of the Palestinians. Their point is that as long as Israel holds millions of Palestinians under military control and extends the occupation, it will be criticised. As long as there are attempts to defuse these criticisms through lobbying and public relations, then there will be a push back on this from Palestinians and their supporters. The propaganda war will therefore continue alongside the actual conflict.

The hasbara apparatus of Israel is actually one of the most developed systems of public relations in the world. The point of such activity is to achieve favourable coverage and influence policy. The role of lobbying and campaign contributions by pro-Israel groups has been the subject of much recent debate. Tom Perkins, writing in the *Guardian*, for example, noted that 'the pro-Israel lobby is highly active and spends heavily to influence US policy' and that 'pro-Israel lobbyists and donors spent more than $22m on lobbying and campaign contributions during the 2018 election cycle' (Perkins, 2019).

In the UK, the Shai Masot case occasioned a good deal of commentary on the possible influence of pro-Israel groups. The *Mail on Sunday* published a commentary by a minister from David Cameron's government, who notes that:

> British foreign policy is in hock to Israeli influence at the heart of our politics, and those in authority have ignored what is going on …
>
> Lots of countries try to force their views on others, but what is scandalous in the UK is that instead of resisting it, successive Governments have submitted to it, taken donors' money, and allowed Israeli influence-peddling to shape policy and even determine the fate of Ministers …
>
> We need a full inquiry into the Israeli Embassy, the links, access and funding of the CFI [Conservative Friends of Israel] and LFI [Labour Friends of Israel], and an undertaking from all political parties that they welcome the financial and political support of the UK Jewish community, but won't accept any engagement linked to Israel until it stops building illegally on Palestinian land. This opaque funding and underhand conduct is a national disgrace and humiliation and must be stamped out. (*Mail on Sunday*, 8 January 2017)

Others have pointed to the rise of the BDS (Boycott, Divestment and Sanctions) movement and suggested it is a key reason for developments in public relations, lobbying and other activity. This is because it is seen as a potential threat to Israel by linking the country to apartheid and questioning its legitimacy. Nathan Thrall examined changes within Israel's Ministry of Strategic Affairs that were intended to counter this threat. He describes the work of Yossi Kuperwasser (referred to as Kuper) and who was a key figure in the Israeli government's efforts against the BDS movement:

> Kuper headed the prestigious research division of military intelligence during the second intifada, and was appointed director general of the Ministry of Strategic Affairs in 2009. It was Kuperwasser who turned the ministry into Israel's command centre for what he calls the battle against BDS. (Thrall, 2018)

One part of the Ministry's work, he writes, was to develop partner groups in foreign countries:

> The Ministry of Strategic Affairs has outsourced much of its anti-BDS activity in foreign countries, helping to establish and finance front groups and partner organisations, in an attempt to minimise the appearance of Israeli interference in the domestic politics of its allies in Europe and the US. Kuper said that anti-BDS groups were now 'sprouting like mushrooms after the rain'. He and a number of other former intelligence and security officials are members of one of them, Kella Shlomo, described as a 'PR commando unit' that will work with and receive tens of millions of dollars from the Ministry of Strategic Affairs. (Thrall, 2018)

This was said to have developed to the point that it was feared it might endanger British Jewish organisations. As he notes:

> In 2016, Israel's embassy in London sent a cable to Jerusalem complaining that the strategic affairs ministry was endangering British Jewish organisations, most of which are registered as charities and forbidden from political activity: '"operating" Jewish organisations directly from Jerusalem

> … is liable to be dangerous' and 'could encounter opposition from the organisations themselves, given their legal status; Britain isn't the US!' (Thrall, 2018)

He also refers to the activities of Shai Masot cited above by Avi Shlaim and notes that he was asked by the Ministry of Strategic Affairs to help establish 'a "private company" in the UK that would work for the Israeli government and in liaison with pro-Israel groups like Aipac"' (Thrall, 2018).

The BDS movement generated intense debate in the UK with some arguing that it was an existential threat to Israel. Lord Jonathan Sacks produced a video saying that it was an attempt to de-legitimise Israel as a prelude to its elimination. But others such as Robert Cohen questioned his account of the history of the conflict, commenting that he had missed out any reference to the Nakba in which Palestinians were forced from their homes and land. In his video, Sacks echoes the point made above by Robert Winston that Israel is being unfairly focused upon and that if BDS is really about human rights, it would be demonstrating about the barbarism of ISIS or against Hamas. Still, as Robert Cohen notes, it is not clear how an economic boycott of ISIS or Hamas would work. He also points out that the international community is already imposing sanctions on Syria and other states that violate human rights (Cohen, 2017).

The BDS movement is clearly a central issue for some supporters of Israel. In the *Jewish Chronicle*, Geoffrey Alderman wrote demanding that the Labour Party expel any who support it:

> The party must expel from its ranks not merely all those who explicitly seek the demise of Israel as a Jewish state, but also those who espouse BDS, which has precisely the same objective. (Alderman, 2016)

Another area where critics of Israel are accused of antisemitism is in relation to the right of the Jewish people to have self-determination. To deny this and the right of Israel to exist, it is argued, is itself a form of racism. This was at the heart of conflicts over the IHRA definition of antisemitism and the examples of statements that could be antisemitic which it had included when published in 2016. In July 2018, the Labour Party NEC had adopted the definition, but left out four examples relating to Israel. These were:

- accusing Jewish citizens of being more loyal to Israel or to the alleged priorities of Jews worldwide than to the interest of their own nation
- denying the Jewish people their right to self-determination, e.g. by claiming that the existence of a state of Israel is a racist endeavour
- applying double standards by requiring of it a behaviour not expected or demanded of any other democratic nations
- drawing comparisons of contemporary Israeli policy to that of the Nazis.

In September 2018, the Labour Party NEC eventually adopted all of the examples. This was after a period of public controversy which included a letter signed by 68 British rabbis and a joint editorial in three Jewish newspapers criticising the Labour leadership. The newspapers claimed that Corbyn posed an 'existential threat' to Jewish life and Labour had 'seen its values and integrity eroded by Corbynite contempt for Jews and Israel' (*Guardian*, 26 July 2018b).

In July, the main objection of the NEC had been to the example that it would be antisemitic to claim that the existence of a state of Israel is a racist endeavor (IHRA, 2016). As the

Guardian reported, the concern of the NEC was that a code that included this could be:

> used to deny Palestinians, including Palestinian citizens of Israel and their supporters, their rights and freedoms to describe the discrimination and injustices they face in the language they deem appropriate. (*Guardian*, 26 July 2018b)

The production of this definition and its examples constituted an attempt to codify what forms of criticism of Israel and Zionism should be deemed antisemitic. These attempts were guided by those who were in sympathy with the notion of the 'new antisemitism', at the heart of which is the idea that 'Israel is the collective Jew among the nations' and was being de-legitimised. As Thrall comments:

> Israel's most powerful tool in the campaign against delegitimisation has been to accuse the country's critics of antisemitism. Doing so required changing official definitions of the term. This effort began during the final years of the second intifada, in 2003 and 2004, as pre-BDS calls to boycott and divest from Israel were gaining steam. (Thrall, 2018)

The new definition came about when the European Union Monitoring Centre on Racism and Xenophobia (EUMC) responded to a proposal by the American Jewish Committee (AJC) and called together a group, broadly supportive of the 'new antisemitism' theory. These were drawn from Jewish defence and antisemitism monitoring organisations, academics working in the field of contemporary antisemitism and anti-racist educators. As Antony Lerman notes in this volume, Kenneth Stern, the AJC's head of antisemitism research, had already drafted such a new definition. It was this, with some small amendments, that surfaced as the EUMC working definition. The draft by Stern was unique in that it singled out various examples of criticism of Israel and Zionism which could be regarded as antisemitic. The definition and examples were then published by the EUMC in 2005.

It was this definition with a list of examples of what could be seen as antisemitic which was substantially reproduced by the IHRA in 2016 (IHRA, 2016). This definition 'has been used, endorsed or recommended, with some small modifications, by a number of other organisations – including the US Department of State' (Thrall, 2018).

The crucial issue, as Thrall notes, is the manner in which the term 'self-determination' has been interpreted in the application of the new definition, such that even asking for equal rights would now be termed antisemitic:

> By the state department's definition, delegitimisation includes 'Denying the Jewish people their right to self-determination, and denying Israel the right to exist'. Thus anti-Zionism – including the view that Israel should be a state of all its citizens, with equal rights for Jews and non-Jews – is a form of delegitimisation and therefore antisemitic. (Thrall, 2018)

The definition and its use have been subject to much debate. Peter Beinart, for example, notes that David Harris, head of the AJC, has said, 'To deny the Jewish people, of all the peoples on earth, the right to self-determination surely is discriminatory' (Beinart, 2019). Beinart then comments that all peoples do not have their own state. In practice, they could not as there are between 6–7000 languages in the world and numberless ethnic groups and sub-groups. Most people live in states that are amalgams of many ethnicities. A central state authority might oppose self-determination of a group because it sees it as impractical and damaging to the country as a whole. The Spanish government oppose Catalan independence, but not on grounds that are seen as racist.

Even if it is accepted that a people have the right to self-determination, whether the resultant state is termed as 'democratic', 'apartheid' or 'racist' depends on the practical form in which it is constituted. A critical point that is made about Israel is that the self-determination of one people has been at the cost of suppressing another. As Nathan Thrall argues, to change this would require a change in the policies which discriminate against Palestinians and inform the structure of the state. It is not racist to attempt to change such a society. As Peter Beinart notes: 'It is not bigoted to try to turn a state based on ethnic nationalism into one based on civic nationalism, in which no ethnic group enjoys special privileges' (Beinart, 2019).

But the defenders of Israel as it is presently constituted would argue that in order for it to be a safe homeland, it is necessary for it to be a 'Jewish state'. In this, Jewish people must have a guaranteed majority and therefore enjoy special privileges. But if this is what is desired, then it is problematic to establish such a state in a place where many other people already live. The left critics of Israel would argue that to do so makes it essentially a settler colonial state. The proper points of comparison would not therefore be with western democracies such as Norway or Holland, but with white South Africa, the French in Algeria or the Protestant plantations in the north of Ireland. In Chapter 5, David Miller shows how he made this comparison in a public lecture and was reported to the Labour Party for antisemitism. The point that he had made was that in his reading of the IHRA definition, to say that 'a' state of Israel would necessarily be racist is not acceptable. This is in the sense of any possible hypothetical state being so. But to say that 'the' state of Israel as it is presently constituted is racist, is not outwith the definition and is therefore acceptable commentary. The accusation of antisemitism was rejected by the Party and he explains the thinking and processes behind this.

It is clear that the above arguments raised extremely complex issues and divisions which made the development of a unified position within the Party close to impossible. In the next chapter, we look at how these conflicts worked out in practice and the response of the leadership to the crisis.

3
What Could Have Been Done and Why It Wasn't, and Will It End?

Greg Philo and Mike Berry

The crisis was explained in many different ways by the contending groups both within and outside the Party. Amongst all these conflicting views, the problem facing the leadership was to navigate a way through them and develop a coherent plan of action. If we look back to the key principles of good public relations, we can assess more clearly the response of the leadership and the difficulties that they encountered. The priorities should have been to establish the scale of the problem, give clear and accurate information, stop exaggerated claims and, crucially, to show that the whole organisation was committed to resolving the issue. It was therefore essential as a first step to establish the number of members involved. But in practice doing this proved elusive.

The claims about antisemitism had begun after the election of Corbyn in September 2015. Then in 2016, both Naz Shah MP and Ken Livingstone were accused of making antisemitic comments and were suspended from the Party. Following this, in April of that year, Corbyn announced an inquiry into allegations of antisemitism and other forms of racism to be led by Shami Chakrabarti. This reported after two months with 20 recommendations, including rule changes to improve the disciplinary process and the formation of a National Executive Committee (NEC) working group for education and training. The investigation concluded that Labour was 'not overrun' by antisemitism, Islamophobia or other forms of racism but there was an occasional 'toxic atmosphere'. Shami Chakrabarti was criticised by the Board of Deputies of British Jews for accepting a peerage from Labour, which was said to undermine the independence of the report. The report was also criticised by the Home Affairs Select Committee on Antisemitism, which itself reported in October 2016. The Committee concluded that the Chakrabarti report had failed to deliver a definition of antisemitism or to suggest effective ways of dealing with it. But it also concluded that there was no reliable evidence of any special prevalence of antisemitism in the Labour Party:

> Despite significant press and public attention on the Labour party and the number of revelations regarding inappropriate social media content, there exists no reliable empirical evidence to support the notion that there is a higher prevalence of antisemitic attitudes within the Labour Party than any other political party. (Home Affairs Select Committee on Antisemitism in the UK, 2016: 45–6)

This conclusion could have been used as part of a coherent public relations campaign, replying to the accusations. It would have to have been accompanied by the statement that one case of racism is too many and that the Party would act urgently to root out the problem. The leadership would then have to show that they were doing so in effective and fair disciplinary procedures and also by new education programmes as suggested in the Chakrabarti report. In an interview with us, John Underwood, a former communications director for the Labour Party, suggested that the hostility of the right wing media means that such a plan plus effective public relations are essential:

> In the circumstances, are the media going to use this as an opportunity to beat up Jeremy Corbyn? And the answer is, of course they are. So you must have a PR strategy. If you are Jeremy Corbyn, you can't hide behind the argument that this is the right wing media. They should have killed it immediately. The only real way to deal with it is to say send us your evidence, and we have to have in the Labour Party an effective, rapid and fair process by which you deal with people who are accused of antisemitism. (3 March 2019)

One Labour activist who we interviewed also raised with us the question of why a more proactive approach to education was not adopted sooner:

> I honestly don't understand why we haven't developed and rolled out self study and group discussion training for members and online resources to help with this. It would have given political and class consciousness a boost and given Corbyn a crutch. (24 February 2019)

But even an issue such as training can be divisive as it raises the question of who is to do it. In 2016, the Party had asked the Jewish Labour Movement to give antisemitism training to branches around the country. This had generated controversy as some on the left saw the JLM as apologetic towards Israel. In March 2019, the Party eventually committed itself to training via a new course to be developed by the Pears Institute for the Study of Antisemitism, Birkbeck, University of London.

In practice, it took a long time to organise the coherent, planned response that was needed. In May 2018, Shami Chakrabarti appeared on the BBC *Daily Politics* programme saying that she was 'incredibly disappointed' at the lack of progress in the implementation of her recommendations. She put this down to 'factionalism' on both wings of the Party and noted the impact of the new Labour general secretary, Jennie Formby, who had 'probably taken more action to implement my report in the last month than has happened in two years' (BBC, *Daily Politics*, 13 May 2018).

It was not until February 2019 that Jennie Formby was able to publish the necessary information for an assessment of the scale of the issue. Following pressure from the Parliamentary Labour Party (PLP), she revealed in a letter to them that 673 complaints alleging acts of antisemitism from Party members had been received between April 2018 and January 2019. Of these, 453 were judged to have a case to answer and to warrant further investigation. The critics of Corbyn in the PLP had assumed that the figures would be much higher. At a heated PLP meeting on the 11 February, MPs were reported as claiming that there were 'thousands of outstanding cases which had been omitted from the figures Formby released' (*Jewish News, Times of Israel*, 11 February 2019).

There had in fact been over 1000 complaints in the period to which Formby referred, but many had proved to relate to people who were not members of the Party. The following day, Formby replied, specifically criticising figures supplied by Margaret Hodge who had given the Party a dossier of 200 examples of antisemitism. Formby noted that just 20 of these had related to people who were Party members. Formby also very vigorously defended the integrity of her staff and the intense work that had been put into assembling the figures. In a reply to the MPs, she wrote: 'The constant and often public criticism of our dedicated and talented staff team is unacceptable and is causing them considerable distress' (*Guardian*, 12 February 2019).

There were other attempts to undermine these figures on antisemitism. *The Sunday Times* reported on 7 April 2019 that internal leaked documents showed that 454 complaints were unresolved including 249 where an investigation had not yet been started. The Party leadership responded by saying the figures quoted by *The Sunday Times* were not accurate and that lines from emails had been 'selectively leaked' to misrepresent their contents and to suggest improper interference in the process (ITV, 7 April 2019). Corbyn had rejected the charge that there were attempts to overrule decisions. But apart from that, 454 cases, around 0.08 per cent of the membership, would hardly match the front page headline of an 'army' of antisemites. The headline read:

> **Labour's hate files expose Jeremy Corbyn's anti-semite army**
> (*Sunday Times*, 7 April 2019a)

There was more criticism of the figures in a report by Alan Johnson of BICOM. He asserted that 'a culture of antisemitism, denial and victim blaming exists in the Labour Party from top to bottom' (Johnson, 2019a: 11). In the report, he details 129 numbered cases. Some of these, as he notes, are not actually about Labour Party members. But he believes that it is 'reasonable to think they have influenced Labour Party members' (p. 82). He thus includes the writings of the *Morning Star* and the *Scottish Left Review*. There is no evidence given that these are first choice reading for Labour Party members, but he thinks they are important. Many of his other cases are already well known and some are highly contested. They include, for example, the case of David Miller which is featured in Chapter 5 of this book.

Johnson also believes that it is problematic to suggest charges of antisemitism have been exaggerated. He begins a section on 'antisemitism denial' with a quote from a YouGov poll saying that 77 per cent of Labour Party members believe 'the charges of antisemitism to be deliberately exaggerated' (p. 73). Johnson blames Labour Party members for believing, 'without any evidence whatsoever', that figures have been manipulated (p. 74). We can agree that to deny the existence of cases of antisemitism would be wrong, but to suggest that figures can be 'politicised and manipulated' in public debate is hardly contentious. In social science, such distortions and their impact on belief is the basis of theories such as 'moral panic'. If the members have seen nothing or just an occasional sporadic case, while media reports describe the Party as being 'riddled' with antisemitism, then how is it not reasonable to doubt the claims of the media? Who is closest to the truth: those in the public who believe that a third of Party members have been reported for antisemitism or actual members who believe the number is much smaller?

Johnson apparently believes that the Labour Party figures understate the number of cases. In suggesting they should be higher, he quotes both Ruth Smeeth and Margaret Hodge and their claim that 'thousands' of allegations have been omitted from the figures. He also reports the claim of Labour Against Antisemitism (LAAS) that they have forwarded to the Party 4000 screen shots, antisemitic comments and images from Labour supporting Facebook groups and Twitter accounts (pp. 57–8). He indicates that just a thousand of these relate to Labour Party members. It is not said how many of this number are the existing cases, or if some are examples from the same person, or if any do not meet the Labour Party criteria for antisemitism. These factors would be likely to reduce the overall number again and move it closer to the existing figures.

In May 2019, it was reported that LAAS had now submitted 'A HUGE dossier detailing 15,000 incidents of Labour anti-Semitism' to the Equalities and Human Rights Commission (EHRC). The text then indicates that the number of people involved is actually 'hundreds' (*Daily Mail, PressReader*, 6 May 2019). Again, it is not clear from the media reports whether these are duplicates of existing cases, whether they are all definitely Labour members, or whether the examples all meet the Party's criteria for antisemitism. There is a need for a cool appreciation of evidence. Writing in *Labour List* in May 2019, Margaret Hodge criticised Jon Lansman, who had defended Labour's new procedures. 'Instead of trading in anecdotes,' she insisted, 'it is important to look at the facts'. But she then notes that 'the Jewish Labour Movement has had countless complaints left unresolved'. If a specific number of complaints have been made, then it must be possible to count them as well as those that remain unresolved. They can't be 'countless'. Margaret Hodge then comments that 'I alone submitted approximately 200 complaints last year and have not heard directly from the party since' (Hodge, 2019). Perhaps Jennie Formby's statement three months earlier, that just 20 of the complaints submitted related to Labour Party members, does not constitute 'hearing directly'. But a small acknowledgement of the difference between 200 and 20 would be helpful.

We can agree that there should be no cases of antisemitism in the Labour Party. But after all these claims, the total identified remains a tiny fraction of its membership. In the end, the strongest argument that this is an accurate assessment is provided by the critics of the Party themselves. This is because the internet and the activities of Party members have been scoured by journalists, researchers, interested individuals and groups searching for examples. The numbers remain stubbornly around those provided by the Labour Party. The vague and unsubstantiated claims that there are thousands more do not impress Harvey Goldstein, a professor of statistics:

> Rivalling even (the debacle over Brexit) is the way in which various politicians and interested parties have sought to utilise allegations of antisemitism within the Labour Party, and the ways in which almost all of the mainstream media have involved themselves ... Needless to say, many of those who were alleging Labour antisemitism continued to press their claims ... referring to 'the scourge of antisemitism' and 'institutional racism'. Remarkably, or perhaps not so remarkably, there happens to be little sound evidence to back any of these claims. (Goldstein, 2019)

There is therefore no reason, on the basis of existing published evidence, to doubt the figures supplied by Jennie Formby and the proportion of members which they indicate. The level of publicity on this issue over three years would be likely to encourage the submission of complaints. This was so much the case that very many were submitted that did not even relate to Party members. The published numbers of cases also make sense in relation to statements made to us by activists, most of whom said they had never seen antisemitism within the Party, but who recognised it quite clearly outside. We tested this again at a meeting of Party members in Leith in March 2019. To do this, we first gave an exhaustive list of examples of antisemitism, including stereotypes and generalisations made about Jewish people. Of 30 members present, just one had seen anything of these in Party circles.

In the case of Formby's figures, even if we assumed a constant level of cases over three years, the number would still come to just 0.3 per cent of the membership. In fact, over that period, it may have been fewer. Corbyn had reported to the Select Committee inquiry in July 2016 that less than 20 members had been suspended since he was elected in 2015. It is clear that the figures from 2019 could have been used for a publicity campaign defending the integrity of the membership and the Party as a whole, saying that over 99 per cent of members were not involved in these allegations.

But the difficulty was that by 2019, the view that the Party was 'riddled with antisemitism' and 'anti-Jewish hatred', as the *Sun* put it, had gained substantial traction in public belief (*Sun*, 22 April 2018). The question remains why did it take so long to develop a coherent response with accurate figures and how did a false perception of the Party's membership become so deeply embedded?

A dysfunctional Party

There was a lack of focus and unified effort in organising public relations and many other elements of the Party apparatus. A key reason for this was that an extraordinary conflict had developed between Corbyn's team, the Parliamentary Party and some elements of Labour's bureaucracy. The issue of Brexit also divided the Party and again made it difficult to have an agreed position.

In the case of the Parliamentary Party, Corbyn had been under attack by his own MPs from the inception of his leadership in 2015. He was criticised on a range of issues including national security, the Trident nuclear programme, air strikes in Syria and Labour's performance in the May 2016 local elections. The Brexit referendum result in June 2016 produced more criticism of his alleged low-key approach to campaigning. This occasioned a major attempt to displace him as over 20 shadow cabinet ministers resigned. On 24 June, Margaret Hodge and Anne Coffey had tabled a vote of no-confidence in Corbyn, which he lost on 28 June by a margin of 172 to 40. He stood firm against this, refusing to resign, but it led to a second leadership election which he eventually won in September 2016.

One result of all this conflict was the complete exhaustion of the leadership inner team who had the appearance of only just surviving permanent attack. In the period after Corbyn's election in 2015, we met John McDonnell and other members of the leadership team to discuss aspects of Labour's communication strategy. McDonnell made the point to us about the exhaustion of the team, but also pointed to the dysfunctional relationship which existed with Labour's permanent bureaucracy. This was not all of it, but he commented that he was 'fighting everyday with Labour HQ bureaucracy'. Decision making and implementation were he said slow. He spoke of the difficulties after the publication of the Chakrabarti report:

> In the months that followed we kept asking the bureaucracy about progress in implementing the Chakrabarti recommendations. I asked in particular about the legal advisory panel.
>
> When Formby arrived, she realised how much work hadn't been done and was therefore still left to do. (21 May 2019)

Other commentators have pointed to the dysfunctional relationship. It is clear that relations between Corbyn's team and some full time staff were very fraught (Marcetic 2017).

In our interviews we were told about how difficult it had been to get basic tasks accomplished, such as appointments. One member of Corbyn's team described it as:

> low intensity warfare ... For whatever reason, the processing of cases of antisemitism went slowly and by the time Jennie Formby came, she inherited a backlog. (8 May 2019)

In this situation both sides blamed each other and staff in Labour headquarters did not accept criticisms that were made (*Guardian*, 12 February 2019). The reasons for the delays were disputed. In May 2019, *BuzzFeed News* reported that the Labour Party's compliance unit had taken 'months to act on some of its most high-profile anti-Semitism cases, according to a cache of hundreds of leaked emails' (*BuzzFeed News*, 11 May 2019). The emails had been given to *BuzzFeed* by a former Labour Party official and a member of the Labour International group, both of whom it was said 'wanted to expose failings in the compliance unit's response to anti-Semitism complaints before Jennie Formby became general secretary in April 2018' (*BuzzFeed News*, 11 May 2019). The essence of this story was that the compliance unit was acting slowly and that Corbyn's staff were pressing for faster action on antisemitism. *BuzzFeed* quotes a source close to the compliance unit giving their side of the story, saying the reason for the delays was that they were overwhelmed by the volume of complaints:

> a source close to the compliance unit at the time accepted that the unit took too long to take action, saying it was overwhelmed by an unprecedented volume of complaints.
>
> The source claimed that compliance unit staff feared ending up on a collision course with NEC members and Corbyn's office over disciplinary cases. (*BuzzFeed News*, 11 May 2019)

Then in the same month, *Private Eye* reported another account which this time suggested that Corbyn's team had tried to protect people accused of antisemitism. The story here was that ex-Labour staffers who were critical of Corbyn's leadership had taken copies of a large number of emails when they left and were now preparing to share these with the EHRC. The *Jewish Chronicle* reported that: 'According to Private Eye, they will include 'tens of thousands' of examples of how the party ignored complaints that supporters were promoting Jew-hate' (*Jewish Chronicle*, 15 May 2019). This is potentially confusing in terms of numbers of cases. *Private Eye* had reported that there were tens of thousands of emails 'showing how the party ignored complaints that supporters were promoting antisemitism' (*Private Eye*, 17–30 May 2019). To be clear, that means there are claimed to be tens of thousands of emails about examples, not tens of thousands of examples of antisemitism. So in principle it could mean that there were a large number of emails relating to a much smaller number of complaints.

Some emails had previously been leaked to *The Sunday Times*. There was then considerable public debate about Corbyn's staff giving views on cases or procedures and whether this was legitimate or indicated an attempt to undermine the struggle against antisemitism. The Buzzfeed story above and the emails they published suggested the opposite.

Jon Lansman makes the point that the leadership did not have effective control over the Party machinery:

> When people talk about the antisemitism problem within Labour, many say that the leadership have had three years to get on top of this issue and the fact that they haven't shows at best complacency and at worst complicity. But of course the leadership did not have control of the party machinery. (*Labour List*, 14 May 2019)

If this is correct, then it does create a potential problem for the view that the Party was made institutionally antisemitic under Corbyn. The question would be how could he have done so if he was not in control of its institutional structures. There are conflicting accounts here of what caused the delays. But none of this points to institutional discrimination against any specific ethnic group. It suggests rather the existence of structures that were overwhelmed and riven with internal disputes.

The conflicts between the Labour leadership and some of its own officials continued at least until the election in June 2017. Tom Baldwin, a former communications director for the Labour Party, described how during the election, Labour officials had 'micro targeted' Facebook adverts at Corbyn and his team. This was a ruse to make them think that the messages they wanted in the campaign were going out across social media. Actually it was only them and a limited group that were receiving them. Baldwin quotes from the officials:

> 'They wanted us to spend a fortune on some schemes like the one they had to encourage voter registration', says one ex-Southsider. 'But we only had to spend about £5,000 to make sure Jeremy's people, some journalists and bloggers saw it there on Facebook. And if it is there for them, they thought it must be there for everyone. It wasn't. That's how targeted ads can work.'
>
> Corbyn's team were receiving 'dark posts' that were tailor-made for them by their own party while most voters saw different content. (Baldwin, 2018: 194–5)

The *iNews* reported the story and quoted a Labour source describing the election period as 'fighting with one hand tied behind our backs by some uncooperative senior staff' (*iNews*, 15 July 2018). The situation then improved after the election as Labour's good showing in it strengthened Corbyn's position.

In February 2019, Jennie Formby wrote to the PLP reflecting on her period of office as general secretary and on previous difficulties with the complaints and disputes processes:

> When I became general secretary of the Labour Party last April, I had been a member of Labour's national executive committee for a number of years.
>
> I had witnessed first-hand that our complaints and disputes procedures were not fit for purpose, with long-standing cases that hadn't been dealt with, alongside new cases coming in, especially in relation to appalling anti-semitic tropes and conspiracy theories, mostly on social media.

She wrote also of the changes that needed to be made:

> It couldn't have been clearer that urgent action was needed to ensure our processes for dealing with complaints were robust, efficient and fair; to resolve outstanding cases; and to establish political education to deepen understanding about, and combat, antisemitism within our movement.
>
> Since then, we've made significant progress to strengthen and speed up our procedures. (*Labour List*, 4 February 2019)

In practice, changes were made including appointing an in-house counsel. The size of the staff team dealing with the investigations was also doubled and the process was streamlined with smaller panels so that cases could be heard quickly. Each of these panels was advised by an independent, specialist barrister.

But these changes were a long time coming and the Party leadership had experienced extraordinary difficulties in developing a coherent approach and clear message on the issue. Another problem was that there were divisions within Corbyn's team on what decisions should be made, for example, whether to adopt the full International Holocaust Remembrance Alliance (IHRA) definition with its examples or to stay with the version of it that had been accepted by the NEC in July 2018. One senior member of Corbyn's team spoke to us of how Jon Lansman, the leader of Momentum, had changed his mind on this:

> He did draft his version of IHRA – his own policy document about dealing with antisemitism and then when it came under severe criticism, he sort of renounced it and then supported adopting IHRA ... In a space of a few months, [he] changed his position where people in the Party were looking to him for a lead. [It] meant that people felt confused naturally and that was then reflected in what happened around the NEC elections ... and that would have affected the whole response of the leadership because he is an influential figure. (16 April 2019)

Corbyn's authority in this was also weakened by attacks on his own history. He had been criticised for the approval which he gave in 2012 to the mural by Mear One, showing an image of Rothschild as an oppressive banker sitting with other financiers and capitalist figures. Corbyn later regretted this saying he had not looked at it properly and had intended only to comment on free speech. He was also criticised because he had referred to members of Hamas and Hezbollah as 'friends' at a meeting in Parliament in 2009. He had said that:

> The idea that an organisation that is dedicated towards the good of the Palestinian people and bringing about long-term peace and social justice and political justice in the whole region should be labelled as a terrorist organisation by the British government is really a big, big historical mistake. (*Guardian*, 2 June 2017)

But the Hamas Charter called for Jihad and was clearly antisemitic. Again, Corbyn later regretted his words and was asked by the MPs in the 2016 Select Committee if he still regarded Hamas and Hezbollah as 'friends'. He replied, 'No' (*Guardian*, 4 July 2016). His supporters would argue that he was naive or careless, but he was wounded by the accusations and given his long history of anti-racism, was not used to being attacked on such grounds. Emily Thornberry pointed to this while speaking at a Limmud event:

> When people accused Jeremy of being an antisemite, he was so upset, and as a result he has found it difficult to deal with the problem. He hasn't dealt with it properly, but to call him antisemitic is wrong. (*Jewish News, Times of Israel*, 27 December 2018)

She made it clear in her view that 'there isn't a racist or antisemitic bone in Jeremy's body', but the attacks on him, she believed, had affected his response (*Jewish News, Times of Israel*, 27 December 2018).

Stimulating the story

Overall, the response was weak. In practice, the leadership did not have the strong public relations infrastructure which was needed as the story was constantly stimulated by interventions from individuals and groups both within and outside the Party. Some interventions were planned, others were simply comments in programmes or news reports which were then amplified in other coverage.

Emily Thornberry, for example, recounted on the *Andrew Marr Show* how someone she had met on the street had turned out to be antisemitic:

> I spoke to someone last weekend and I was really shocked to suddenly see the way in which the conversation turned and she thought she was supportive of Labour and she thought she was supportive of me and I had to make it clear that actually that was really not acceptable. (BBC One, *Andrew Marr Show*, 22 April 2018)

This was then turned into a *Sun* headline and commentary on the Labour Party being 'riddled with hate' – without evidence that the person who Thornberry met was even a member:

> LABOUR is so riddled with anti-Semitism that party activists have stopped Emily Thornberry in the street to make vile comments, she admitted today. (*Sun*, 22 April 2018)

Earlier that month, Jon Lansman and Momentum had issued a statement saying that antisemitism was 'more widespread' in the Party than previously thought. No figures were offered, but the claim was based on saying that the bias was 'unconscious'. Jon Lansman was reported as saying on the *Victoria Derbyshire Show* that 'a big programme of education and training' was needed to confront this unconscious bias. When asked if this should include the Party leader, he replied, 'I think we all should'. The *iNews* thus concluded:

> Prominent Labour figures including Jeremy Corbyn should take part in training courses to combat unconscious anti-Semitic prejudice, the founder of Momentum has suggested. (*iNews*, 3 April 2018)

The web link for this actually reads:

momentum-founder-jon-lansman-calls-on-jeremy-corbyn-to-attend-anti-semitic-prejudice-course

Leaving aside how such a story grows in media reports, the suggestion of a bias which is unknown, unrecognised and widespread means that intrinsically it cannot be quantified. Those who have it won't know. It is somehow lurking in the collective unconscious of the Labour Party. The members of the Party might be forgiven for asking what special power anyone has to identify what is going on in their minds when they don't know it themselves. The following year, just after Jennie Formby had published actual figures, Jon Lansman spoke again on Radio 4 and was reported as saying: 'It's now obvious that we have a much larger number of people with hardcore anti-Semitic opinions which unfortunately is polluting the atmosphere in a lot of constituency parties and in particular online'. Again, no alternative evidence is given, but he is quoted as saying that there is a 'major problem' and 'a lot' of constituencies are polluted. The headline in the *Evening Standard* read:

> **Momentum founder and Corbyn ally Jon Lansman: Labour has 'major problem' with anti-Semitism**
> (*Evening Standard*, 25 February 2019)

Such a message is especially powerful since it is presented as being from an 'ally' of Corbyn. Because it is from such an unexpected source, it carries greater legitimacy. We found in other research on food panics that a statement which appears in this way is likely to have a very dramatic impact (Miller and Reilly, 1994).

Other high-profile cases attracted extensive media coverage such as those of Ken Livingstone, who resigned from the Party in May 2018, and Jackie Walker, who was eventually expelled in March 2019. The controversy over Livingstone's remarks originally made in April 2016, that Hitler had supported Zionism, went on intermittently with a sequence of attacks on him, statements and hearings until he finally left the Party. In May 2018, Shami Chakrabarti had appeared on the *Sunday Politics* programme saying that he had brought it into disrepute and should not be allowed to remain:

> He has repeated really, really incendiary remarks. To compare somebody who was trying to escape Nazism, with Nazis themselves and to do so again and again and again, even when you know that this has caused the deepest hurt and upset and embarrassment to the party is completely unacceptable. (*PoliticsHome*, 13 May 2018)

The story was also amplified by major interventions from MPs who were critical of Corbyn. In March 2018, there was the sight of Labour MPs speaking at a demonstration against antisemitism in the Party outside of Parliament, to chants of 'Enough is enough'. This protest was strongly criticised by some on the left for its political timing. David Rosenberg, for example, wrote that:

> Many Tory politicians were present … The timing of this event on Parliament Square, a few weeks before local government elections, was transparently about damaging Corbyn in particular and Labour in general just weeks before those local elections. (Rosenberg, 2019)

The lack of discipline in the Party came to a head when Margaret Hodge publicly attacked Jeremy Corbyn in Parliament, an event which was again very widely reported:

> Corbyn's party faced yet more criticism from Jewish groups yesterday when its ruling body approved a new code of conduct on anti-Semitism. The document was slammed by Labour MPs and peers, with senior MP Dame Margaret Hodge calling the leader a 'fucking anti-Semite' during an angry tirade in the House of Commons. (*Metro*, 18 July 2018)

Margaret Hodge was not disciplined or suspended for this, which created a strange situation where it appeared that people on the left could be disciplined for bringing the Party into disrepute, but this was not applied equally across all groups. One reason for this was that the leadership had decided to avoid a split in the Party at virtually any cost. McDonnell made it clear in private and also in public statements that the priority was to avoid, or at least minimize, a split if it did occur. He makes the point in an interview in the *New Statesman*:

> 'If you're having people like the SDP standing in particular constituencies, it takes votes away from Labour ... And what does that mean? It means the Tories getting in.' He added: 'So the issue for me is I'd want to avoid at all costs a split if we can.' (Maguire, 2018)

The strategy was to hold together a party that in reality was bitterly divided. But the consequence of this was that it became impossible to have a coherent or united message on the scale of antisemitism, to limit exaggeration, or explain the new procedures. It was difficult even to defend the basic integrity of the Party and its membership. In terms of the key principles of public relations, it was a perfect storm.

Will it end?

The Labour leadership lived constantly in the hope that a line could be drawn under the crisis. McDonnell told us in April 2018 that he thought this might come after the parliamentary debate to be held that month. But in practice it simply amplified the criticism as the Conservatives attacked Corbyn for lack of leadership and Labour MPs spoke of the abuse directed at them. The NEC later attempted a resolution with their version of the definition of antisemitism in July 2018, then again by accepting the full IHRA examples in September 2018. In February 2019, Jennie Formby published the figures on cases of antisemitism, but as we have seen, this was followed by yet more attacks and controversy.

So is the story and issue likely to subside? This depends on the motives of those involved. If the intention is to reduce antisemitism in the traditional sense of an irrational hatred of Jewish people, then with goodwill and some respect between different groups in the Party, it conceivably could. A united party could point to the progress that has been made, to the changes in disciplinary procedures and the new education programme. There could be a serious discussion about how more could be done. With the current level of controversy over the issue, the message is very clear to Party members that racist statements will be reported. That in itself has an effect and the issue would recede.

But if the motive is to displace Jeremy Corbyn because of the internal politics of the Party, then the conflict will go on. For different reasons, it will continue if the intention is to reshape the definition and understanding of antisemitism to argue that movements such as BDS and contemporary criticisms of Israel are illegitimate. In those circumstances, there is unlikely to be any process which the leadership could come up with that would be seen by all groups as acceptable. We will examine these two issues in turn – first, the nature of the internal politics and second, the arguments over Israel and what constitutes legitimate criticism.

We can look, for example, at how the internal politics of the Party affected the reception of the new processes developed by Jennie Formby. As we have seen, she had made statements about these in two meetings on 4 and 11 February 2019 as well as on the number of cases. The level of 'heat' in the first meeting is described in this account in the *Independent*:

> The row over antisemitism in the Labour Party reignited last night after furious MPs condemned party leaders. (*Independent*, 4 February 2019)

We are told that it was a 'heated showdown' and that Jennie Formby had 'sparked fury' (*Independent*, 4 February 2019). In a commentary on the meeting, the Jewish Voice for Labour (JVL), who are supportive of Corbyn, point to what they see as the political reasons behind the continual conflict: 'Nothing is good enough for the anti-Corbyn diehards, who choose the height of the Tory crisis over Brexit to launch a new attack' (JVL, 6 February 2019). Such meetings can generate fury whether or not antisemitism is being discussed. Here is an account of an earlier one from March 2017:

> Labour's civil war has erupted in furious clashes at a 'brutal' meeting between leader Jeremy Corbyn and the party's MPs and peers.
>
> As the Westminster meeting ended in a shouting match, angry Labour MPs rounded on Mr Corbyn (Sky News, 21 March 2017)

These 'furious' clashes and brutal meetings apparently relate to the internal struggles over Jeremy Corbyn's leadership. The

Skwawkbox noted that 'right-wing back-benchers do seem to have trouble recognising that they are not in control of the party' (Skwawkbox, 5 February 2019). Len McCluskey, general secretary of Unite the Union, went so far as to say that Labour MPs who criticise Jeremy Corbyn should leave the Party and 'go and do something else' (*Independent*, 10 September 2018).

In the PLP, the outrage at how the leadership was dealing with the antisemitism issue continued after the 'heated showdown' of 4 February 2019. A week later on 11 February, Jennie Formby provided the actual figures on cases. We have seen above that these figures were disputed, as the *Independent* reports:

> **Labour MPs condemn party leaders after admission that just 12 members have been expelled over antisemitism**
> (*Independent*, 11 February 2019)

In fact, a further 49 people had left the Party after being presented with the evidence against them. But a central concern at the meeting for some MPs was to attack the process and query 'why so few members had been suspended' (*Independent*, 11 February 2019). In all this heat, there was little attention to the possibility that the process might be working better with the appointment of the in-house counsel and an independent specialist barrister attached to each panel. Almost a third of the cases had been dismissed but to have so many instances where it is found there is no case to answer indicates that people have been accused who were innocent. There is no outrage reported about this. In the current climate, the consequences of such accusations can be very serious.

One activist who we interviewed described being suspended and the effects of this.

Although the suspension was lifted, the accusation made against the activist had dramatic impacts. These included the loss of work, debt, hate mail and death threats. This account was given to us:

> The accusation that one is antisemitic, followed by months of investigation, accompanied by hate mail from strangers in many countries and even death threats, followed by the lifting of one's suspension followed by the repeated allegation that one is a vile antisemite whose reinstatement indicates merely that the party is institutionally antisemitic, cannot be the best way to root out antisemitism. (13 April 2019)

The only help offered from the Party to this person was to suggest contacting the Citizens Advice Bureau or the Samaritans.

The Wirral Labour councillor, Jo Bird, also commented to us on her suspension in March 2019. This was for making a play on words in a speech. Because she is Jewish, she said that for her 'due process' would be 'Jew process'. It was a reference to the Woody Allen joke where he mixes up the words 'do you' with 'Jew'. The suspension was lifted after nine days following public protest, but as with the above case, she also received hate mail and abuse. As she told us: 'I'm still getting some. I had about a dozen hate emails in the first week, saying I'm a Nazi and an antisemite.' She also believes that the current climate in which inappropriate accusations are made actually weakens the struggle against real racism. As she comments: 'A self deprecating joke or a play on words by a Jewish person is not antisemitism, and it devalues the real fight against antisemitism' (4 May 2019). Such situations are in part a result of the frenzied atmosphere that has been generated. Inasmuch as this is about criticising the current leadership and the ongoing civil war in the Party, then it is unlikely to recede until there is a greater correspondence between the purpose and beliefs of the PLP, the leadership and the mass of Party members. This is unlikely to happen until either a great part of the membership leaves or there is re-selection of MPs at local level. In the meantime, the struggle and conflict will continue.

Of course it is correct to be angry about racism, but we can see that the level of response varied with who was being abused. Luciana Berger MP suffered very serious antisemitic abuse, and the most extreme examples of it from the far-right were pursued by the police resulting in custodial prison sentences. The attacks on her were highlighted both in the Party and in the media, but the racism directed at Diane Abbott, Shadow Home Secretary and a prominent supporter of Corbyn, received less attention. Research by Amnesty showed that she received 45 per cent of all abusive tweets sent to female MPs in the six weeks before the 2017 election (Dhrodia, 2017).

Other forms of racism also received comparatively little comment nationally or in the Party. It was reported in a local paper in Wales, for example, that a post from the Facebook account of a local councillor had referred to 'gas canisters' in relation to a Traveller's camp:

> A post claiming 'Hitler had the right idea' was made from the Facebook account of a Prestatyn councillor during a discussion about Travellers.
>
> The post, from the account ... also asked 'anyone got any gas canisters?' (Brennan, 8 April 2019)

Racism against the Roma does not attract a great national outcry. The *Daily Mail*, which had pursued Jeremy Corbyn and antisemitism in the Labour Party with such vigilance, appeared untroubled by these headlines:

Villagers threaten vigilante action as 200 travellers descend on leafy Surrey common stealing boules sets and lawn tennis kits and defecating in gardens of £2m houses

(*Mail Online*, 6 August 2018)

A credit to the nation! British traveller family hang around shirtless and swigging Red Bull outside New Zealand hotel as they say they will SUE mayor who declared them 'worse than pigs'

(*Mail Online*, 25 January 2019)

British gypsies are banned from every Burger King in New Zealand for scamming free meals by taking customers' leftovers to the counter and claiming they'd been served cold food

The unruly 'gypsy' British tourists terrorising New Zealand have been banned from all Burger Kings across the country (*Mail Online*, 14 February 2019)

To hang around shirtless scarcely qualifies as terrorising a nation. But imagine the outcry if the headlines had read 'Black family hang around shirtless and swig Red Bull' or 'Jews are banned for scamming meals'. In June 2019, the *Independent* reported a poll of Conservative Party members showing that two thirds believe parts of Britain operate under Sharia law and 43 per cent agreed with the statement that: 'I would prefer to not have the country led by a Muslim' (Dearden, 24 June 2019). Imagine the outcry if this had been the result for Labour Party members speaking of a Jewish person. But outrage can clearly be selective when it comes to the struggle over racism.

And then Israel

Arguments about antisemitism and Labour policy towards Israel certainly precede Corbyn's leadership and are likely to continue. Here, for example, is a report in 2014 by Dan Hodges in the *Telegraph*, of Maureen Lipman's comments, complaining that Ed Miliband, the Labour leader, wants to recognise the state of Palestine. Lipman is quoted as saying:

> Just when you thought it couldn't get any worse ... just when the anti-Semitism in France, Denmark, Norway, Hungary is mounting savagely, just when our cemeteries and synagogues and shops are once again under threat. Just when the virulence against a country defending itself, against 4,000 rockets and 32 tunnels inside its borders, as it has every right to do under the Geneva Convention, had been swept aside by the real pestilence of IS, in steps Mr Miliband to demand that the government recognise the state of Palestine alongside the state of Israel. (Hodges, 2014)

On this, Hodges concludes that 'the Labour party's support within the Jewish community is now on the brink of collapse' (Hodges, 2014). This does produce a slight double take as we have heard so often since, that it is Corbyn who has brought this support to the point of collapse.

In practice, arguments over antisemitism can move swiftly into criticism of those perceived to be acting against the state of Israel. We have seen the view that supporters of BDS should be expelled from the Labour Party. The BDS website in fact states that it is an 'inclusive, anti-racist human rights movement that is opposed on principle to all forms of discrimination, including anti-semitism and Islamophobia' (BDS, 2019). But this is not good enough for its critics. Alan Johnson, for example, asserts that the movement contains 'demented anti-Israeli sentiment' and that Israel is presented as 'uniquely malevolent, full of blood lust'. This, for him, is a new version of old-fashioned antisemitism. He argues this in *Prospect* magazine in a two-way debate with Johnathan Rosenhead who is chair of BRICUP (British Committee for the Universities of Palestine). As Johnson comments:

> Old-fashioned Jew hatred still exists, but anti-Semitism today is often found – as the Labour Party is discovering – in the smelly borderlands where an anti-Israeli sentiment of a particularly excessive, demented kind, commingles with and updates – often unthinkingly – older anti-Semitic tropes, images and assumptions.
>
> I call this 'anti-Semitic anti-Zionism' ... [BDS] bends the meaning of Israel and Zionism out of shape until both become receptacles for the tropes and ideas of classic anti-Semitism …
>
> The BDS movement has taken this demonising discourse into every nook and cranny of civil society and has poisoned all it comes into contact with, from the churches to the trades unions to the Labour Party. (Johnson and Rosenhead, 2016)

Rosenhead replies that Johnson's rhetoric confuses two categories, first antisemitism and second, anti-Zionism. He suggests that Johnson is mixing up:

> the question of anti-Semitism as a pathological and distorted dislike of a certain kind of Other, with anti-Zionism which is a legitimate political concept. Zionism was and is a nationalistic and political movement to establish a Jewish homeland. But there were people already settled on that bit of land. The outcome has been a steadily

> escalating programme of discrimination, dehumanisation and violence against the Palestinians …
>
> The accusation of a 'new anti-Semitism' is a political project, developed as a shield against the many legitimate and indeed compelling criticisms of Israel. Boycott is by far the most effective tactic to impress on the Israelis that their actions have consequences. That is why it has become such a priority to try to brand it as anti-Semitic. (Johnson and Rosenhead, 2016)

But Johnson is worried that criticisms of Zionism and Israel can involve antisemitic assumptions about plots and conspiracies. We have seen above his views on Labour Party members who believe that figures on antisemitism have been exaggerated. He is especially bothered that they see it as a 'politicised and manipulated thing' by 'Zionists'. If by this is meant that people believe a world conspiracy of Jews is behind it, then of course that would be antisemitic. But if the belief is that the argument on antisemitism in the Labour Party and attacks on Jeremy Corbyn are linked to the defence of Israel and its policies, then it is a legitimate opinion. We can assume that Benjamin Netanyahu, the Prime Minister of Israel is a Zionist and he has publicly attacked Jeremy Corbyn. In August 2018, he criticised Corbyn for 'attending a Palestinian wreath-laying ceremony'. Netanyahu's attack was also linked to Corbyn's views on the Israeli occupation of the Palestinian West Bank:

> Mr Netanyahu's second claim is likely tied to a 2013 video that emerged last week, in which Mr Corbyn said occupation of the Palestinian West Bank was 'of the very sort that would be recognised by many people in Europe who suffered occupation during the Second World War'. (Sky News, 14 August 2018)

Within Israel, Corbyn is seen as a major threat. An article in Israel National News is headed:

> **A UK Corbyn government will be a major existential threat to Israel**
> (*Israel National News*, 20 November 2018)

Another by Caroline B. Glick in the *Jerusalem Post* has as its illustration a front page from the UK *Jewish Chronicle* which has the headline, 'Antisemitic and a racist' over a picture of Corbyn. Beneath it are the words:

> UK Labour MP calls Jeremy Corbyn 'racist', 'antisemite' over party's new antisemitism definition, July 19, 2018.

The article in the *Jerusalem Post* speaks of the dangers to Israel's bilateral relationships with Britain, noting that the UK is Israel's largest European trading partner. Glick comments that:

> All of this will be jeopardized if and when Corbyn comes to power. In a speech in 2015, Corbyn expressed support for the boycott, divestment and sanctions campaign against Israel. In his words, 'I think the boycott campaign, divestment campaign, is part and parcel of a legal process that has to be adopted.'

She also points to the issue of weapon sales to Israel and how Corbyn has called for a review of these: 'From 2015 through 2017, UK weapons sales to Israel totaled $445 million. Much of Britain's arms exports are not stand-alone systems.' Another crucial point for her is that Britain is a global power and she notes that 'The first place his impact will be felt is among members of the British Commonwealth, particularly

Australia and Canada' (Glick, 2018). The perceived level of the threat to Israel posed by Corbyn perhaps explains the high-profile response from Netanyahu.

Johnson and others are concerned that Israel is singled out among nations for special attention. Still, as the BBC notes, the public argument between Netanyahu and Corbyn is fairly unique and would therefore attract considerable coverage and comment:

> It is highly unusual for a foreign prime minister to get involved in a British political row. It's even more unusual for that to happen on a public forum like Twitter. Add in the fact the Jeremy Corbyn replied to Benjamin Netanyahu's tweet and you're looking at a unique political moment. (BBC News Online, 14 August 2018)

Such a moment is part of the ongoing public relations and propaganda war to which we have referred above. There is nothing intrinsically antisemitic about describing such relationships. There are geopolitical struggles for power and influence in which very many nations and interest groups engage. They can be discussed without endorsing antisemitic assumptions about a world conspiracy by Jewish people. It is not therefore illegitimate to ask if Israel or its agencies might be involved in the antisemitism issue in Labour. Such a question is not in itself antisemitic. To say that it is racist would imply that Israel alone among nations cannot be said to be acting openly or covertly to defend its interests. In fact, this is what nations typically do. In the case of Israel, there is evidence that it has been involved in arguments over the nature of antisemitism as part of opposition to BDS and has also been linked to covert operations in British politics. Neither of these prove any covert involvement in the current Labour Party arguments. But the question can be posed and it does not follow of itself that anyone who does so has an irrational hatred of all Jewish people or believes there is a conspiracy to control the world. But Johnson is still concerned that Israel is being accused of behaving badly and that such criticisms can embody a new antisemitism. They would include the suggestion that it is 'always acting in bad faith' (Johnson and Rosenhead, 2016). In his report, he quotes approvingly from Dave Rich, communications director for the Community Security Trust, who argues that antisemitism in the Labour Party 'usually involves language that draws on old racist lies about Jews, but reforms the bigotry in a modern "anti-zionist" setting that has nothing to do with what zionism is or how Israel actually behaves' (Rich, cited in Johnson, 2019a: 19). If a statement about 'not acting in good faith' is based on a view that it is characteristic of Jewish people in general, then that would clearly be antisemitic. But if the statement relates to an appraisal of actual events, then it would either be correct or not without any racist implications. For example, it has been argued that the period after the acceptance of the Wye Accords and the Oslo peace process was used by Israeli leaders such as Ariel Sharon to encourage the expansion of illegal settlements on occupied land. As we noted in our history of the conflict:

> Although both parties to the agreement had agreed not to undertake 'unilateral actions' to change the status of the occupied territories, members of Netanyahu's coalition publicly called on settler groups to take as much land as possible to keep it out of Palestinian hands. Ariel Sharon, the infrastructure minister, told a Tsomet Party gathering on 15th November that 'Everyone should take action, should run, should grab more hills ... We'll expand the area. Whatever is seized will be ours. Whatever isn't seized will end up in their hands'. (BBC News Online, 16 November 1998, cited in Philo and Berry, 2004: 80–1)

But Johnson goes beyond attacking what he sees as unacceptable criticisms of Israel. He wishes to advocate a specific policy approach for the Labour Party and a whole way of thinking about the Israeli/Palestinian conflict. As he writes:

> Rescuing the party will need more than changes to administrative structures, disciplinary processes and educational programmes, important as they will all be. And the state can't be expected to do the work of political rethinking.
>
> For that is what the party needs more than anything: a new approach to the Israel-Palestinian conflict. (Johnson, 2019b)

The Party, he argues, 'needs a new mindset' and to do away with 'two camps activism'. Instead of seeing Israelis and Palestinians as diametrically opposed, they are to be seen as 'two peoples who are both the victims of a tragic history' (Johnson, 2019a: 28). This is a 'complex, tragic and as yet unresolved national question'. In order for them to get along better, there needs to be much more contact with pro-Israeli, pro-Palestinian peace organisations instead of 'dead end, polarising "two camps" activism' (Johnson, 2019a: 103–4).

But as some critics of Israel would point out, this is not just a situation of two peoples living side by side, both victims of a difficult, tragic history, wanting to resolve their desires for self-determination and needing better peace negotiations. One of them is actually living under military occupation and control imposed by the other, in a system of structural discrimination based on ethnicity. To change such a structure requires ending state policies which discriminate against Palestinians. As Nathan Thrall writes:

> In the case of Israel, these could be found not just in the occupied territories, but everywhere Palestinians came into

> contact with the state. In the West Bank, Palestinians were denied the right to vote for the government controlling their lives, deprived of free assembly and movement, forbidden from equal access to roads, resources and territory, and imprisoned indefinitely without charge. In Gaza, they could not exit, enter, import, export or even approach their borders without the permission of Israel or its ally, Egypt. In Jerusalem, they were segregated from one another and encircled by checkpoints and walls. In Israel, they were evicted from their lands, prevented from reclaiming their expropriated homes, and blocked from residing in communities inhabited exclusively by Jews. In the diaspora, they were prevented from reunifying with their families in Israel-Palestine or returning to their homes, solely because they were not Jews. (Thrall, 2018)

Johnson accepts that the occupation and the expansion of settlements can be criticised (2019a: 12). The problem for him comes when people try to change the policies with the practical action of a boycott. This is, as we have seen, because he believes that some in the BDS movement are racist, even though the organisation itself has declared that it opposes antisemitism. But the question raised by Rosenhead remains. What would actually work as an effective tactic to change the current situation? Johnson advocates much closer connections with peace groups. Of course, to discuss peace even in small fringe groups is laudable, but we are still left with the issue of what is going to alter the approach of the Israeli state. Some point to the election in Israel in April 2019 as indicating that it does not intend to change and is committed very much to the status quo. As Joseph Dana puts it:

> What we have learned from Mr Netanyahu's victory, however, is that Israelis now firmly believe the status quo

> is the solution to the conflict. Tel Aviv used the Oslo peace process to entrench its occupation to a virtually permanent degree. In so doing, Israel destroyed any prospect for an equitable two-state solution. It managed to do this while growing its economy and winning recognition for its aggression in Washington. As such, Israel today is exactly the country most of its citizens want. For the overwhelming majority of voters, the ultimate peace solution is one whereby the country has to sacrifice nothing to gain everything. (Dana, 2019)

He notes that this is a substantial change from a decade ago when most Israelis 'might have said that the occupation was unsustainable and a peace agreement was the only way to secure the country's future' (Dana, 2019). The view is further expressed here by Hanan Ashrawi, the Palestinian legislator and diplomat who served as an official spokesperson in the Middle East peace process:

> Israelis overwhelmingly voted for candidates that are unequivocally committed to entrenching the status quo of oppression, occupation, annexation and dispossession in Palestine and escalating the assault on Palestinian national and human rights. They have chosen an overwhelmingly right-wing, xenophobic and anti-Palestinian parliament to represent them. Israelis chose to entrench and expand apartheid. (Ashrawi, cited in Dana, 2019)

Palestinian voices appear rather sparsely in Johnson's report on antisemitism in the Labour Party. He is critical of Momentum for making a video which states: 'Palestinians need to have the right to define their oppression in whatever terms they see fit.' Johnson is scornful, saying 'Really?' and asks, 'What if Jews are "apes and pigs", to be slaughtered by divine edict as

Hamas believes?' (Johnson, 2019a: 25). Of course, we should oppose all racism, but a conflict so bitter and protracted as this is likely to produce stereotypes and abuse on both sides. This is not a theme which Johnson pursues in his report. He could have pointed for example, to the commentary by Odeh Bisharat in Israeli newspaper *Ha'aretz*, who notes that: 'It's hard to fight racism against Jews all over the world when there's such terrible racism among Jews in Israel' (Bisharat, 2017). Bisharat reports the words of Rafael Eitan speaking in 1984 of the future of the occupation and describing Palestinians as roaches:

> 'If 100 settlements will exist – and they will – between Nablus and Jerusalem, all the Arabs will be able to do about it is to scurry around like drugged cockroaches in a bottle,' then-Chief of Staff Rafael Eitan said in 1984. He was talking about the occupied territories, but in Israel itself the matter has already been tested on Arab citizens. (Bisharat, 2017)

The full quote from Eitan is given in *Honest Reporting* as:

> The Arabs will never win over us by throwing stones. Our response must be a nationalist Zionist response. For every stone that's thrown – we will build ten settlements. If 100 settlements will exist – and they will – between Nablus and Jerusalem, stones will not be thrown. If this will be the situation, then the Arabs will only be able to scurry around like drugged roaches in a bottle. (Plosker, 2014)

Eitan was a member of Parliament, the founder of the Tzomet political party and later joined Yitzhak Shamir's government as a minister in 1990. In an interview in 2004, he speaks of how 'it will never be possible to make peace with the Arabs'. His view is that:

> The Arabs wage negotiations with us in three ways: pretense, deception, and violence. (Hanley, 2005)

Such a generalisation directed at 'Arabs' recalls Johnson's critical comments about Israel being described as 'always acting in bad faith'.

In another commentary on racism in Israel, Bel Trew writes of it in the Israeli election of April 2019. She reports the comments of Samir al-Sharif, a Palestinian TV producer from East Jerusalem: 'The right wing feels they have the power in the government in the street – they don't care how racist they are. Especially (with) the American government supporting it' (Trew, 2019).

She also points to the content of campaign videos during the elections:

> The campaign videos which have been flooding social media suggest he (Samir al-Sharif) could be right. Elizabeth Tsurkov, research fellow at the Forum for Regional Thinking, a progressive Israel think tank, said that many of the videos are centred around competing over which candidate killed the most Palestinians. (Trew, 2019)

Of course, racism in one place does not justify its existence elsewhere. But the highlighting of the racism of one side can be another dimension of the propaganda war.

It is clear that the deep and bitter divisions over how Israel is understood as well as policy towards it are unlikely to recede until the conflict between Palestinians and Israelis is itself resolved. Within the Labour Party, it would help if the leadership made clear to members what is acceptable commentary. For example, that it is antisemitic to say that all Jews are in a worldwide conspiracy to support Israel. But it is not antisemitic to argue, on the basis of evidence, about whether

Israel as it is presently constituted is a racist state. Neither is it antisemitic to say that some groups, Jewish and non-Jewish, organise and lobby to defend it.

We can also note that some groups, Jewish and non-Jewish, organise and lobby to *criticise* Israel, but there is no necessary racial stereotype in pointing to that either. If pro-Israel groups claim that Palestinian groups give incorrect accounts, then that claim is either true or false on the basis of evidence. It does not imply by itself a racial stereotype that Arabs are 'devious' and 'manipulate' the truth. Such arguments are not about racial stereotyping – they are just politics.

But even clear guidelines and education on the nature of racism will not resolve the controversy. The propaganda war will continue and there will be constant attempts to redraw the boundaries of acceptable discourse as well as to change policy by, for example, outlawing BDS. The key issue for the Labour Party is how can it function as an effective political organisation in the face of this and the other conflicts outlined here.

4

Media Coverage of the IHRA Definition and Its Adoption by the Labour Party

Justin Schlosberg

This chapter examines media representations of the Labour and antisemitism issue. It focuses on the coverage of the International Holocaust Remembrance Alliance (IHRA) working definition of antisemitism and its eventual adoption by the Labour Party in 2018.

Recent research has evidenced systematic distortions and inaccuracies in mainstream coverage and it seems highly likely that this played some role in shaping (mis)perceptions of the issue. This chapter drills down into that evidence, as produced by the Media Reform Coalition in a real-time study in 2018 (Schlosberg and Laker, 2018). Overall, the research documents a catalogue of reporting failures across the mainstream media; failures that were consistent with a disinformation paradigm. The term 'disinformation' here refers to systematic reporting failures that privileged a particular ideological or political agenda (Bennett and Livingston, 2018). The term 'paradigm' reflects the broad scope of these failures which transcended divides between broadcasters and newspapers, between 'quality' and tabloid news, and across the political spectrum of the mainstream press. We reflect not just on the reporting failures themselves, but also a wholesale failure of accountability, with publications and broadcasters responding to the evidence with a mix of blanket silence and dismissal.

A word on methodology

This research was carried out against the backdrop of a sensitive and complex public controversy, which called for a particularly cautious approach in both the design and analysis framework. Of course, no research in the field of media and communications can be entirely free of subjective influence. But in this case, the researchers went to extraordinary lengths in order to minimise the scope for interpretative judgement. This necessarily limited the horizon of inquiry, with categories of analysis restricted to observable manifest content (text or speech), and qualitative dimensions minimised. In particular, the research avoided questions of slant or sentiment in relation to a given news article or piece.[1]

1. The reliability of the framework was tested using a subsample that was analysed and coded separately by two researchers. This yielded a 93 per cent agreement rate across the most contentious coding categories. Using Cohen's kappa statistic (which takes account of random chance agreement), this resulted in a score of 0.91, which is considered near perfect agreement and indicative of highly reliable findings (Landis and Koch, 1977).

In relation to sourcing, the analysis was restricted to directly quoted or speaking sources in order to ensure consistency and comparability across the units of analysis, and avoid potential anomalies when dealing with anonymous and/or paraphrased sources. This also had the advantage of capturing the power of 'voice' given to particular individuals or groups. Direct quotations and appearances on television reflect voices and perspectives of salience – those judged by journalists to be important (Zoch and Turk, 1998; Jullian, 2011). The sample of analysis was drawn from a cross-section of the largest online news providers in the UK, as well as flagship television news bulletins and programmes, based on recent survey data measuring top news brands across plat-

Closing down debate

As with public belief, the dominant media narrative has rested on a twofold premise. First, that antisemitism under Corbyn has become endemic to the Party ('institutional antisemitism'). Second, that there has been a wholesale failure – principally by the leadership – to deal with the problem. The logical conclusion is that the Party has been lost to extremists and hate-mongers with Corbyn a figurehead, if not chief among them.

This provides the conceptual linkage to a wider 'threat' narrative that has surfaced repeatedly in mainstream media discourse since the summer of 2015 in varied contexts: that under Jeremy Corbyn, Labour has become a party of entryists, Trotskyists, terrorist sympathisers and, above all, racists (Cammaerts et al., 2016; Cartwright, 2016; Schlosberg, 2016; Piazza and Lashmar, 2017; Schlosberg and Laker, 2018). The antisemitism controversy cannot therefore be understood in isolation from this broader narrative which simultaneously positions Corbyn's Labour as irrelevant (beyond the pale of consensus politics and common sense) *and* as an imminent threat to public safety and security.

---

forms (Newman et al., 2018). The sample therefore captured the leading news brands across the two most widely used platforms for news (television and online). This reflects our particular concern with media that individually and collectively reach a critical mass of the public and thus have the greatest potential to influence public belief. The sample duration was from 5 July 2018 (the day that Labour announced proposed revisions to its code of conduct) through to 4 September 2018 (the day the NEC decided to adopt the IHRA definition in full. The sample of analysis was derived using a combination of key-word searches on Google.co.uk and the broadcast news archives held at the British Library. After refinements to ensure comparability, this yielded a total and final sample of 193 news articles across both television and online platforms.

There is, however, one important distinction of the antisemitism controversy in respect of this wider threat narrative. In contrast to other contexts, the antisemitism controversy by its very nature inhibits the development of a counter-narrative. This is because much of the discursive framing serves to pre-emptively de-legitimise any defensive response as 'part of the problem'.

When the *Sun* newspaper claimed that Corbyn was a former Czech spy in early 2018, the story was quickly and comprehensively debunked, and a counter-narrative was able to gain a foothold on the agenda. The *Guardian* ran two pieces in the days that followed the *Sun*'s exclusive, one focusing on the leadership's rebuttal of the claims and the other focusing on the contradictory evidence as presented by intelligence experts.[2]

It was not long after this episode that the antisemitism controversy began to saturate headlines. But in contrast to the Czech spy story, barely any of the rebuttals or contradictory evidence in relation to antisemitism allegations attracted mainstream media attention. Indeed, those pushing antisemitism allegations in columns and comment pages actively invoked terms such as 'whataboutery' and 'denial' in such a way as to close down the possibility of debate. As Labour MP Chuka Umunna put it in a piece for the *Independent*: 'Sadly, even when there is an admission that antisemitism is a problem, too often it is followed by an avalanche of "whataboutery" by people in the party.'[3] The message was clear:

2. See, for instance, R. Tait, L. Harding, E. MacAskill and B. Quinn (2018), 'No evidence Corbyn was a communist spy, say intelligence experts', *Guardian* [online], 20 February. Available from: www.theguardian.com/politics/2018/feb/20/no-evidence-corbyn-was-spy-for-czechoslovakia-say-intelligence-experts, accessed 1 June 2019.

3. C. Umunna (2018), 'Labour can't talk with credibility about racism until we tackle the antisemitism in our ranks', *Independent* [online],

those who deny or defend against allegations of antisemitism are, by default, complicit in the problem.

This foreclosure of legitimate debate surrounding the politicisation of antisemitism invokes a fundamental and unresolved question at the heart of the IHRA controversy: What can we legitimately say in critical discussion of Israel, Zionism or the issue of antisemitism within Labour itself, which ought to be protected from charges of antisemitism?

(Re)framing consensus

As Chapters 2 and 3 show, this is a deeply contested and unavoidably political question. Those who lean towards the right of Labour politics tend to draw the boundaries of acceptable debate much more narrowly compared to those who lean towards the left. It forms the crux of the controversy surrounding the IHRA definition and its incorporation into Labour's code of conduct. But it is also a question that confronted journalists and editors who covered that controversy and the issue of antisemitism within Labour more broadly.

Indeed, drawing the boundaries of legitimate public debate is integral to the process of news construction (Tuchman, 1978; Schlesinger, 1987). For some, this process amounts to the ideological force of *legitimation*, according to which the media play a defining role in marginalising voices outside of the consensus framework (in other words, suppressing dissent). But the key question for critics of media power has always been the nature and origins of that consensus. As Stuart Hall (1982: 82) put it:

---

23 April. Available from: www.independent.co.uk/voices/labour-party-antisemitism-jeremy-corbyn-chuka-umunna-windrush-a8318436.html, accessed 1 June 2019.

> 'who produces the consensus?' 'In what interests does it function?' 'On what conditions does it depend?' Here, the media and other signifying institutions came back into the question – no longer as the institutions which merely reflected and sustained the consensus, but as the institutions which helped to produce consensus and which manufactured consent.

The IHRA controversy in particular provides a useful and important test case for examining the degree to which the mainstream media can *intervene* in the formation of consensus, as suggested by Hall and others. It compels us to ask a simple but far-reaching question at the outset: What role did professional news-makers play, if any, in redrawing or reinforcing the boundaries of what is considered acceptable debate?

To be clear, unlike Labour's NEC, it is not the job of professional journalists to determine whether or not a given statement or action is antisemitic. But it is their job to determine whether a given statement or action is *unquestionably* antisemitic. The consensus framework is thus not reducible to a rigid conception of right or wrong, but rather a wider orientation or understanding of which or whose perspectives *count*, and the degree to which they ought to be subject to attention, challenge or scrutiny.

This is a subtle but important distinction. Consciously or otherwise, all professional journalists covering the IHRA controversy would necessarily have confronted the substance of that controversy: a contested area of discourse which is considered by some to be expressions of anti-Jewish hatred, and by others to be legitimate political speech.

It is against this backdrop that the Equalities Sub-committee of Labour's governing body announced proposals to adapt the IHRA definition of antisemitism on 5 July 2018, for incorporation into Labour's disciplinary code of conduct. Contrary to the ascendant narrative that quickly took hold in the coverage, initial signs suggested that these changes were broadly consensual and the product of substantive consultation with a range of Jewish groups. According to an official response from the Labour Party, this consultation was 'open and inclusive' in which 'a range of Jewish communal organisations, rabbis, academics, lawyers, trade unions, Palestinian groups, local Labour parties and members took part'.[4]

Indeed, the Jewish Labour Movement appeared ready to welcome the proposed changes with its then co-Chair Ivor Caplan remarking just prior to the announcement: 'There have been extensive discussions about how we deal with antisemitism and get it right and I am already starting to see the small steps that I wanted to see … I think we are starting to see the progress that I wanted to see.'[5]

The *Sun* ran a story on 5 July which reported that

> Figures from the Jewish Labour Movement (JLM) met with the party's general secretary Jennie Formby to discuss the new rules earlier this week, and Labour sources said they were 'positively received'[6]

Remarkably, no other reference to this consultation was found within the sample of coverage analysed. Instead, both news reports and comment pieces made repeated reference to the Party's alleged *failure* to consult, without qualifica-

4. Email response from Labour's press office, 25 September 2018.
5. LBC, *The Nick Ferrari Show*, 3 July 2018.
6. N. Clark (2018), '"A toothless document": Jeremy Corbyn's new antisemitism rules slammed as a "racists' charter" by Jewish groups', *Sun* [online], 5 July. Available from: www.thesun.co.uk/news/6701818/fury-as-it-emerges-labour-anti-semites-could-escape-punishment-if-they-tell-party-they-didnt-mean-to-be-offensive/, accessed 1 June 2019.

tion. *Guardian* columnist Jonathan Freedland, for example, wrote on 27 July that Labour 'drew up its code of conduct itself, without consulting the organized Jewish community at all'.[7] And the BBC's Andrew Neil responded with incredulity when Peter Dowd MP pointed out that Jewish groups were in fact consulted:

> Andrew Neil: Who were these Jewish organisations? It wasn't the Board of Deputies was it?
> Peter Dowd: Yes they were.[8]

As part of the case research a comment was sought from the Board of Deputies in response to this point but, despite repeated attempts, no reply was received. What does seem clear at the very least was that the NEC was intent on further consultation prior to implementing any changes to the code of conduct. As an article in the *Jewish Chronicle* made clear on 4 July:

> The *JC* has seen copy of the letter sent by Ms Formby on behalf of the Labour Party on Tuesday to the Board of Deputies, the Jewish Leadership Council and the Community Security Trust in which she confirmed the 'positive' nature of Monday's meeting and invited representatives of the three organisations to attend a 'feedback' meeting on July 17.[9]

---

7. J. Freedland (2018), 'Yes, Jews are angry – because Labour hasn't listened or shown any empathy', *Guardian* [online], 27 July. Available from: www.theguardian.com/commentisfree/2018/jul/27/jewish-anger-labour-listen-antisemitism-opinion, accessed 1 June 2019.
8. BBC Two, *Daily Politics*, 18 July 2018.
9. L. Harpin (2018), 'Jewish Labour Movement Chair condemned over Labour antisemitism meeting', *Jewish Chronicle* [online], 4 July. Available from: www.thejc.com/news/uk-news/jlm-chair-ivor-caplin-

Barely a month later, Peter Mason, national secretary of the JVL, stated on Sky News that

> Since the Labour Party adopted its own code of practice a month ago there have been no formal conversations with the Jewish community, there have been no invitations offered.[10]

Whatever the degree of consultation surrounding the proposed IHRA adaptation, the 5 July announcement precipitated a marked shift in the consensus framing which quickly positioned the Labour Party as an extremist outlier. Central to that narrative was the premise that the IHRA definition was itself consensual and broadly accepted internationally, among public bodies, and across the Jewish community. In the words of former Prime Minister Gordon Brown, 'the strength of the definition is the unanimity behind it'.[11] Labour MP John Mann put it even more starkly in an unchallenged exchange with a BBC anchor: 'It's never happened before. And it's quite extraordinary to have that unanimity across the Jewish community.'[12]

Of course, what such assertions failed to take account of was the controversy that had surrounded the history of the IHRA definition. Indeed, prevailing academic and legal opinion had long been that the definition was not fit for purpose – at least for incorporation into any kind of legal statute or disciplinary code – and it had been rejected by dozens of Jewish organisations around the world.[13]

---

faces-criticism-over-labour-antisemitism-meeting-1.466577, accessed 1 June 2019.

10. *Sunrise*, Sky News, 4 August 2018.

11. *Channel 4 News*, 2 September 2018.

12. *Daily Politics*, 18 July 2018.

13. R. Vilkomerson and R. Kuper (2018), 'As Jews, we reject the myth that it's antisemitic to call Israel racist', *Independent* [online], 22 July.

Not surprisingly then, the announcement on 5 July precipitated a range of outspoken and contesting voices attacking and defending the proposed changes to the code as well as the IHRA definition. They included senior rabbis and 'mainstream' representatives of the Jewish community; a progressive alliance of dissenting Jewish groups both within the UK and around the world; representatives of Black and Asian minorities and migrant communities within the UK; Arab leaders in Israel's Parliament; as well as contesting views on all sides and within all sections of the UK's Labour movement. In contrast to preceding antisemitism controversies, the party's official line against inquiries was a defensive one: the changes were designed to strengthen and expand the code in an effort to enable a swifter and more effective disciplinary process, as previously demanded by mainstream Jewish groups and many Labour MPs.

What was perhaps most significant about the coverage was the relative, and in some cases complete, invisibility of sources outspokenly critical of the IHRA definition, or defensive of Labour's proposals. The *Guardian* online was a particularly problematic example in this respect, given its disproportionate coverage of the issue relative to others within the sample. Overall, sources critical of Labour's proposed amendments to its code of conduct were three times more likely to be quoted in *Guardian* news reports compared to those defensive of the Party on this issue, or critical of the IHRA definition.

There was, however, some variance within the sample. The *Independent*, for instance, produced the second highest number of news reports focused on this issue, but was considerably more balanced in its sourcing compared to the

---

Available from: www.independent.co.uk/voices/antisemitisim-jews-israel-labour-party-bds-jewish-coalition-palestine-a8458601.html, accessed 1 June 2019.

Guardian. Here, quoted sources attacking the proposals outnumbered those defending them by 1.8 to 1. Even the *Sun*'s online coverage was more balanced than the *Guardian*'s on this measure, with 2.8 quoted sources attacking the Party for each one defending it.

There was a tendency in *Guardian* news reports to quote the leadership or official party sources only on related issues such as the controversy surrounding Corbyn's attendance of the 2014 memorial at a Palestinian cemetery in Tunisia, or in relation to the Party's movement towards accepting the IHRA in full. But in relation to the Party's earlier explicit defence of the proposed revisions, reports frequently made only a passing and paraphrased reference. Similarly, prominent sources outspokenly critical of the IHRA definition tended to attract only a brief mention if at all. For instance, in a report headlined 'Labour MP labels Corbyn an "antisemite" over party's refusal to drop code' there was a single reference in the article's final sentence of a letter published on behalf of 36 Jewish groups critiquing the IHRA definition.[14]

The language adopted by reporters in framing the issue was also highly contentious. In keeping with the wider threat narrative discussed earlier in the chapter, journalists made repeated use of 'failure' terminology in respect of Labour's proposed revisions:

> The rows over the summer about the party's handling of antisemitism complaints were sparked by a decision to

---

14. H. Stewart and J. Elgot (2018), 'Labour MP labels Corbyn an "antisemite" over party's refusal to drop code', *Guardian* [online], 17 July. Available from: www.theguardian.com/politics/2018/sep/02/gordon-brown-labour-ihra-antisemitism-definition-nec-vote, accessed 1 June 2019.

> implement a code of conduct that *failed* to adopt four of the 11 examples of antisemitism given by the IHRA.[15]
>
> Corbyn and the Labour party have been engulfed in controversy after *failing* to endorse the International Holocaust Remembrance Alliance's (IHRA) definition of antisemitism in its entirety.[16]
>
> The shift comes after weeks of discord between Labour's national executive committee (NEC) and the Jewish community after the party *failed* to adopt all 11 examples of antisemitism given by the IHRA, arguing that under one of them legitimate criticism of Israel could be deemed antisemitic.[17]

On other sourcing indicators, problems were observed across the sample of news stories analysed. Perhaps the most serious was the almost complete omission of prominent interventions by significant figures and interest groups critiquing the IHRA definition. For instance, in August 2018 a legal opinion was published by Geoffrey Robertson QC, arguing that the IHRA definition was not fit for purpose. *The Times*

---

15. J. Elgot (2018), 'Antisemitism row risks chances of Labour government, *Guardian* [online], 1 September. Available from: www.theguardian.com/politics/2018/sep/01/antisemitism-row-risks-chances-of-labour-government, accessed 1 June 2019.
16. Press Association (2018), 'Antisemitism row: Corbyn has to change, says Gordon Brown', *Guardian* [online], 15 August. Available from: www.theguardian.com/politics/2018/aug/15/antisemitism-row-corbyn-has-to-change-says-gordon-brown, accessed 1 June 2019.
17. H. Stewart and J. Elgot (2018), 'Labour prepares the ground for compromise on antisemitism code', *Guardian* [online], 15 August. Available from: www.theguardian.com/politics/2018/aug/15/labour-prepares-to-amend-antisemitism-code-ihra-israel, accessed 1 June 2019.

online was the only outlet within the sample to report on this.[18] In the same month, 84 groups representing migrant and minority communities issued a joint statement claiming that the IHRA definition risks 'silencing public discussion' over Palestinian rights. Again, this was picked up by only the *Independent* (which was also the only title to give voice to the 36 Jewish groups who published a letter critiquing the IHRA definition).[19] In contrast, a published letter condemning Labour over the IHRA definition signed by 68 rabbis attracted headline or sub-headline attention in seven outlets within the online sample.

Spotlight on TV

One of the most striking and unexpected findings concerned the difference in performance between the online and television news coverage of this issue. Online, the ratio between sources attacking and defending the Party was 2.6 to 1. In contrast, television news programmes were nearly four times more likely to feature sources attacking the Party compared to those defending it. Far from offering a more balanced alternative to their commercial rivals, BBC anchors and presenters were notably partisan in their treatment of sources. In particular, the claims of those attacking Labour on this issue were

18. The Brief (2018), 'Government definition of antisemitism not fit, says Geoffrey Robertson, QC', *The Times* [online], 31 August. Available from: www.thetimes.co.uk/article/government-definition-of-antisemitism-not-fit-says-geoffrey-robertson-qc-htx6trnmq, accessed 1 June 2019.

19. P. Stubley (2018), 'Antisemitism definition at heart of Labour row "will silence public discussion", say minority groups', *Independent*, 18 August. Available from: www.independent.co.uk/news/uk/politics/labour-antisemitism-row-jeremy-corbyn-ihra-definition-bame-group-a8496906.html, accessed 1 June 2019.

routinely accepted almost entirely without challenge, while those few contesting voices given airtime were subjected to sustained and aggressive questioning.

Consider, for instance, the approach taken by Andrew Neil on the BBC's *Daily Politics* show when questioning John Mann MP over his party's reputation on antisemitism:

> Andrew Neil: The Chief Rabbi in the United Kingdom says that your party is treating Jews with contempt. Margaret Hodge, one of your fellow Labour MPs … has said that Jeremy Corbyn himself is an antisemite and a racist. What do you say to that?
>
> John Mann: It's not just the Chief Rabbi. For the first time ever we've had rabbis across the entire Jewish – from the liberal rabbis through to the ultra-orthodox rabbis – combining together in one letter.[20]

Here Neil appears notionally to 'challenge' a Labour MP over the Party's performance. But he was presumably aware that the MP in question had long been an outspoken critic of the Labour leadership, including on antisemitism. Far from constituting a challenge in any meaningful sense, Neil's line of questioning serves the opposite purpose: effectively granting Mann a blank cheque to put forward his views without interruption or come back.

In the same programme, Neil subjected Peter Dowd – a Labour backbencher who *had* been broadly supportive of Jeremy Corbyn's leadership – to considerably more pointed and aggressive questioning such as '[in respect of the IHRA definition] why wouldn't you just do what everyone else does? What's different about Labour?'[21]

20. *Daily Politics*, 18 July 2018.
21. Ibid.

What's most significant here is not just the distinction in tone between the two interviews, but the fact that Margaret Hodge (referenced in Andrew Neil's opening question to John Mann) had adopted a relatively extreme position among Labour MPs while Peter Dowd was comparatively moderate. He had not, for instance, been as outspokenly defensive of Labour's revised code of conduct as other MPs, including Richard Burden and Chris Williamson.

This is important because we would expect journalists to be especially probing in relation to sources that adopt relatively extreme positions in a political controversy (Manning, 2001). But here the inverse appeared to be the case, and this pattern was broadly observed across the television sample. So, for instance, edited clips from an exclusive Radio 4 interview of Margaret Hodge were replayed on several programmes but without any of the critical questioning by Radio 4 presenter Martha Kearney that *did* take place in the original live interview. And when Sky News aired their own recorded interview with Hodge, she was given an entirely unchallenged platform to express her views.[22] Indeed, in spite of Hodge's acknowledgement that she called Corbyn a racist and antisemite, on several occasions, anchors and correspondents still qualified the charge as 'alleged'. References to her outburst were also routinely prefaced with deferential descriptions of her stature as a 'senior' and 'long-standing' MP as well as someone who had lost relatives in the Holocaust. In spite of her relatively extreme views and aggressive verbal attack on Corbyn, Hodge was consistently framed as herself being under attack by the Party's 'high command'. As one BBC anchor remarked on 23 July: 'Hodge has been told she can expect disciplinary action within 12 hours ... very promptly.'[23]

22. *Sunrise*, Sky News, 13 August 2018.
23. *Daily Politics*, BBC Two, 23 July 2018.

The relative performance of television compared to online news also raises troubling questions regarding media diversity more broadly. Much has been made in academic and policy discourse about the 'explosion' of news sources in recent years (e.g. Compaine, 2005; McNair, 2012), and especially the rise of partisan online news outlets on both the left and right of the political spectrum (Bennett and Livingston, 2018). But the reality is that television remains not only the largest platform for news consumption, but uniquely capable of transcending polarised and fragmented online audiences.[24] Even within the online sphere, partisan news sites like the *Canary* and *Skwawkbox* still have only a tiny fraction of the reach commanded by 'legacy' news brands like the *Daily Mail* and *Guardian*. The latter also enjoy significant leverage over broadcast agendas, not least in the regular spots on prime-time news programmes dedicated to reviewing 'the papers'.

Falsehood

Given the marked skews in sourcing, the agenda built by sources attacking the Party on this issue (both from within and without) achieved near complete ascendancy. This agenda was founded on a dual premise: that the IHRA definition was broadly and internationally 'consensual' and that Labour had 'failed' to adopt it. Assertions by sources along these lines occupied the spotlight in virtually every article within the sample.

---

24. According to the UK's media regulator Ofcom, television is used by 79 per cent of adults for news compared to 64 per cent who use the internet and 40 per cent who use newspapers. See Ofcom (2018), *News Consumption in the UK: 2018*. Available from: www.ofcom.org.uk/__data/assets/pdf_file/0024/116529/news-consumption-2018.pdf, accessed 1 June 2019.

But the consequence was not just that the coverage leaned in favour of a particular point of view, but that the ascendant narrative was based on a fundamentally false premise. As we have already glimpsed, the IHRA definition did not have consensual support by any measure. Prevailing academic and legal opinion had been strongly critical of the definition since its earliest formulation.[25] In the UK, as we have seen, the definition was also opposed by a number of Jewish groups as well as other ethnic minorities, and had been publicly rejected by a number of institutions, including the School of Oriental and African Studies.[26]

As for UK local authorities, by July 2018 less than a third had formally adopted the definition (in spite of a call for them to do so from central government in 2016) and of these, at least two had chosen not to include any of the illustrative examples appended to the definition, meaning that their adoption was significantly more restrictive than what was proposed by Labour (Schlosberg and Laker, 2018).

The degree of consensus surrounding the IHRA definition formed the crux of the controversy and evidence of widespread *dissensus* was overwhelming. Accordingly, assertions that the definition was 'widely', 'broadly' or 'internationally' accepted were clearly contentious. Where these claims were made by journalists or sources without any qualification or

---

25. D. Feldman (2016), 'Will Britain's new definition of antisemitism help Jewish people? I'm sceptical', *Guardian* [online], 28 December. Available from: www.theguardian.com/commentisfree/2016/dec/28/britain-definition-antisemitism-british-jews-jewish-people, accessed 1 June 2019.

26. S. Oryszczuk (2017), 'SOAS director rejects new "contentious" antisemitism definition', *Jewish News* [online], 13 March. Available from: http://jewishnews.timesofisrael.com/soas-director-rejects-new-contentious-anti-semitism-definition/, accessed 1 June 2019.

challenge, they were considered (for the purposes of this research) to be examples of misleading reportage.

On the other hand, statements that amounted to assertions of fact or statistical claims about the degree to which the definition was supported included absolute quantifiers such as 'universally supported', 'unanimous' and 'the global definition'. Some included numerical values especially regarding the number of countries that had adopted the definition, including 31, 42 and in more than one instance, 'every country in the world'. Where these sorts of statements surfaced in news discourse without any challenge or counter-view, they were considered examples of inaccurate reporting.

It's important to highlight the distinction here between news reports and comment pieces. Clearly, we would not consider the latter to be 'misleading' if they featured unchallenged opinion, however questionable or contestable. Accordingly, statements alluding to relevant consent (e.g. 'widely', 'broadly', 'internationally') were discounted from the analysis of comment pieces. But professional news values and standard editorial codes of conduct dictate that commentary and opinion editorials are not immune to judgements of accuracy. Editors are therefore responsible for subjecting any statements of fact or statistical claims in such pieces to the same checks and balances for *accuracy* as they would for standard news reports.

Adopting this framework for the sample as a whole, the research uncovered a total of 28 examples of inaccurate reporting and 27 instances of misleading coverage. In practice, this reflected a conventional wisdom in mainstream journalism that the IHRA definition was widely or universally supported principally amongst the international community, the Jewish community and UK public bodies. Stock phrasing in this respect surfaced repeatedly in news discourse. For instance, Sky News television anchors tended to describe the IHRA definition as 'widely accepted':

> The widely accepted definition[27]

> The widely accepted definition put forward by the IHRA[28]

> The IHRA's widely accepted definition[29]

Others went further, with repeated references in both headlines and news copy to the 'global definition of anti-semitism'[30] or 'the globally recognised definition'.[31]

Jonathan Freedland, writing in his *Guardian* column, referred to the 'near universally accepted' definition of anti-semitism,[32] while one of the title's headline news reports on the issue featured a quote referring to 'this universal definition' without any mention of groups or prominent figures who had opposed it.[33]

---

27. *Sunrise*, Sky News, 30 July 2018.
28. *Sunrise*, 13 August 2018.
29. *Sunrise*, Sky News, 4 September 2018.
30. C. Hope (2018), 'Labour Party's biggest union backers aim to force Jeremy Corbyn into global definition of antisemitism', *Daily Telegraph* [online], 11 August. Available from: www.telegraph.co.uk/news/2018/08/11/labour-partys-biggest-union-backers-aim-force-jeremy-corbyn/, accessed 1 June 2019.
31. M. Smith (2018), 'Union boss Len McCluskey calls on Labour to adopt full antisemitism definition', *Daily Mirror* [online], 16 August. Available from: www.mirror.co.uk/news/politics/union-boss-len-mccluskey-calls-13092188, accessed 1 June 2019.
32. Freedland, 'Yes, Jews are angry'.
33. J. Elgot (2018), 'Labour Jewish affiliate in row with party over antisemitism code', *Guardian* [online], 11 July. Available from: www.theguardian.com/world/2018/jul/11/labour-jewish-affiliate-in-row-with-party-over-anti-semitism-code, accessed 1 June 2019.

Perhaps not surprisingly, the *Sun* produced some of the most striking falsehoods with reports asserting that Labour were 'the first to refuse to accept' the definition[34] and that it had been 'accepted by every local authority'.[35] Columns and comment pieces were especially liable to produce random falsehoods including one in the *Daily Mail* which claimed the definition had been 'accepted around the world by organisations such as the United Nations'.[36]

But it was BBC television which performed the worst in this respect, with anchors and presenters repeatedly asserting the universal quality of the definition:

> The definition accepted by more or less every country in the world[37]

> It isn't just adopted by Jewish groups it's adopted by pretty much everybody[38]

---

34. M. Dathan (2018), 'CORBYN RACE RULE SLAMMED Labour leader Jeremy Corbyn rapped over his party's new definition of anti-semitism', *Sun* [online], 7 July. Available from: www.thesun.co.uk/news/6717937/jeremy-corbyn-anti-semitism-definition-blast/, accessed 1 June 2019.
35. S. Hawkes (2018), 'LABOUR RACE ROW Labour MPs demand Corbyn ditch rules on anti-Semitism which "let bigots off scot-free" as dozens of rabbis slam party over its Jewish problem', *Sun* [online], 16 July. Available from: www.thesun.co.uk/news/6795469/labour-mps-demand-corbyn-ditch-rules-on-anti-semitism-which-let-bigots-off-scot-free-as-dozens-of-rabbis-slam-party-over-its-jewish-problem/, accessed 1 June 2019.
36. N. Pearlman (2018), '"How sickening that, as a British Jew, I'm now being told to 'go home' – and it's Corbyn who must take the blame": One mother reveals her sickening experience of the rise in anti-Semitism on our street', *Daily Mail* [online], 4 September. Available from: www.dailymail.co.uk/news/article-6131925/How-sickening-British-Jew-Im-told-home.html, accessed 1 June 2019.
37. *Victoria Derbyshire*, BBC One, 4 September 2018.
38. *Daily Politics*, BBC One, 19 July 2018.

> why wouldn't you do what everyone else does, what's different about Labour?[39]

Sources were also given free rein to espouse the myth of consensus surrounding the definition. In a clip from an earlier radio interview shown on BBC One's *Victoria Derbyshire* show, Margaret Hodge MP spoke of 'the universally used definition of antisemitism which everybody else had adopted, every other institution'.[40]

Accountability failure

Why did professional journalists allow and amplify this flagrant mischaracterisation of the controversy? It is hard to accept that they were simply not aware of the contesting views and voices on the IHRA definition. One explanation offered in off-the-record responses to the research is that there was confusion over whether or not the 31 member countries of the IHRA had themselves adopted the definition by default. But this hardly seems an adequate justification even for the subset of false claims in which reference was made to adoption by '31 countries'. In September 2016, the BBC was forced to acknowledge – albeit buried on its 'corrections and clarifications' web page – the following essential facts in relation to this pivotal issue:

> In this edition of [the Today Programme] it was stated that the IHRA definition of antisemitism had 'been accepted by almost every country in the world'. In fact, 31 member countries of the International Holocaust Remembrance Alliance (IHRA) supported the adoption of a non-legally

39. *Daily Politics*, BBC One, 18 July 2018.
40. *Victoria Derbyshire*, BBC One, 23 July 2018.

> binding Working Definition of Antisemitism to guide the organisation in its work on 26 May 2016.
>
> To date, according to the IHRA, the working definition has been adopted and endorsed by the following governments and bodies: The United Kingdom (12 December 2016), Israel (22 January 2017), Austria (25 April 2017) Scotland (27 April 2017), Romania (25 May 2017), City of London (8 February 2017), Germany (20 September 2017), Bulgaria (18 October 2017), Lithuania (24 January 2018), and the former Yugoslav Republic of Macedonia (6 March 2018).[41]

These facts were not hard to come by. Indeed, the IHRA had already published a fact sheet in March 2018 confirming and clarifying that just eight countries had adopted the definition to date.[42] But even if we were to accept that reporting failures were the result of a common misunderstanding, this begs the even more important question of what was done to correct the errors. The BBC's published 'correction' as quoted above was wholly inadequate even by the standards of press self-regulation. Indeed, guidance published by the Independent Press Standards Organisation (which regulates the majority of UK national newspapers) places a strong emphasis on 'due prominence' in respect of corrections and remedies.[43] The BBC's

41. E. Apple (2018), 'The BBC admits that John Humphrys got a crucial fact wrong in the antisemitism debate', The *Canary*, 21 September. Available from: www.thecanary.co/uk/2018/09/21/the-bbc-admits-that-john-humphrys-got-a-crucial-fact-wrong-in-the-anti-semitism-debate-2/, accessed 1 June 2019.

42. The International Holocaust Remembrance Alliance (2018), *Fact Sheet: Working Definition of Antisemitism*, 16 March. Available from: www.holocaustremembrance.com/sites/default/files/inline-files/Fcat%20Sheet%20Working%20Definition%20of%20Antisemitism_1.pdf, accessed 1 June 2019.

43. Independent Press Standards Organisation, *Guidance for Jour-*

online published correction would not have reached even a tiny fraction of the audience commanded by Radio 4's flagship Today Programme, where the original error was made. When the Media Reform Coalition published evidence of similar inaccurate statements made by television news anchors and presenters, the BBC failed to respond to media inquiries.[44]

This 'silence' by mainstream media outlets in response to the research findings was partly reflected in the complete absence of any editorial coverage.[45] This was in spite of it attracting considerable attention on social media platforms, in the progressive online press, and from senior academics and public figures around the world.[46] But perhaps more serious was the improper and inadequate response to formal complaints. This was notably the case with the *Guardian* which, like the BBC, is one of the most trusted news sources in the UK.[47] Yet persistent efforts to engage constructively with editorial

---

nalists: Due Prominence. Available from: www.ipso.co.uk/media/1486/promience_v8.pdf, accessed 1 June 2019.

44. F. Lockley (2018), 'Damning evidence of "misleading", "distorted" and "inaccurate" reporting on the Labour antisemitism row', *The Canary*, 28 September. Available from: www.thecanary.co/uk/2018/09/28/damning-evidence-of-misleading-distorted-and-inaccurate-reporting-on-the-labour-antisemitism-row-2/, accessed 1 June 2019.

45. Media Lens (2018), 'Blanket silence: Corporate media ignore new report exposing distorted and misleading coverage of Corbyn', 3 October. Available from: www.medialens.org/index.php/alerts/alert-archive/2018/883-blanket-silence-corporate-media-ignore-new-report-exposing-distorted-and-misleading-coverage-of-corbyn.html, accessed 1 June 2019.

46. N. Chomsy, B. Eno, F. Martinez et al. (2018), 'Flawed reporting on antisemitism in the Labour Party', *Guardian* letters, 30 September. Available from: www.theguardian.com/politics/2018/sep/30/flawed-reporting-on-antisemitism-claims-against-the-labour-party, accessed 1 June 2019.

47. Ofcom, *News Consumption in the UK: 2018.*

and public affairs staff did not bear any fruit.[48] Furthermore, a protracted formal complaints process resulted in a blanket dismissal of the research by the *Guardian*'s 'Reader's Editor'.

Conclusion

Underlying the evidence presented here was a persistent subversion of professional news norms. There were three in particular.

First, we have seen how the journalistic convention of giving voice to contesting sources did not produce any measure of balanced reporting in the controversy surrounding the IHRA definition. To reiterate, this is not a question of balance in an equal sense. On the surface at least, the story centred on prominent voices in a minority community accusing a major political party of harbouring racism directed towards them, and supported by many high-profile MPs within that party. In such circumstances we would expect journalists to take these concerns seriously, view them as inherently newsworthy, and not necessarily afford equal time and attention to contesting views. But we would at least expect that prominent sources challenging the views of right wing Labour MPs and mainstream Jewish groups be given some degree of a hearing. In large swathes of the mainstream coverage, their voices were entirely absent.

Second, where contesting sources *were* featured in broadcast news coverage there was a marked distinction in the nature of questioning directed towards them. In particular, Labour MPs adopting relatively moderate positions

48. Media Reform Coalition (8 November 2018), An open letter to the Guardian's Reader's Editor. Available from: www.mediareform.org.uk/blog/an-open-letter-to-the-guardian-readers-editor, accessed 1 June 2019.

were subjected to pointed and aggressive questioning by anchors and presenters. On the other hand, those Labour MPs attacking the leadership over this issue – in several cases using extreme language – were paradoxically treated on a number of occasions as being under attack from the Party's 'high command'.

Third, and above all, mainstream coverage of the controversy surrounding the IHRA definition all but entirely eschewed widespread criticism of that definition, and routinely characterised it as consensual and unanimous. In this way, mainstream news discourse effectively established a 'regime of truth' predicated on a demonstrably false assumption: that there was nothing controversial about the IHRA definition itself, but everything controversial about Labour's attempts to deal with it.

The problem was especially pronounced on television where two thirds of the news segments sampled revealed at least one inaccuracy or substantive distortion. This raises particular concerns since television news programmes typically reach audiences that dwarf their online counterparts and rivals, let alone the considerably smaller reach of partisan news sites like the *Canary* and *Skwawkbox*. They are also likely to include audiences who may have relatively little prior knowledge or understanding of the issue and may therefore be more vulnerable to the effects of misreporting and misrepresentation.

It is not clear why television performed so badly in this respect. It is conceivable that some of the additional reporting failures were a function of the relatively constricted news space as well as the spontaneity of live television. But the analysis also suggests that inaccuracies were intimately linked to skews in sourcing: the failure to adequately challenge or counter particular source agendas resulted in journalists accepting certain maxims and claims uncritically and, in many cases, repeating them without qualification. A perceived authority of sources attacking the Party and leadership over this issue may go some way to explaining why their claims were not identified as contentious and not duly checked for veracity.

All this matters because such controversies bring into sharp relief the news media's role and responsibilities in nurturing inclusive public debate and contributing to an informed citizenry. In this case the definition controversy, as we have seen in earlier chapters, had a direct bearing on public debate about Palestinian rights.

It also matters because the misreporting of antisemitism risks normalising or distracting attention from certain forms of antisemitic discourse. Distortions may also provoke counter-outrage that may be misdirected at Jews on either the left or right of the political spectrum. It is notable in this respect that in 2016, a *Daily Mail* columnist who has been outspoken on this issue described one Corbyn supporter as a 'useful Jewish idiot';[49] while in 2018, the UK Prime Minister's warm congratulatory words offered to her Malaysian counterpart – a leader who has openly described himself as an 'antisemite' – received virtually no attention at all in mainstream news, despite antisemitism being such a salient issue on the news agenda at the time.[50]

In sum, although our findings do not tell us a great deal about their causes, we can say with some certainty that there have been prevalent errors, omissions and skews in the mainstream coverage of this issue. Furthermore, this was no anomaly – almost all of the problems observed in both the

49. D. Hodges (2016), Twitter, 22 August. Available from: https://twitter.com/AudreyAurus1/status/1021834371001708544, accessed 1 June 2019.

50. T. May (2018), Twitter, 11 May. Available from: https://twitter.com/10DowningStreet/status/994968670609780737, accessed 1 June 2019.

framing and sourcing of stories were in favour of a particular recurrent narrative: that the Labour Party has been or is being lost to extremists, racists and the 'hard left'. During the summer of 2018, this controversy reached fever pitch amid claims that the Party had become 'institutionally racist' under the leadership of Jeremy Corbyn, and that the prospect of a Corbyn-led government posed an 'existential threat' to Jewish life in Britain.

5
Weapons in the Labour Antisemitism Wars?
The IHRA Working Definition and the Accusation of 'Institutional Antisemitism'

*Antony Lerman**

Introduction

We can and must make every effort to take antisemitism out of politics. But we'll never take the politics out of antisemitism.

While the first statement – which applies to any and all forms of racism – must be a priority for an avowedly anti-racist Party like Labour, putting it into practice does not immunise the Party, or any party for that matter, against the complicated, troubling and challenging politics of antisemitism: the difficulties of tackling it as a recurring political problem and the politicisation of the problem to serve partisan political ends. Both manifestations of politics in antisemitism have been with us at least since the end of the nineteenth century, but their concatenation in one political party since Jeremy Corbyn was elected leader of Labour in 2015 is possibly unique.

In this chapter I examine two closely interrelated and particularly significant manifestations of the criticism levelled at Labour for its handling of its perceived problem of anti-

* This chapter is based on three articles written for openDemocracy in 2018 and 2019.

semitism with a view to drawing some conclusions about their consequences for the Party. First, the eventual adoption of the International Holocaust Remembrance Alliance's (IHRA) 'working definition'[1] of antisemitism, a move Labour was put under severe pressure to take in mid-2018. Second, charges levelled against Labour for institutional antisemitism, which have been formalised in the shape of an investigation launched by the Equality and Human Rights Commission (EHRC) on 28 May 2019 (Sky News, 28 May 2019) to determine whether 'the Party unlawfully discriminated against, harassed or victimised people because they are Jewish'. This followed representations made to the EHRC by the Jewish Labour Movement (JLM) and the Campaign Against Antisemitism (CAA). Both cases have the potential to create more difficulties for Labour going forward, with the second perhaps more serious since legal sanctions may be imposed on the Party. What might be done to mitigate further damage?

Both are connected to the question of how antisemitism today should be defined and understood. On one level this has been about conflicting views of formal definitions. On another level it's a reflection of a more visceral, experiential reality: the widespread public confusion about what comprises antisemitism today. A confusion also apparent in the Labour Party's response to the antisemitism 'crisis'.

It's highly relevant that in both of these cases the underlying approach taken by critics of Corbyn and the Party to how antisemitism today should be defined and understood was heavily influenced by referencing what the report of the Macpherson Inquiry into the conduct of the police in investigating the 22 April 1993 killing of the black teenager Stephen Lawrence, published on 24 February 1999, was alleged to have

1. Subsequent references to the IHRA 'working definition' will simply read: IHRA definition.

said about defining racist incidents and institutional racism. Even though antisemitism does not figure directly in Judge William Macpherson's Report, he was often and has continued to be cited in support of the range of antisemitism accusations made against Labour. At the very least, this has been of doubtful value, obscuring rather than aiding understanding. Even more troubling, it could be argued that referencing this landmark report in the history of striking at the very roots of racism in the UK was not in the spirit of the need to address all forms of racism in the Party, but rather an appropriation of, at best, misunderstood concepts for the purposes of validating the exceptionalism of anti-Jewish racism.

Part I: The International Holocaust Remembrance Alliance working definition of antisemitism: a triumph of symbolism over substance

The demise of Labour's new code of conduct on antisemitism

The Labour Party released the text of the National Executive Committee's (NEC) new code of conduct on antisemitism on 5 July (*Jewish Chronicle*, 5 July 2018). This sought to implement the June 2016 Chakrabarti Report's recommendations (Report, 30 June 2016), fulfil commitments made by Jeremy Corbyn to speed up disciplinary procedures after meeting representatives of Jewish establishment organisations in April 2018, to deal more robustly and efficiently with alleged expressions of antisemitism by Party members and 'to produce a practical code of conduct that a political Party can apply in disciplinary cases' (*Guardian*, 11 July 2018). After the battering Labour received over the issue of antisemitism in the Party since Corbyn was elected leader and the fact that nothing the Party had done had succeeded in fully placating its critics, it seems unlikely that the new general secretary, Jennie Formby and her officials expected anything approximating to universal approbation. But the barrage of outrage, vilification and accusations of bad faith and betrayal that greeted the new code was extraordinary. It had barely seen the light of day before it was being condemned in the harshest terms by all and sundry. JLM, the official Jewish affiliate to the Party, initially appeared positively disposed towards the new rules (see Schlosberg, this volume) but later complained that they had been misled by the NEC and were never properly consulted over the new code.

In some ways it was of little consequence whether or not there was anything in the slightest controversial in the new text. Numerous politicians, media commentators, Jewish organisations and anti-antisemitism groups were by now permanently primed to respond to each and every moment of antisemitism 'news' relating to the Labour Party.

Two assertions were fundamental to the arguments of those attempting to trash the NEC's new code. First, that the NEC rejected the IHRA definition and second, that the NEC code contravened what was said to be the 'Macpherson principle' giving Jews the exclusive right to determine for themselves what antisemitism is.

Putting the record straight on these two assertions is quite straightforward. In both cases the evidence is easy to marshal. But what needs further explanation is the reverence in which the IHRA definition seemed to be held, as if it were holy writ, untouchable and possessing almost magical powers. In fact, it came into existence in highly controversial circumstances and the way it was adopted by the IHRA remains shrouded in mystery. First, I present the working definition; second, I deal with the two critical assertions; finally, I explain the origins of, and politics behind, the production and adoption of the IHRA's definition.

What is the IHRA working definition of antisemitism?

The IHRA began life as the Task Force for International Cooperation on Holocaust Education, Remembrance and Research (ITF), which was created by the Stockholm International Forum on the Holocaust (SIF) in 2000. It was institutionalised permanently as the IHRA in 2012. Of its 31 members, four are not European. Two of the remaining 27 are not full members.

The IHRA adopted its definition at the organisation's plenary meeting in Bucharest on 26 May 2016. The definition is contained in a single document divided into two parts: a box within which is a heading, 'non-legally binding working definition of antisemitism', followed by 38 words. All this text is in bold type.

> **Antisemitism is a certain perception of Jews, which may be expressed as hatred toward Jews. Rhetorical and physical manifestations of antisemitism are directed toward Jewish or non-Jewish individuals and/or their property, toward Jewish community institutions and religious facilities.**

This definition is accompanied by additional text in roman type running to 468 words, prefaced by the following sentence:

> To guide IHRA in its work, the following examples may serve as illustrations:

After which comes this paragraph:

> Manifestations might include the targeting of the state of Israel, conceived as a Jewish collectivity. However, criticism

> of Israel similar to that levelled against any other country cannot be regarded as antisemitic. Antisemitism frequently charges Jews with conspiring to harm humanity, and it is often used to blame Jews for 'why things go wrong.' It is expressed in speech, writing, visual forms and action, and employs sinister stereotypes and negative character traits.

There then follows another prefacing sentence:

> Contemporary examples of antisemitism in public life, the media, schools, the workplace, and in the religious sphere could, taking into account the overall context, include, but are not limited to ...

which is followed by eleven such examples, seven of which relate to Israel and/or Zionism.

Did the NEC 'reject' the IHRA's definition?

On whether the NEC rejected the IHRA's definition, the code could not have been clearer. Clause (or paragraph) 5 unequivocally stated:

> To assist in understanding what constitutes antisemitism, the NEC has endorsed the definition produced by the International Holocaust Remembrance Alliance (IHRA) in 2016.

Moreover, it reproduced the 38-word text of the definition in full.

Some critics spoke of 'Labour's refusal to adopt antisemitism definition *in full*' or that 'the code *does not fully adopt*' (*Jewish Chronicle*, 2018, emphases added) the IHRA definition. So given that the code *did* endorse the 38-word definition in full, what can it then mean to claim that the NEC *did not* adopt the definition 'in full'?

By 'full', critics were referring to the additional text, principally the eleven examples, seven of which relate to Israel and/or Zionism. And while the NEC code was content with seven of them, omitting four, in discussing these four it endorsed their content and strengthened their language with the aim of protecting freedom of speech on Israel-Palestine and simplifying the process for Labour officials conducting disciplinary hearings reaching judgements as to whether or not the code had been breached. It also added two more examples. In defending these changes for a 17 July openDemocracy article, Dr Brian Klug remarked:

> I have not yet come across a critic of the NEC Code – I mean a critic who places a premium on combating antisemitism – who acknowledges [the points that significantly enhance the IHRA text], let alone welcomes them as the enhancements that they are. They are passed over in silence, as if the IHRA document were a sacred text whose words may not be tampered with – not even if the text can be improved. (Klug, 17 July 2018)

Was it therefore true to say that the IHRA definition had not been fully adopted? The vast majority of people reading this document and all the comment surrounding it are not in a position to divine any undisclosed motivations of those who devised and drafted it. So we have to begin by taking the entire document at face value. And as my extracts from the text above show, it could not be clearer as to what is and what is not part of the definition. So Community Security Trust's (CST) Gardner is simply wrong when he claims that 'the definition is a single document, but Labour treats it as having two parts'. It has two parts. Period.

Where the language of the definition is definitive – it could hardly qualify as a definition if it wasn't – though also problematic, the language of the additional text providing examples is more circumspect, more conditional, using phrases such as: 'might include', 'could include', 'taking into account the overall context', 'not limited to'. In other words, the manifestations or examples of antisemitism given may or may *not* qualify as antisemitic, and they do not constitute an exclusive list. There may be more, perhaps many more, categories. These are very important caveats, but they are hardly the stuff of a definition.

It seems reasonable to assume that had the IHRA wanted the examples to be *formally* part of the definition, it would have said so in May 2016. Nevertheless, the fact that only these eleven examples of possibly antisemitic expressions are listed also suggests that the IHRA wanted them to be *seen* as antisemitic, but the body seems to have been canny enough to understand that statements, the meaning of which depend on the 'overall context' in which they appear, can hardly be part of a definition that seeks to be definitive. So the document containing the working definition is a single entity, but it is unequivocally separated into two parts: definition and supporting, conditional examples.

Is there a 'Macpherson principle'?

> Labour's decision means a break from the Macpherson standard, which held that a minority was best placed to define prejudice against it. (Freedland tweet, 5 July 2019)

The second assertion about the NEC code was also based on an accusation of Labour's alleged rejectionism: critics claimed that the NEC had rejected the alleged universally accepted Macpherson definition of racism, the notion of the absolute right of a minority to define for itself what constitutes prejudice against it. 'It is for Jews to determine for themselves what antisemitism is', stated Board of Deputies of British Jews (BoD) President Marie van der Zyl and Jewish Leadership Council (JLC) Chair Jonathan Goldstein on 5 July (BoD, 5 July 2018). But critics went further. In Nick Cohen's words, it was 'the Party's decision to make Jews the only ethnic minority Labour denies the right to define the racism they face' (Cohen, 7 July 2018).

In a letter sent to Jennie Formby on 10 July, the professional heads of the CST, the BoD and the JLC stated: 'It is for the Jewish community to decide what does and what does not constitute racism towards us, just as any other group has the right to do' (JLC, 10 July 2018). 'This attempt at defining prejudice on behalf of the Jewish community in the face of our clear advice constitutes a significant departure from established anti-racist [principles] that will worry all minorities'. On 17 July the JLM presented to the Party legal advice claiming that Labour may have breached the Equalities Act by ignoring the so-called Macpherson principle in its new NEC code of conduct on antisemitism (*Guardian*, 16 July 2018).

The problem with this apparent 'iron rule' is that Macpherson produced no such definition. And yet it continues to be made indignantly and insistently by Jewish groups no matter how often it is clearly proven to be a misreading of the 1999 report.

As I explained in a piece for openDemocracy in June 2011 (Lerman, June 2011), in connection with accusations levelled at the time against the Universities and Colleges Union (UCU), that by rejecting the European Union Monitoring Centre on Racism and Xenophobia's (EUMC) 'working definition of antisemitism' (which I will refer to in greater detail below) they were denying Jews the Macpherson-conferred right to define it for themselves, the only definition of racism Macpherson produced was of institutional racism. However, he did also define a racist *incident*, describing it as 'any incident which is perceived to be racist by the victim or any other person'. But this was a specific instruction to the police that the victim's perception of the motive for an attack is what the police must record as the motive for the attack. The intention of providing this definition was to change police culture prevailing at the time, which systematically failed to take heed of the experience of victims. But there is nothing in the report suggesting a move from a specific and very important rule about recording the victim's perception of what occurred to a general rule that only the victim can define the racism they experience.

That this elision is highly problematic was in fact recognised by the CST. Its *Antisemitic Discourse Report 2009* states:

> The Stephen Lawrence Inquiry definition of a racist incident has significantly influenced societal interpretations of what does and does not constitute racism, with the victim's perception assuming paramount importance. CST, however, ultimately defines incidents against Jews as being antisemitic only where it can be *objectively shown* to be the case [emphasis added], and this may not always match the victim's perception as called for by the Lawrence Inquiry. CST takes a similar approach to the highly complex issue of antisemitic discourse, and notes the multiplicity of opinions within and beyond the Jewish community concerning this often controversial subject. (ADR, 2009: 12)

This is of course perfectly logical, because if an incident results in a prosecution being brought against the alleged perpetrator, judges and juries listen to the evidence and make objective judgements as required by the law of the land. They do not say: 'Well, if the victim says the attacker was motivated by antisemitism, that's all the evidence needed to convict.'

Professor David Feldman, director of the highly respected Pears Institute for the Study of Antisemitism, Birkbeck University of London, in a 22-page sub-report for the Parliamentary Committee Against Antisemitism published in 2015, concurred: 'Macpherson's report has been misinterpreted and misapplied ... In short a definition [of antisemitism] which takes Jews' feelings and perceptions as its starting point and which looks to the Macpherson report for authority is built on weak foundations' (Feldman, 2015). Feldman continues:

> More fundamentally, if we rest our definitions of racism on the perceptions of minority groups then we open the way to conceptual and political chaos. For if the identification of racism becomes a matter of subjective judgment only, then we have no authority other than the perception of a minority or victim group with which to counter the contrary subjective opinions of perpetrators who deny they are racists. Without an anti-racist principle which can be applied generally we are left in a chaotic situation in which one subjective point of view faces another. (p. 7)

Note the measured tone of the CST's statement in 2009 and compare it with this June 2019 damning indictment from the CST's Gardner: 'IHRA rejection is now fundamental to [Labour's culture]. It represents and repeats the same far left ideological, emotional and systematic rejection of our concerns that we have faced for decades.' It is what moved *Jewish Chronicle* editor Stephen Pollard to accuse Labour of 'institutional antisemitism' (Pollard, 5 July 2018) – a tone echoed also in BoD and JLC statements. Pollard's contributions to ratcheting up this rhetoric are legion. Musing on who 'would be on the shortlist of the least suitable people to draw up a definition of antisemitism', Pollard implies that the Labour Party would not be much better than the Nazis.

Is reverence for the IHRA definition justified? Backstory and context

It would be naive in the extreme to think that this kind of politicisation of antisemitism, which was engulfing Labour and looking to some like an orgy of self-destruction, was a new phenomenon. I first started writing about the use and abuse of antisemitism in Jewish communal politics back in 1985 and was, to say the least, not thanked by official communal bodies for doing so. But even after almost 40 years engagement in studying contemporary antisemitism, it was clear to me that this level of politicisation, going well beyond the organised Jewish community, was unprecedented in its reach and ferocity.

In the last three decades of the twentieth century, politicisation mostly expressed itself in the form of differences in the organised Jewish community over how to deal with the problem of antisemitism on the political level and whether it should be given minimum publicity or openly discussed, and no efforts made to suppress news about desecration of cemeteries and other antisemitic attacks – the default position of the BoD for many years, which feared that publicising such incidents would make matters worse.

There was hardly any political controversy over how antisemitism should be defined. A broad consensus understanding of what it was prevailed – in the organised Jewish community, among mainstream political parties, across countries in the west. Once that consensus had clearly broken down by the first years of the twenty-first century, almost entirely over the issue of Israel-Palestine and how far anti-Israel rhetoric can be defined as antisemitism – and dubbed the 'new antisemitism' – the politicisation of antisemitism was taken to another level. Until that time, Israeli governments had not always made engagement with the problem of antisemitism for diaspora Jews a top priority. Zionism and the establishment of the state were all about overcoming antisemitism. To become too involved, certainly publicly, in this diaspora problem would have meant admitting that, in one of its key aims, Zionism failed. But when Israel was placed at the centre of the antisemitism issue, Israeli state policy changed. Leading the Jewish fight against antisemitism, under the banner of promoting the notion of the 'new antisemitism', became a core strategic task of government. And the IHRA definition has become a key weapon in that effort.

Contrary to the narrative spread by the IHRA itself and some of the more enthusiastic members of country delegations to the organisation, the working definition was not something freshly minted in 2016. It is a marginally revamped version of the working definition of antisemitism developed in 2004 in controversial circumstances under the auspices of the now defunct EUMC based in Vienna and published on its website on 28 January 2005 (EUMC wd, 2005). The American Jewish Committee's (AJC) International Affairs Director, Rabbi Andrew Baker, persuaded the EUMC Director Beate Winkler to call a meeting of representatives of Jewish groups to discuss framing a new antisemitism definition as a way of extricating the EUMC from a damaging public controversy over a suppressed, and then leaked, antisemitism report, produced in 2002 by the Centre for Research on Antisemitism, Berlin Technical University, purporting to show that rising attacks on Jews in Europe were principally the responsibility of young Muslims. The AJC's antisemitism research head, Kenneth Stern, had already drafted such a new definition and it was this, subject to some small amendments made by a group comprising only Jewish representatives sympathetic to the notion of the 'new antisemitism', that surfaced as the EUMC working definition (Lerman, 2011). What marked Stern's draft definition as unique was his structured singling out of various examples of criticism of Israel and Zionism which he regarded as antisemitic.

The draft working definition was never subjected to proper scrutiny. On Stern's own admission, only five people signed off on the final text: Winkler, Stern, Baker, Mike Whine (from the CST, the defence body of the Jewish community) and Deidre Berger (head of the AJC's Berlin office).

However, it undoubtedly made an impact. For example, the US State Department, the Organization for Security and Co-operation in Europe (OSCE), the All-Party Parliamentary Inquiry into Antisemitism (2006), either used, cited or recommended adoption of the definition. Many referred to it erroneously as *the* EU definition. From the start, the definition and examples were deliberately conflated. The conditionality of the examples was described by Professor Dina Porat of Tel Aviv University, a key figure in the initial discussions about the draft, as 'a list of acts and statements that *are anti-Semitic*' (emphasis added).

But institutional and public reception was patchy, and as inappropriate attempts to use it to suppress freedom of speech became known, criticisms mounted. The EUMC began to make it clear that the working definition had 'no legal basis', 'did not necessarily reflect the official position of the EUMC' and was not adopted by it. It should be viewed as 'a work in progress', Winkler said, 'with a view to redrafting'.

When the Agency for Fundamental Rights (FRA) replaced the EUMC, it dropped the working definition, did not display it on its website, said that no public authority in the EU applied the document in any way and that the FRA had 'no legal competence to develop itself any such definitions'.

Despite this quite definitive abandonment of the EUMC working definition, which was never adopted as an official EU definition, it was never likely to disappear. The FRA did not go out of its way to publicise what it had done. News of its action only became public following enquiries made by researchers. It suited many Jewish groups, some international bodies, the Israeli government's institutions set up to combat antisemitism and some research and monitoring organisations to continue using the EUMC formulation. After all, 'new antisemitism theory', as it was becoming known, had a significant and growing following and the European institutional imprimatur was very useful in extending the definition's reach. But those who regarded the EUMC definition as deeply flawed were encouraged and made efforts to publicise the FRA's position. So the battle between proponents and opponents of 'new antisemitism theory' continued apace.

And the fact is that at the heart of the notion of the 'new antisemitism' is a simple and easily understood idea, one which had instinctive appeal to Zionist groups and supporters of Israel increasingly concerned about what they saw as ever more extreme attacks on the Jewish state. One of the earliest figures who conceptualised 'new antisemitism' and assiduously publicised and promoted the notion internationally at numerous conferences and international forums was Irwin Cotler, a Canadian human rights law professor who was justice minister in the 2003–06 Liberal government. He summed it up in 2010 in these words:

> In a word [*sic*], classical anti-Semitism is the discrimination against, denial of, or assault upon the rights of Jews to live as equal members of whatever society they inhabit. The new anti-Semitism involves the discrimination against, denial of, or assault upon the right of the Jewish people to live as an equal member of the family of nations, with Israel

> as the targeted 'collective Jew among the nations.' (Cotler, 9 November 2010)

From the outset, this notion was disputed, contested and criticised, but also found support among many, including individual academics, some antisemitism monitoring and research bodies and antisemitism research institutes (some of which were specifically created to develop research and analysis grounded in the 'new antisemitism' idea). But it brought most solace to Israel advocacy groups, Israel lobbying organisations and an Israeli government that was now convinced of the usefulness of using antisemitism as a defensive shield against external criticism of its actions. As Neve Gordon writes: 'The Israeli government needs the "new anti-Semitism" to justify its actions and to protect it from international and domestic condemnation. Anti-Semitism is effectively weaponized, not only to stifle speech ... but also to suppress a politics of liberation' (Gordon, 2018). And although the demise of the EUMC definition of antisemitism was a blow to those who had worked to develop it and promote it, the effort to promote the notion or theory of the 'new antisemitism' continued apace – and successfully.

However, one crucial consequence was to turn discussion and reasoned argument about the idea, which was just about still discernible in the first years of the twenty-first century, into an all-out verbal and rhetorical war over the nature of contemporary antisemitism. As I wrote in *The Nation*, it

> diluted the allegation of antisemitism. To warrant the charge, it is sufficient for someone to hold any view ranging from criticism of the policies of the current Israeli government to denial that Israel has the right to exist, without having to subscribe to any of the beliefs historians have traditionally regarded as constituting an anti-Semitic worldview. This

> is a fundamental redefinition of the term 'anti-Semitism' for political purposes, one consequence of which is that if almost everything is antisemitic, then nothing is. The word is rendered useless. (Lerman, 2010)

Or as Brian Klug put it: 'when anti-Semitism is everywhere, it is nowhere. And when every anti-Zionist is an anti-Semite, we no longer know how to recognize the real thing – the concept of anti-Semitism loses its significance' (Klug, 2004).

The promoters and supporters of the EUMC definition were never reconciled to it being set aside by the FRA. And in a climate of growing, murderous jihadi terrorism and perceived worsening antisemitism they found a sympathetic hearing among European political leaders. In tracing the path to the revamping and adoption of the definition by the IHRA, Ben White writes: 'At the Israeli-government convened GFCA [Global Forum for Combating Antisemitism] in Jerusalem in 2015, a working group recommended "that the Working Definition of Antisemitism be reintroduced into the international arena with the aim of giving it legal status"' (White, 2018). However, it's not immediately obvious why a body ostensibly dedicated to Holocaust remembrance should have been the chosen vehicle for the EUMC definition's rehabilitation.

The truth is that the almost exclusively European IHRA is not so international, not so exclusively focused on Holocaust remembrance and not at all above responding to political pressure. The AJC and the Simon Wiesenthal Centre (SWC) in Los Angeles worked assiduously behind the scenes to get the ITF institutionalised, with the express idea of using it as a vehicle to revive international promotion of the EUMC working definition. Acting for the AJC, once again, was Rabbi Baker. Acting for the SWC was its Director of Government Affairs, Mark Weizman, who, conveniently, also chaired the Antisemitism and Holocaust Committee of the IHRA. And it was through that committee that Weizman drove adoption by the IHRA of a slightly amended version of the EUMC definition. Some reports suggest that this was the work of two years of hard drafting. The Experts of the UK Delegation to the IHRA on the Working Definition of Antisemitism called the result 'a clear "gold-standard" definition of what contemporary antisemitism consists of'. Yet the IHRA text is so similar to the EUMC one as to be, on first glance, virtually indistinguishable – especially the actual 38-word definition which is indeed identical.

I've been informed that members of some country delegations felt that adoption of the working definition on 26 May 2016 was 'railroaded through'. The head of one of the state delegations to the IHRA participating in the Plenary, who wishes to remain anonymous, stated:

> The discussions, as I remember them, were quite intense and lengthy, both in the couloirs and in the plenary hall, until a decisive step was taken by the presidency, on the demand by some member states. Namely, the original draft text was cut into two, and only the first two-sentence part was to be the *working-definition to be adopted*, while the other part, the examples, remained what they were: *examples to serve as illustrations, to guide the IHRA in its work*. From then on, the plenary was able to move quickly on, and the non-legally binding working definition was unanimously adopted. The relevant press release of 26 May 2016 ... states it very clearly ... This is why I really do not quite understand the reason of the ongoing and apparently heated debate in the UK on adopting the definition (actually, rather, the illustrative examples) in full, without caveats nor amendments [emphases added].

As for what adoption meant: only 6 of 31 governments whose countries are members of IHRA have formally endorsed/adopted the definition, and it's not clear whether they adopted the examples or not.

However, we do know that (Gould, 2018):

- the UK government adopted the definition but not the list of examples;
- the LSE adopted the IHRA definition but clarified that it 'does not accept ... all the examples';
- the European Parliament adopted the definition without the examples in June 2017.

Deliberate obfuscation of what is and what is not the IHRA definition

The dilution of any sense that the definition of antisemitism has any boundaries was evident even in the way the first incarnation of the working definition by the EUMC was promoted and treated. Its advocates engaged in deliberate obfuscation as to what did or did not constitute the working definition. When accused of encouraging the chilling of free speech and endorsing the notion that anti-Zionism and antisemitism are one and the same – by including statements such as the 'state of Israel is a racist endeavour', 'denying the Jewish people their right to self-determination' and 'drawing comparisons of contemporary Israeli policy to that of the Nazis' as examples that could be antisemitic – protagonists would insist that the examples were not part of the definition and were a work in progress. But when Zionist and Israel advocacy groups, and 'new antisemitism' theorists treated the entire text as the definition, very little was done to disabuse them of this error. So as with the EUMC version, the same process has applied to the IHRA text – only more so.

One of the differences between EUMC and IHRA is the way the definitions are set out. As explained above, in the former, the 38-word working definition is distinguished from the rest of the text by being set in bold type. The same text in the IHRA definition is not only also in bold type, it's enclosed in a box which contains the longer part of a prefatory sentence that begins outside the box:

> On May 2016, the Plenary in Bucharest decided to: [in the box] **Adopt the following non-legally binding working definition of antisemitism.**

As we see from the Corbyn-Labour antisemitism affair, critics like John Mann MP, Louise Ellman MP, Dame Margaret Hodge, Gordon Brown, Chuka Umunna MP and more aggressively demanded that Labour adopt the entire text and often claimed that the entire text *was* the working definition. And when they proclaimed that the definition had universal acceptance, they further imply that the examples are an integral part of what was universally accepted. But given that there is *no* evidence of 'universal acceptance', there can hardly be evidence that the examples are folded into that.

Moreover, the administration of the IHRA itself confirmed unequivocally that the definition and the examples were separate things. Its permanent office in Berlin issued the following statement on 12 September 2017 (Gould, 2018): 'The working definition, like all IHRA decisions, is non-legally binding. The working definition is the text in the box.' This statement makes a nonsense of the statement issued by Experts of the UK Delegation to the IHRA on 7 August 2018 that 'Any "modified" version of the IHRA definition that does not include all of its 11 examples is no longer the IHRA definition' (UK IHRA Experts, 2018). How they were induced to make this untrue statement remains a mystery.

Analysis of the full text: deeply flawed and by definition, not a definition

The 38-word definition is vague and tells us very little. It's a linguistic mess. If antisemitism is a 'certain perception', what is that perception? If it's a 'certain' one, why not spell it out? We're barely five words into the definition and instead of clarity we get opacity. This antisemitism '*may be* expressed as hatred towards Jews', which means it also *may not*. So if it may not be expressed as hatred, how else might it be expressed? If the next sentence is designed to answer this question, it's surely incomplete and inadequate. 'Rhetorical' seems to imply that it's just for effect, for show, to make an impression. Surely it's an inappropriate word. Then to say that antisemitism is 'directed toward Jewish or non-Jewish individuals', you might as well just say 'everyone', but that doesn't seem to tell us anything of any use at all.

Professor Feldman criticised the definition's key passage, calling it 'bewilderingly imprecise' (Feldman, 2016). And this is what he said about the eleven examples:

> Seven deal with criticism of Israel. Some of the points are sensible, some are not. Crucially, there is a danger that the overall effect will place the onus on Israel's critics to demonstrate they are not antisemitic. The home affairs committee advised that the definition required qualification 'to ensure that freedom of speech is maintained in the context of discourse on Israel and Palestine'. It was ignored.

Four prominent and respected lawyers who have written opinions on the definition are also unimpressed. Hugh Tomlinson QC described it as 'unclear and confusing' and said it 'should be used with caution' (Tomlinson, 2017). In Sir Stephen Sedley's view, it 'fails the first test of any definition:

it is indefinite' (Sedley, 2017). Sir Geoffrey Bindman wrote: 'Unfortunately, the definition and the examples are poorly drafted [and] misleading' (Bindman, 2018). And Geoffrey Robertson concluded: 'It is imprecise, confusing and open to misinterpretation and even manipulation' (Robertson, 2018).

At first glance, the sentence introducing the examples is reassuring, since it establishes their conditionality: they 'could be' manifestations of antisemitism, 'taking into account the overall context'. Moreover, the list is not limited.

However, if they 'could be' antisemitic, they also 'could *not*'. But you could say that about any number of statements and sentiments. For example, why not include 'support for Zionism and the existence of the state of Israel', since leading Zionist thinkers, including Herzl, used antisemitic tropes to describe their diaspora Jewish opponents. And there have always been antisemitic advocates of Zionism, most well known perhaps being Lord Balfour, author of what became known as the 1917 Balfour Declaration. In 1904 he spoke of 'the undoubted evils that had fallen upon the country from an immigration that was largely Jewish'. Better that they have a homeland of their own than bring misfortune to Britain. Yet, if we look at the examples in the definition document in light of the intentions of the drafters, we see sleight of hand at play. In the same way as we are not discouraged to see the entire text as the working definition, we are invited to entertain only one possibility – that 'could be' means 'are'.

The whole idea of adding examples to a definition of antisemitism is suspect. If a definition needs clarification using such simplistically formulated examples, it's not a definition worth its salt. Certainly, the recording, analysis and interpretation of incidents, events, social media posts, statements by politicians, news programmes – of human activity in short – that is suspected of being antisemitic needs to be done, but that is the work of experts and not pre-prepared crib cards. Sometimes that work might involve legal examination, sometimes the writing of political essays, sometimes extended historical research and so on.

When there was a general consensus about what constituted antisemitism, there was never a need for a handy list of examples.

Legal dangers: chilling free speech and silencing Palestinian voices

Although the document categorically states that it is 'non-legally binding', the urge to make it so is very strong. In the US, where the equivalent of the IHRA definition is the US State Department definition – which, being partially based on the EUMC working definition, bears more than a passing resemblance to the IHRA text – a determined effort to give it legal force is underway at both state and federal level. The House Judiciary Committee has held hearings on the Antisemitism Awareness Act where witnesses presenting testimony have clashed with congressmen and with each other (JTA, 8 November 2017). At one of those hearings, the original author of the IHRA definition, Kenneth Stern, who in recent years has become a prominent critic of how the definition is being applied, warned against making it legally binding because he feared it would restrict freedom of speech.

In the UK, Dr Rebecca Gould, who has written the first thorough legal study of the adoption and implementation of the IHRA working definition (Gould, 2018), has argued that it has come to function as what she calls a 'quasi-law, in which capacity it exercises the de facto authority of the law, without having acquired legal legitimacy'. 'Adoption' of the IHRA document occurred in the form of a governmental press release, not through a process of democratic deliberation. Had the government sought 'legal ratification of adoption within a regulatory regime that would formally sanction Israel critical speech', this would have been a troubling development among scholars and activists concerned with safeguarding freedom of speech. This would surely have amounted to the establishment of an adjudicative standard, something Geoffrey Robertson refers to when he concludes that: 'The IHRA definition of antisemitism is not fit for any purpose that seeks to use it as an adjudicative standard.'

All of the legal experts quoted above either referred directly or indirectly to the government's obligation, and the obligation of all institutions, including universities and colleges, to abide by Article 10 of the European Convention on Human Rights, which protects freedom of speech. But, wrote Robertson, 'a particular problem with the IHRA definition is that it is likely in practice to chill free speech, by raising expectations of pro-Israeli groups that they can successfully object to legitimate criticism of their country and correspondingly arouse fears in NGOs and student bodies that they will have events banned or else have to incur considerable expense to protect themselves by legal action' (Jewish Voice for Labour, 2018).

Hugh Tomlinson said Article 10

> does not permit the prohibition or sanctioning of speech unless it can be seen as a direct or indirect call for or justification of violence, hatred or intolerance. The fact that speech is offensive to a particular group is not, of itself, a proper ground for prohibition or sanction. The IHRA Definition should not be adopted without careful additional guidance on these issues. (Tomlinson, 2017)

Geoffrey Bindman argued that the definition and examples 'in practice have [already] led to the suppression of legitimate debate and freedom of expression' (*Guardian*, 27 July 2018).

And Gould provided evidence that the IHRA definition played a role in successfully getting Israeli Apartheid Week events at Manchester University and the University of Central Lancashire re-titled and cancelled, and an ultimately unsuccessful role in a complaint of antisemitism against the author herself in connection with an article she had written. Sedley described an event in 2013, when a replica of Israel's separation wall was erected in the churchyard of St James, Piccadilly. The *Spectator* denounced it as an 'anti-Israeli hate-festival', 'a description', Sedley (2017) suggests, 'now capable of coming within the IHRA's "working definition" of anti-Semitism. In such ways the official adoption of the definition, while not a source of law, gives respectability and encouragement to forms of intolerance which are themselves contrary to law.'

Especially troubling is the impact NEC adoption of the full IHRA definition and examples is very likely to be having on Palestinian members of the Labour Party and on Palestinian voices more widely. There is a clear danger that adopting IHRA will further marginalise public discussion of the Palestinian experience of Zionism and the discriminatory policies of the Israeli state, and suppress Palestinian voices even more than they are now. This may not be a result of Palestinians in the Party, or non-members invited to be on platforms at local meetings and conferences, being accused of contravening IHRA guidelines by claiming, for example, that Israel is a racist state – even though they should be fully entitled to describe their personal experiences of dispossession in this manner and Labour has explicitly confirmed that such a statement does not fall foul of the IHRA definition (see Miller, this volume) – but rather a result of self-censorship.

This problem is starkly highlighted in a statement from Palestinian unions, NGOs and movement organisations, calling on Labour to reject the 'biased IHRA definition that stifles advocacy for Palestinian rights', released on 28 August 2018 and published on openDemocracy (Appeal, 2018). Its second paragraph reads as follows: 'This non-legally binding definition attempts to erase Palestinian history, demonize solidarity with the Palestinian struggle for freedom, justice and equality, suppress freedom of expression, and shield Israel's far-right regime of occupation, settler-colonialism and apartheid from effective measures of accountability in accordance to international law.' These words could easily have their authors condemned as antisemites according to the IHRA definition.

When I asked John McDonnell[2] about the reactions of Palestinian Labour members to adoption of the IHRA definition, he said they 'are a bit subdued at the moment. A bit quiet because of the atmosphere. Palestinian members of the Party of course want to have their say, like everyone else, but in the current situation they don't want to be seen as provoking any disputes.'

A painful adoption: Labour succumbs

In politics, neutralising a toxic controversy and moving on by taking a strategic decision to retreat, withdraw or compromise may be a prudent course of action. So it is easy to understand if this is what members of the NEC hoped would be the result of the decision they took when they met on 4 September 2018 to ditch the amendments they made to some examples of antisemitism in the guidance notes of the IHRA definition of antisemitism, and embrace the entire text lock, stock and barrel. I strongly suspect that there was acute awareness among Labour's leadership of the overwhelming evidence I have summarised in this chapter of the IHRA definition being not fit for purpose. Also, perhaps, that this

2. This and subsequent quotes by the Shadow Chancellor of the Exchequer John McDonnell are from an on the record interview I conducted with him on 21 May 2019.

definition – or any definition for that matter – offers Jews no credible refuge from antisemitism. It has deepened intra-Jewish conflict over the question of the relationship between anti-Zionism and antisemitism, further institutionalised the notion of the 'new antisemitism', thereby further degrading both Jewish and public understanding of the nature of contemporary antisemitism. If Israel is 'the collective Jew among the nations', the underlying antisemitism of right wing populists who profess admiration for Israel and of Christian evangelicals whose 'love' for the country and the right of Jews to have a state is driven by their vision of the Rapture, which would result in the death of all Jews, is something the self-proclaimed leader of the Jewish people, Israeli Prime Minister Benjamin Netanyahu, is more than happy to live with. What value can a definition have if it effectively legitimises actual promotion of classic antisemitism by the Prime Minister of the Jewish state?

Eventually, the relentless pressure from inside and outside the Party to get the NEC to abandon its amendments to the examples, coupled with a constant stream of attacks on Jeremy Corbyn for allegedly associating with antisemites and even allegedly being an antisemite himself, now paid off. As widely expected, on 4 September the NEC reversed its decision, making the entire, un-amended IHRA definition and examples an integral part of its code of conduct on antisemitism.

Not only is there now overwhelming evidence that it's not fit for purpose, but it also has the effect of making Jews *more* vulnerable to antisemitism, *not less*, and exacerbating the bitter arguments Jews have been having over the nature of contemporary antisemitism for the last 20 to 25 years. Arguments that are inextricably linked to the Israel-Palestine conflict and generated by two questions: Are there forms of criticism of Israel which equate to antisemitism? If so, where is the line between 'legitimate' criticism and criticism that spills over into antisemitic hate speech?

Part II: 'Institutionally antisemitic': a wounding indictment

Among the daily repetition of many charges of ugly and systemic antisemitism in the Labour Party, the claim that the organisation was 'institutionally antisemitic' was surely the most serious and wounding indictment. The accusation has been current since 2016, but it was given unprecedented publicity during and after the 18 February 2019 press conference at which seven Labour MPs resigned from the Party to form what they initially called the Independent Group (TIG), but subsequently established as a political Party, Change UK, citing institutional antisemitism as one of the main reasons for their departure (*Guardian*, 18 February 2019).

On 7 March the charge dramatically ceased to be a mere allegation. The EHRC announced that: 'Having received a number of complaints regarding antisemitism in the Labour Party, we believe the Labour Party may have unlawfully discriminated against people because of their ethnicity and religious beliefs' and would now be 'engaging with the Labour Party to give them an opportunity to respond', with the likelihood that it would begin a statutory investigation (EHRC, 7 March 2019). Such an inquiry would, in other words, lead to the determination of whether the Party was institutionally antisemitic. Adam Wagner, a barrister at Doughty Street chambers, who acted for one of the two complainants, the Campaign Against Antisemitism (CAA), was in no doubt about this (Wagner, 7 March 2019). The other complainant was the JLM, the official Jewish Labour Party-affiliated socialist society.

The charge was particularly damaging – not principally because it had been made repeatedly by commentators and politicians as if it were indisputable holy writ. But rather because of the huge symbolic significance of the term 'institutional racism', of which institutional antisemitism is understood to be a component, in the dominant discourse around reasons for the persistence of racial discrimination and hatred in the UK. It should be noted, however, that in the 28 May announcement by the EHRC that it was going ahead with an investigation (see above) no mention is made of the terms 'institutional antisemitism' or 'institutional racism'.

In Part II of this chapter, I explain the significance of the concept; assess the validity of the accusation; discuss the consequences that the relentless focus on Labour's alleged institutional antisemitism has for BAME people who urgently need to bring their current experience of racism and discrimination to public attention; and consider whether the needs and concerns of Jewish people are met by this onslaught on Labour.

The central concept in the 1999 report of the Macpherson Inquiry into the murder of Stephen Lawrence

The concept of institutional racism was central to the conclusions of the 1999 inquiry (to which I have already referred above in relation to the fact that it has erroneously been credited with affording minorities the exclusive right to define what constitutes racism against them) headed by Sir William Macpherson, a retired high court judge, into the way the Metropolitan police investigated the 22 April 1993 murder of the black teenager Stephen Lawrence by a group of white youths. Macpherson's 350-page report (Macpherson, 1999) concluded that the police investigation had been 'marred by a combination of professional incompetence, institutional racism and a failure of leadership'. It made 70 recommendations designed to show zero tolerance for racism among police and in the civil service, NHS, judiciary and other public bodies.

As Barbara Cohen, former head of legal policy at the Commission for Racial Equality, noted in a Runnymede Trust report, *The Lawrence Inquiry 20 Years On* (Cohen, February 2019), 'The concept of institutional racism was not new; it had been developed over several decades by activists and academics in the US and Britain who had given a name to the phenomenon that was part of black people's routine encounters with public and private organisations' (p. 1).

As Cohen wrote: 'the Report [was] expected to change permanently the shape of race relations in Britain'. And, indeed, the broad acceptance of the relevance of the term seemed to reflect an understanding of the depth and persistence of racial discrimination in a society that had become so visibly multicultural and in which, on the surface, major advances had been made in reducing the impact of racially prejudiced attitudes.

But Cohen says: 'Is it not a sad finale to this anniversary of a Report expected to change permanently the shape of race relations in Britain that patterns of race discrimination have altered very little ... racism and racist violence have increased.'

The accusation of institutional racism remains a powerful and sensitive touchstone for assessing the scale of debilitating prejudice and discrimination in British society. When a lawyer for some Grenfell families in September 2018 said the public inquiry must ask if the 72 deaths were 'a product of institutional racism', firefighters said it was an offensive slur, reports the *Guardian* (*Guardian*, 22 February 2019). But at least 34 victims were nationals of African, Middle Eastern or Asian countries. Could unwitting actions have delivered a racist outcome? Did institutional racism affect firefighters' behaviour? asked Imran Kahn, who represented the Lawrence family at Macpherson.

From damaging political accusation to grounds for a statutory inquiry

The cross-Party Home Affairs Committee examined antisemitism in the UK and reported on its findings in October 2016 (Home Affairs Committee report, October 2016). The Committee acknowledged that there was 'no reliable, empirical evidence to support the notion that there is a higher prevalence of antisemitic attitudes within the Labour Party than any other political Party' (*Guardian*, 16 October 2016). But in what the *Guardian* called 'a damning indictment of the Party and its leader', the Committee claimed that Corbyn's lack of action 'risks lending force to allegations that elements of the Labour movement are institutionally antisemitic'. The *Guardian* added: 'it is withering about the Labour leader's response to antisemitic attacks on his own MPs, and his understanding of modern forms of racism'.

Chuka Umunna, one of the founders of Change UK, was a Labour member of the Committee and in a personal statement took issue with the charge: 'Some have suggested that there is institutional antisemitism across the whole of the Labour Party, this is not a view I share, not least because I have not seen one incident of antisemitism in almost 20 years of activism within my local Labour Party in Lambeth' (Labour List, October 2016). Nevertheless, just over two years later, on 24 February 2019, Umunna told Sophy Ridge in a Sky News interview: 'I've been very clear, the Labour Party is institutionally antisemitic, and you either put your head in the sand and you ignore it or you actually do something about it.'

Whatever caused Umunna to change his mind, or heart, his volte face is a reflection of how repeating the charge has come to be used as a political sledgehammer, ostensibly to bring about the eradication of antisemitism from the Party but more commonly to justify public opposition to the leadership, or the act of resigning from the Party. This is highly damaging to the Party and wittingly or unwittingly promotes outcomes that really have nothing to do with combating antisemitism in the Party or anywhere else. Among other Labour MPs who have either led in making the accusation or endorsed it subsequently are Luciana Berger, Mike Gapes, Louise Ellman, Margaret Hodge, John Mann, Wes Streeting and more. The charge is almost always made without any clear explanation as to how institutional antisemitism manifests itself in such a way as to correspond to the definition of institutional racism as formulated by Macpherson.

There is no doubt whatsoever that some Jewish Labour MPs have received communications – especially online – containing antisemitic abuse, some of which appear to come from Labour Party members or supporters. Claims have been made that some Labour MPs have wittingly or unwittingly used antisemitic tropes; that senior Labour figures have appeared on panels in discussion with people who have a track record of expressing antisemitic views; and that criticism of Israeli government policies and of Zionism has at times been couched in terms using antisemitic tropes. The rather unfairly criticised Chakrabarti Report quite comprehensively and frankly covers this ground very well. The Party's leaders, officials and the Party membership more broadly acknowledge that more needs to be done to rid the Party of manifestations of antisemitism, that the Party and its members should operate a zero tolerance policy towards such manifestations, report them when they occur and have them dealt with within the investigatory and disciplinary procedures of the Party. John McDonnell told me that the Chakrabarti Report 'was not a whitewash and made sensible proposals regarding process'.

But it is also true that there are many members of the Party – now a massive entity, the character of which cannot be reduced to stereotypes – whose experience of antisemitism in the Party mirrors that of Umunna's in 2016. They haven't witnessed it. They feel that the Party is being tarred with the brush of a very small minority expressing antisemitic views. And some strongly feel that the problem of antisemitism is being used as a weapon in internal battles over Corbyn's leadership and the direction in which the Party is moving ideologically.

It is surely only sensible and realistic to acknowledge the validity of this mixed picture. But whether it can fairly, usefully or objectively be called a 'crisis' takes us into the realms of value-laden, highly subjective opinion of dubious expediency in that whatever truth such a judgement may contain, the word is immediately tainted from being used with abandon by the Party's enemies who have no particular interest in seeing Labour overcome its 'crisis'. For a Party that sees itself as a bulwark against all forms of racism, grappling with a very different public image was always going to be experienced as a crisis. But whether the crisis is one of antisemitism itself is another matter. Of course, no level of antisemitism is acceptable. But the Party exists in a society in which antisemitic attitudes are endemic. Making sense of these contradictory realities requires maintaining a balanced perspective, one that should be grounded in evidence. A useful source for this is the conclusions of a major 2017 study of UK antisemitism undertaken by the respected Jewish community think tank, the Institute for Jewish Policy Research (JPR), together with the Community Security Trust (CST), the private charity that monitors and combats antisemitism for the organised Jewish community: that 'antisemitism is no more prevalent on the left than in the general population' (JPR, September 2017). A conclusion that echoed the finding of the 2016 Home Affairs Committee report on UK antisemitism quoted above. Nevertheless, while this finding is important to note for the sake of a balanced perspective, it is not one with which Labour can feel comfortable. It must constantly strive to be much less racist, much less antisemitic than any overall measure of these phenomena in society as a whole.

Given this picture, the EHRC's decision to conduct an investigation signifies a – brave or foolhardy – willingness to enter a highly politicised and complex environment, ensuring that any conclusions it reaches, though no doubt intended to bring about improvements in ways of dealing with racism, will face unavoidably severe political reaction. They could be seen as endorsing exaggeration by some or justifying denialism by others. Either way, they are stepping into a minefield and must be able to demonstrate squeaky-clean impartiality.

Can the Macpherson definition of institutional racism/antisemitism apply to the Labour Party?

So what precisely is institutional racism/antisemitism and can it apply to the Labour Party? The Macpherson report defined it as:

> the collective failure of an organisation to provide an appropriate and professional *service* to people because of their colour, culture or ethnic origin. It can be seen or detected in processes, attitudes and behaviour which amount to *discrimination* through unwitting prejudice, ignorance, thoughtlessness and racist stereotyping which *disadvantage* minority ethnic people. (paragraph 6.34)

There are three crucial words in the definition, which I have italicised: *service*, *discrimination* and *disadvantage*. Presumably, all three must apply to any organisation accused.

'An appropriate and professional service'

Macpherson's principal target was the Metropolitan police: a public body, the employees of which provide a *service* to the public, who are in effect 'clients' or 'customers'. And there is a clear distinction between the service providers and the customers. The same applies to the other principal organisations Macpherson was thinking of when framing the definition: the civil service, NHS, judiciary and so on.

In the Labour Party there is no such clear distinction between service providers and customers. Indeed, such terms are manifestly inappropriate when describing the Party. As the political scientist Iain McLean, Professor of Politics at Nuffield College, wrote in a 1978 study, it is 'a complex organism' (McLean, 1978). It does have employees of course, but they are not providing services in the same way that the Met and the NHS do. There is some centralised control to ensure that the rules and regulations of the Party are adhered to, and a small administrative staff to implement this control and ensure the proper functioning of the Party. But, as McLean said, there are three main interdependent elements: the parliamentary leadership, the paid-up members outside the parliamentary elites and the mass of ordinary Labour voters – which makes this complex organism predominantly a voluntary organisation. Without the last element, the first two could not exist; although it's arguable that all three are interdependent, and that the absence of any one of them would reduce the Party to a fiction.

Within the interdependent structure, a high degree of autonomy is exercised by some of the Party institutions. Powers are devolved to local CLPs; complex committee structures exist at local and national levels; and numerous affiliated and semi-affiliated organisations participate in the affairs of the Party. This does not mean that some practices within the Party, at these various levels, are not racist; that lists of alleged expressions of antisemitism cannot be compiled. And it may well be that the evidence the complaining organisations, the CAA and JLM, present relates to how the affairs of local CLPs are run. We certainly know that documentation of this kind exists since Jennie Formby has provided details of the scale of it in her reports. But this does not automatically equate to evidence of institutional antisemitism. It involves a very small fraction of the Party. Furthermore, presenting proof of systemic, unwitting, institutionalised antisemitism on a wide scale would be immensely difficult, especially when you consider that much of the currency of disputes and heated arguments is the free expression of different political views, and is clearly not taking place on the basis of racist or antisemitic assumptions. And, as I established in Part I when discussing the so-called 'Macpherson principle', there are no grounds for the CAA and JLM being allowed to define for themselves what is racist and antisemitic. There would have to be a definition acceptable to all parties.

As far as the minimal services provided within the organisation are concerned, apart from the procedures for dealing with complaints of bullying, racist abuse and so on, I don't recall seeing any accusations that these services are in any sense systematically antisemitic. So even though the very fact that the Party is not a service organisation per se disqualifies it from being institutionally racist or antisemitic, on the basis of what we know about its day-to-day operations, Mike Gapes's accusation, made in an interview with LBC on 18 February, that 'the Party' – yes, the entire Party – is 'racist and antisemitic' is groundless.

'Discrimination'

But as we know from the EHRC's formal announcement of its decision to investigate Labour, the key word in the definition is *discrimination*. It's the discrimination that resulted from an organisation's failure to provide an appropriate and professional service to people because of their colour, culture or ethnic origin that Macpherson was so concerned about. The Lawrence family suffered hideous discrimination as a result of the failures of the Met. But this was just the tip of the iceberg of decades of unrelenting discrimination against black people. So let's set aside for the moment the conclusion of the previous section and simply ask whether, on the currently publicly available evidence – I of course have no access to the data being presented to the EHRC by the complaining organisations – Jewish people in the Party, at whatever level, experience and suffer discrimination?

- *In elections to Party posts?* To start at the top: in the election for leader following the resignation of Gordon Brown, the two front runners, brothers Ed and David Miliband, were self-identifying Jews. Ed Miliband was elected and held the post without challenge until the 2015 election.
- *In parliamentary representation?* Eleven of the Party's 261 MPs elected in 2017 were Jewish. The UK Jewish population makes up approximately 0.5 per cent of the total population (BoD, 2014), which means Jewish MPs were overrepresented in the Parliamentary Labour Party by a factor of 4.
- *In seeking to be a member of the Party?* There's no way of knowing how many Jewish people are members of the Party, but an educated guess, bearing in mind the rightward shift of the Jewish voting population over the last few decades, puts it between 3–3500, which gives a proportion of a little above 0.5 per cent of the total membership. Certainly, judging by the prominence of Jewish voices in many constituencies and at the parliamentary level, there is no barrier systematically holding Jews back from not only becoming members, but also

playing their part in the variety of positions of responsibility within the Party at local and national levels.

- *In formal recognition of Jewish identity within the Party?* There are opportunities for self-defined minority groups to maintain their own socialist organisations within the Party as affiliates. For example, Labour Party Irish Society 'aims ... to promote the interests of the Irish community to and within the Labour Party and to promote the Labour Party to Irish citizens in Britain. The Society is open to all people of Irish heritage and anyone who simply has an interest in Irish affairs' (labourirish.org.uk).

  BAME Labour grew out of 'black sections' to articulate the distinctive needs of people of colour within the Party. It is open to all Labour members who identify as BAME (labourbame, n.d.).

  As for self-identifying Jews, the organisation designated as fulfilling a similar function is the Party-affiliated JLM, from 1903 to 2004 known as Poalei Zion (Workers of Zion), which claims a membership of 3000 (jewishlabour.uk). It's recognised as a socialist society and you do not need to be Jewish to be a member. Naturally, you do need to share JLM's aims, which are to 'maintain and promote Labour or Socialist Zionism as the movement for self-determination of the Jewish people within the state of Israel', and its belief in 'the centrality of Israel in Jewish life'. But this leaves Jews in an anomalous position. On the one hand, it demonstrates that Jews face no discrimination if they wish to assert publicly, within the Party, the importance of the link between their Jewish identity and their socialist principles. On the other hand, membership is not an option for anyone – Jews included – with a different view of Zionism or Israel. So, while JLM claims to speak for all Jews in the Labour Party, and to be treated as such by Labour, given that a significant proportion of Jewish members are not Zionists or are anti-Zionists, JLM's claim is simply incorrect.

This does constitute a kind-of de facto discrimination: discrimination in *favour* of Zionist Jews; discrimination *against* non-Zionist or anti-Zionist Jews – a situation all the more strange, however, given that a sizeable proportion of Party members, I suspect, would hold similar views. And it's Jews of a Zionist persuasion who are accusing the Party of institutional antisemitism.

The privileging of Zionism has deep historical roots in the Party. JLM's predecessor, Poalei Zion, affiliated to the Party back in 1903, a time when a very positive view of Zionism, then only of minority interest among Jews, prevailed in the Labour movement. So today, the Party acquiesces to the fact that, as far as I can ascertain, no other affiliated society makes membership dependent on the individual expressing support for the official, nationalist ideology of another state.

- *In recognition of alternative Jewish identities?* An alternative framework for self-identifying Jews, but not as yet affiliated to the Party, is Jewish Voice for Labour (JVL) (jewishvoiceforlabour.org.uk), established in July 2017, whose 'mission is to contribute to making the Labour Party an open, democratic and inclusive Party, encouraging all ethnic groups and cultures to join and participate freely'. It has a formal membership structure and non-Jews can join as Solidarity members.
- *In Jewish participation across the range of Party activities?* More broadly, there is no attempt to prevent Jews in the Party – whether as MPs, constituency party chairs, members – playing a prominent part in making contributions to the discussion of Party policy in any area, with the antisemitism question, the Israel-Pales-

tine conflict and the link between the two the focus of sharpest debate, controversy and sometimes bitter disagreement. Indeed, it seems at times as if this is primarily an intra-Jewish battle, reflecting differences in the Jewish world and in Israel, the intensity of which is at its ideological and political height within the Party. It's no secret that there is no love lost between JLM and JVL, whose ideological differences are reflected in the views of many non-Jewish members of the Party and remain unresolved.

- *In the procedure for dealing with complaints about alleged manifestations of antisemitism?* The EHRC's investigation is likely to focus principally on this question. It has certainly become a matter of considerable controversy. But even if we assume for the moment, judging by reports in the media, whose reliability is not impressive in this area, that some cases have not been handled as they should have been, it would be highly unlikely that this practice was systemic and absurd if it alone led to a judgment of institutional antisemitism, given that the overwhelming evidence points to no systemic discrimination against Jews at all.

Nevertheless, while this is the case, the fact that some Jews have left and some are contemplating leaving – though quantifying this is not possible – because, at the very least, they feel an atmosphere of 'tolerance towards antisemitism' that makes it impossible for them to stay, or more disturbingly they experience direct abuse, or they find the discourse around the Israel-Palestine conflict to be unbearably toxic, has to be accounted for. The Luciana Berger case is emblematic of this as she claimed that racist bullying by Labour members and supporters was responsible for her decision to leave. (It should be acknowledged that the accuracy of her claims is disputed: see Bob Pitt, 2019.) So can Jews leaving for such reasons be seen to suffer from a systemic institutional culture that permits this? Are they institutionally disadvantaged?

'Disadvantage'

While instances of antisemitic abuse directed at Jewish Party members can be categorised as 'racial stereotyping', a term used in the definition of institutional racism, there is no justification for jumping to the conclusion that there is substantive systemic *disadvantage* for Jewish members, as understood by Macpherson.

A fog of controversy has settled over the statistics revealing the progress made by the Party's compliance team in processing complaints of antisemitic abuse. Allegations of irregularities and inappropriate political interference surfaced over the weekend of 2–3 March 2019 and were published in the *Guardian* (*Guardian*, 2 March 2019), with responses reported by the BBC and other media outlets on 5 March (BBC, 5 March 2019). But even from what chief critic of the process Margaret Hodge has said, the number of what she claims are 'suspicious' cases is very small. So it is highly unlikely that the overall picture which emerged from General Secretary Jennie Formby's report, which she made public on 11 February, would change. The level of abuse as reported to the compliance team is very low indeed. Barry Gardiner gave a full and robust account of these figures to Sophy Ridge on Sky News on 25 February (Skwawkbox, 25 February 2019), while not for one moment denying that there is a problem of antisemitism still needing treatment. And Glyn Secker and Dr Alan Maddison summarised them in 'The truth behind the stats' in the March 2019 *Labour Briefing* (*Labour Briefing*, March 2019).

What does not figure in reports are claims that barriers are being put in the way of people who want to complain about alleged antisemitic incidents. Such incidents have been tweeted about, recorded – on audio and video – and in the public domain in short order. There are reports of apparent irregularities in the handling of these complaints, but is this to be ascribed to discriminatory bad faith rather than administrative disarray?

For someone to claim, or to have claims made on their behalf, that they were bullied out of the Party by racist abuse is a very serious matter. But while this is what Luciana Berger and her supporters say happened to her, other MPs, such as Margaret Hodge and Louise Ellman, fierce critics of Corbyn's leadership and uncompromisingly vociferous in accusing the Party of being riddled with antisemitism, who are also subject to online abuse, have remained, vowing to fight back against it, refusing to tolerate. Staying or leaving is still a matter of choice.

Moreover, away from the high-profile individuals, it's clear that many Jewish members are determined to remain in the Party and give a variety of reasons for doing so: some simply do not experience an antisemitic atmosphere, some feel the scale of the problem is exaggerated, some have faced it but refuse to be intimidated, some are channelling their loyalty to the Party and its leadership by growing a pro-Corbyn left voice in JVL. And even JLM, despite threatening to split from the Party, presents a combative stance on its website and through its tweets, and on 7 April 2019 decided to remain, for now (*Guardian*, 9 April 2019).

The very existence of this variety of responses, both at the parliamentary and membership levels of the Party, surely confirms that there is really no justification for leavers blaming their experience on processes that leave them 'disadvantaged', in the sense meant by Macpherson. For sure, none of this leaves the Party in a good place. But people leave and join parties all the time, especially parties where there is continuous struggle over clashing political ideologies. And we know that this is a key feature of the current malaise. Insofar as we are talking about losing a political argument, this is not to be disadvantaged, and certainly not in the sense in which Macpherson used the term.

Preoccupation with institutional antisemitism overshadows racism against BAME people

Whatever is the precise nature of the problem of antisemitism in the Labour Party it does not constitute institutional antisemitism; it does not correspond with Macpherson's definition of the concept of institutional racism. It is, however, only fair to acknowledge an opposing documented view (as opposed to the expression of a political or journalistic opinion lacking substantive supporting evidence): the 128-page 'report' by Alan Johnson published in early 2019 by the journal *Fathom*, which he edits, titled 'Institutionally Antisemitic: Contemporary Left Antisemitism and the Crisis in the British Labour Party' (Johnson, 2019a). *Fathom* is the house journal of BICOM, the Britain Israel Communications and Research Centre (www.bicom.org.uk/), the main Israel lobby group in the UK (Johnson finds Labour guilty as charged on the basis of a list of 'over 130 examples of antisemitism or antisemitism denial in the Party').

There are three fundamental weaknesses in Johnson's report. He fails to establish that Labour is the kind of institution covered by the Macpherson definition of institutional racism; he makes up his own, highly contentious definition of antisemitism; and his list of examples of antisemitism in Labour is riddled with unproven assertions.

Crucially, in my view, the so-called evidence of antisemitism in Labour that Johnson and other prominent accusers claim is institutional plainly does not parallel the experiences of those the Macpherson inquiry was set up to address. Given the specificity of the case which Macpherson was asked to examine and the ethnic group primarily affected by institutional racism, it would seem to me obviously necessary to refer to the Lawrence experience and the consequences of Met institutional racism for black communities when attacking Labour over antisemitism. Not once in 128 pages does Johnson do this. The result of this is to overshadow – at the very least – those who are BAME and have been and still are victims of institutional racism and those who are BAME who experience racism and abuse within the Labour Party. In my discussion of institutional racism 20 years after Macpherson (above), I made it plain that there are strong feelings in black communities that the Met police still have a long way to go in rooting out 'unwitting prejudice, ignorance, thoughtlessness and racial stereotyping'.

Doreen Lawrence, Stephen Lawrence's mother, said in February 2019 that progress in reforming institutions was stagnant. 'As time moved on, it's as though they changed the word from "racism" to diversity, and then "diversity doesn't exist anymore"', Lady Lawrence told MPs (*Guardian*, 22 February 2019).

In a series of tweets on 26 February, Dr Alan Maddison contrasted the fact that 'Racism in society accounts for 76% of hate crime', with '1% attributed to antisemitism'. 'Surveys show BAME MPs get more abuse than Jewish MPs, despite media noise for the latter and not the former.' He continued: 'Nineteen per cent of Labour voters are BAME, you are letting them down, and feeding Tory lies' by excessive concentration on antisemitism.

In another tweet he wrote: 'There is no evidence that antis. is more prevalent in Labour, or even far left, than elsewhere. Antisemitism prevalence is 4x higher on the far right, 62% vote Tory. One study into Party members suggests greater prejudices amongst Tory members. Nobody seems bothered.'

None of this is cause to dismiss one form of racism for the sake of prioritising another. Nor is it to endorse any notion of a hierarchy of racisms. All must be fought consistently and concertedly. But those affected do not all experience racism in the same way. So to a significant degree, those different experiences require differentiated solutions. But it is of no help to Jews for Jewish leaders and their prominent non-Jewish supporters to seek a differentiated method of tackling antisemitism on the grounds of a false accusation of institutional antisemitism in the Labour Party that derives from a misguided sense of Jewish exceptionalism. Especially when made by high-profile figures, these accusations damage the fight against antisemitism. There is already cause to regret allowing this narrative of institutional antisemitism to run and run, undoubtedly influencing public belief about antisemitism, without determined challenge.

Racism in Brexit Britain is here and now, and getting seriously worse. Disproportionate and unacceptable numbers of black people have died in police custody. BAME people continue to suffer appalling levels of day-to-day discrimination in education, jobs, housing, health, the justice system. Immigrants, asylum-seekers, 'foreigners', Roma, Muslims, Jews, people of colour, all face various levels of abuse. The Windrush scandal and Grenfell Tower disaster showed just how ingrained in our administrative culture is the treatment of people in a hostile fashion and as second class citizens based on race and class. It is a terrible misjudgement when so-called friends of the Jews exceptionalise Jewish suffering today.

The wrong diagnosis – and a trap for the EHRC?

Institutional antisemitism is the wrong diagnosis of Labour's antisemitism problem. Were it to be judged correct by the EHRC, in the form of a conclusion that the Party has been tolerating and promoting systemic discrimination against Jews, is there any evidence, on the basis of the EHRC's past actions, that the medication and surgery likely to be prescribed would improve matters, rather than make them worse? The Party has openly acknowledged that its methods of handling complaints were imperfect, and even since these were changed, there have been difficulties. Were the EHRC, without pre-judging the state of antisemitism in the Party, able to offer help and advice on better practice, then perhaps its involvement might be useful. But the auguries do not look good. The EHRC itself does not start from an uncommitted position. Of course, by definition it opposes racism in all its forms, but in 2017, its chief executive Rebecca Hilsenrath responded to accusations against the Labour Party with these words: 'Antisemitism is racism and the Labour Party needs to do more to establish that it is not a racist Party. A zero-tolerance approach to antisemitism should mean just that' (Hilsenrath twitter, 26 September 2017). Prior to investigation, is it not worrying that the CEO already claims to know what the Labour Party needs to do? Furthermore, only two years ago the EHRC was subjected to withering criticism for itself targeting disabled and ethnic minority employees and denying them work opportunities in other agencies (*Guardian*, 5 March 2017).

Concluding thoughts

This examination of these two major stories in Labour's antisemitism trials offers no prospect of any respite from continued external assaults and internal battles. Whatever the

EHRC concludes, further damage to the Party is inevitable. I very much doubt that any such inquiry could be conducted behind closed doors, so there would be ample opportunity for the Party's detractors to make hay with either leaked or openly available evidence of alleged antisemitic manifestations and dysfunctional procedures for dealing with the issue. Presumption of guilt seems to be the default position of external and internal critics. If suggestions from the EHRC itself are accurate, that any inquiry could take two years to complete, further periodic bouts of turmoil over antisemitism for the Party are inevitable.

As for the IHRA working definition, even though it may not have loomed large in recent antisemitism controversies, its potential for use in restricting freedom of speech on Israel-Palestine issues is very great. Ominously, the JLM, which is still considering disaffiliating from Labour, has been pressing for reaffirmation of NEC adoption of IHRA; that any Labour candidate standing for office must affirm acceptance of IHRA; and that IHRA must be mandatory for all Labour groups. It might be a slight exaggeration, but IHRA and institutional antisemitism can be likened to ticking time bombs. Labour has no control over when they might go off or very much power to defuse them, but can be sure that they are liable to cause havoc.

One of the particularly distinctive features of Labour's antisemitism controversies is just how much is out of Labour's hands to control. From the start, the obvious path was to get ahead of the game. However, while there were many within the leadership who were so appalled and hurt by what they saw as the deliberate mischaracterisation of their Party and could not get beyond passionate and angry condemnations of antisemitism and declarations of good faith, there were others who wanted a harder-headed approach, anticipating crises and seizing control of the narrative through proactive positive action.

When I asked John McDonnell about the Party's handling of the issue, he was quite clear. Speaking, I believe, in the name of the leadership as a whole, he said:

> I'd have taken more control ... If I'd have known more about the lack of implementation [of Chakrabarti] ... the failure to set up a legal panel and the nature of the problem, I'd have made sure that we had proper legal advice; been more ruthless and increased the pace of the process. We were let down by the system and the bureaucracy. We took it as read that Chakrabarti was being implemented, because why wouldn't it be? I'd have erred more on the side of being firmer on some cases ... We should have been more transparent. We were never told the exact numbers regarding cases [before Formby's reforms].

McDonnell and others in the leadership team believe there is more that could be done to make the process both efficient and transparent. The procedures for referrals and final adjudications in serious cases can still be cumbersome. The Labour Party was not designed to be a centralised body for dispensing justice. It developed as a complex and diffuse political organisation comprising local branches, affiliated societies and a range of committees overseeing governance of the Party. In addition, there are parliamentary representatives with their own office arrangements plus a full- and part-time staff to manage those elements of Party affairs which are not devolved to CLPs.

This complexity can have some negative effects on the efficient management of Party processes and decision making, but are clearly not intended to produce systematic discrimination against any racial or ethnic group, nor can it simply be assumed that they would unwittingly do so. To be institutionally dysfunctional, or even at times chaotic, is very different from being institutionally racist.

Post-truth

First, the way Labour's antisemitism controversies have played out provides copious evidence that we live in a post-truth age. When it comes to antisemitism, expertise and experience seem to count for little. Celebrity status, emotional 'authenticity' and the loudest voice on social media trump them. No matter how many times fatal flaws in the IHRA working definition and brazen distortions about its origins, international reach and misuse are pointed out, no one wants to know. So-called UK antisemitism 'expert' delegates to the IHRA assure us that it's the 'gold standard', when the truth is that it's more like a ponzi scheme.

Constantly reiterate that respected scholars and analysts agree there is no Macpherson principle handing absolute rights to minorities to determine what is racism against them: no one wants to know. Draw attention to the fraudulent use of the institutional antisemitism charge, when it fails to apply the criteria for it in Macpherson's thoroughly considered and carefully constructed definition: no one is listening.

When the default position is to double down on what is untrue, is it any wonder that actual cases of antisemitic manifestations in the Party are hard to handle effectively.

Confusion about what antisemitism is

Second, 40–50 years ago there was consensus about what antisemitism was. Now, confusion about it is rife, not only among the general public, but also among Jews.

Asked to explain what antisemitism means in a Populus 2015 survey, 45 per cent of respondents were not confident that they could explain to someone else what antisemitism means. Among respondents aged between 18 and 34, more than 60 per cent felt unable to explain what antisemitism is.

On specific issues, opinion is not merely uncertain but divided. A 2016 Populus survey revealed wide disagreement about the relationship between antisemitism and anti-Zionism and 'hatred of Israel' – 48 per cent were confident that hating Israel and questioning its right to exist is antisemitic, which means that nearly half disagreed.

In 20 per cent of cases respondents thought the opposite, that 'hating Israel' and questioning its right to exist was not antisemitic.

A JPR and IPSOS-MORI poll conducted among Jews for the FRA in 2014 showed even greater division (FRA Survey, 2014). When asked whether Jews believed that antisemitism is a problem in the UK, respondents were split – 48 per cent reported that antisemitism is 'a fairly big problem' or a 'big problem', but a small majority said it is 'not a very big problem' or 'not a problem at all'. So it's reasonable to conclude from this that they held widely divergent opinions on what antisemitism is.

Finally, a Deltapoll for the *Jewish Chronicle* in March 2019 (*Jewish Chronicle*, March 2019) revealed that 40 per cent of British adults said they did not know what the term antisemitism meant, rising to more than half among under 25s.

This confusion must partly be put down to the effect of labelling various forms of criticism of Israel as antisemitic.

Post-truth, confusion and ignorance: a more fertile ground for hyperbole, outrageous accusations, unbounded scaremongering and the weaponising of antisemitism could hardly exist. So is there a name for the third contextual factor that creates a sense that we are on the verge of an antisemitic apocalypse? How can we explain the transformation of someone regarded even by his traditional political opponents as fundamentally a good man, if somewhat inflexible and tin-eared perhaps, into a monster? By all objective measures, the UK must be one of the safest places for Jews to live, yet we are told that Labour represents an existential threat to Jewish life, that 30 per cent of Jews are thinking about leaving the country and the president of the BoD, Marie van der Zyl, announces in August 2018 that: 'Jeremy Corbyn has declared war on the Jews.' (The only person such an extreme statement calls to mind is Hitler.) These reactions cannot be explained away just by showing how absurd they are.

Moral panic

When similar bouts of collective emotional reaction around antisemitism have appeared in the past 20 years, the sociological concept of *moral panic* has seemed to me an accurate way of describing what's happening. And never before has it seemed as apt as it does now. I'm not alone in using the term in this context. Jonathan Cook, Bob Pitt and others who have addressed various aspects of the Labour antisemitism story have reached for the same term. The leading theorist of the concept, the late Professor Stanley Cohen, describes it as 'happening when "a condition, episode, person or group of persons emerges to become defined as a threat to societal values and interests"'.

While in my experience the moral panic around Labour and antisemitism is unprecedented in being so clearly focused on a person and a group, if you examine headlines relating to reports of outbursts of antisemitic activity going back 20 or more years, the hyperbolic language used is uncannily similar each time.

It seems that antisemitism and moral panic are natural bedfellows, which, when history is taken into account, is not so strange perhaps. But using the concept to help explain the particular nature of the Labour antisemitism crisis does not for one moment imply that there are no manifestations of antisemitism in the Party, or that antisemitism is not a real and growing problem in our society. It's a salutary reminder of the danger of getting the problem out of proportion. Doing so does not help in the combating of real antisemitism and it tends to suck up the oxygen needed to fight racism in general.

The counterproductive discourse of 'eradication'

Moreover, if the problem is as existentially threatening as it's painted, only an equally draconian solution can be the answer. And this is why we constantly hear what I call the *discourse of eradication*; the absolutist demand that antisemitism be 'eliminated' from Labour, from British society, from everywhere. Anything less is simply unacceptable. This was the clear message of the organised Jewish community demonstration in March 2018. But I don't think any serious person working in the field of racism as an academic or as an activist believes that racism can be completely eliminated from human society. Sad as it is to say: it's endemic. Yes, we can do an immense amount to combat it, shrink it, push it to the margins, even create 'zones' where you would have difficulty identifying its existence. But it will always be with us and every generation has to learn the lessons of its consequences. And the danger in falling for the discourse of eradication is that it sets the bar too high and promises only disappointment. It hinders the fight against racism because reaching for the impossible crowds out working for what is practical. By all means set high standards – zero tolerance of racism for example – yet Jews of all people should know that prejudice will always arise from time to time and in every generation the tools for combating it will need sharpening and made ready for use.

Labour as the anti-racist Party: an obligation, not an accolade

And it seems to me fairly obvious that even a small amount of proven expressions of antisemitism is going to have heightened significance because Labour sees itself as *the* anti-racist Party and will be more sensitive to criticism in this area and more vulnerable if there is evidence. If you set high standards, it's hard to complain if you are taken to task for falling short, to whatever degree. It's therefore incumbent upon Labour to focus relentlessly on political education about racism in all its forms, on ensuring that its procedures and practices with regard to minorities are beyond reproach and never to develop a mindset that suggests complacency in any form whatsoever.

It's a Jew-on-Jew war

Jews make up less than 0.5 per cent of the UK population though there may be a higher percentage – perhaps up to 1.00 per cent – making up Labour Party membership. And yet, very much at the heart of the antisemitism controversies in the Party is a Jew-on-Jew war; a battle between members who identify themselves as Zionists and those who do not. Some of the most controversial cases of alleged antisemitism involve Jews. Some of the most vociferous opponents of Corbyn's leadership are Jews; some of his most loyal and ardent supporters are Jews. On social media there is a constant flow of accusation and counter-accusation about who is and who is not a 'legitimate' Jew, who is judged a member of 'the community' and who isn't, who is a 'self-hating Jewish kapo' and who knows how to recognise a Jewish antisemite. It's no secret that the bitter arguments between Jewish factions in the Party are, at root, about the rights and wrongs of the Israel-Palestine conflict. And of course this is a subject of major concern for a large swathe of the Party, very many of whom feel equally passionate about the issue as the Jewish activists: Zionists or not Zionists. But rather than prominence being given to rational discussion about solutions to the conflict, the public space in the Party is dominated by the fraught question of where to draw the line between what you can say in criticism of the Israeli state and government that is or is not antisemitic.

My sense is that this intra-Jewish war in the Party is an inordinate influence on the antisemitism controversies and needs to be resolved. When I raised this issue with John McDonnell he frankly admitted: 'It's very difficult especially with the in-fighting within the Jewish community.' He recounted going to a meeting in support of prospective parliamentary candidate Jenny Manson. He walked into the room alongside Rabbi Danny Rich and they both received terrible abuse from some of the Jewish people who were in the audience. 'I haven't seen a community this divided since the Irish back in the day. It was pretty violent – pushing and shouting ... I didn't fully understand this. The level of antagonism from both sides has come as a shock.'

This brings me, finally, to two practical proposals.

Investigatory and disciplinary procedures

The first relates to the vexed issue of procedures for dealing with complaints about and accusations of antisemitism. This has vastly improved under Jennie Formby since quasi-legal procedures were introduced. But from my own observations, these new procedures are creating their own problems, leading to long delays. A court-like process demands an unequivocal decision: guilty/not guilty, antisemitic/not antisemitic. But all the research on antisemitism shows that a person can be a little bit antisemitic, not necessarily aware of it, harbouring both positive and negative views of Jews, susceptible to a process of learning and leniency. It is not, after all, illegal to harbour antisemitic views, express them in your own home, share them with close friends. It would rightly disgust us, of course, but it only becomes actionable if it's inciting racial hatred or contravenes the Equality Act.

The current approach requires, in many cases, the gathering of mountains of documentation – evidence and counter-evidence – and adversarial encounters. This should change. Disciplinary procedures are necessary, of course. But primary use should be made of the methods of mediation, non-accusatory clarification through dialogue and education that does not belittle. A leading, highly respected Jewish, Labour supporting lawyer with whom I discussed this issue, and who has discussed antisemitism in the Party with Corbyn, was himself sure that this kind of approach would be more productive. This would be in line with the Chakrabarti Report which advised dealing with some concerns informally, without the need to set in train a formal investigation, recommending also that expulsion should only be the last resort.

A managed and open debate about new principles for achieving peace with justice in Israel-Palestine

In a piece I wrote in 2018 for openDemocracy, I set out a practical proposal for a way of defusing the antisemitism issue for the longer term. The intra-Jewish war and the poisonous atmosphere around Israel-Palestine generally must be brought to an end. It's a festering sore. It's a boil that needs to be lanced. With the two-state solution dead in the water, Labour's policy on bringing peace with justice to Israelis and Palestinians is not fit for purpose. Start a managed but open debate in the Party on how to achieve equal rights for all, setting to one side all discussion of state-based paradigms and draw opposing voices into dialogue with each other – a dialogue that will certainly be made difficult if it was policed by misusing the

IHRA working definition. Nevertheless, the opportunity to be seen to be helping pave a new path, putting demonising, insulting and abusive language aside, could well encourage people to gently park IHRA in the name of free speech. At the end of the process, the conclusions may alienate some at the far ends of the spectrum of views. Some may deem it impossible to stay in a Party that reached what for them are unacceptable conclusions. But plenty of Party members may tolerate some policies they don't fully agree with for the sake of achieving the majority of the policies they do favour.

Defusing the antisemitism furore for the long term is one aim of this proposal, though it's a proposal that Labour needs to implement irrespective of the antisemitism issue. In any event, it's offered in the spirit of the argument that: the answer to hate speech is more speech.

6
'A' State of Israel or 'The' State of Israel: The Politics of the IHRA Definition

David Miller

This chapter is on the vexed question of the International Holocaust Remembrance Alliance (IHRA) definition of antisemitism and the way in which it has been used to attempt to silence or discipline critics of the Israeli state or the Zionist movement, especially, but not only in the Labour Party.

What follows is a case study of what happened after I addressed a small meeting of Palestinian students at Friends House in London in late 2018. At the meeting I discussed criticisms of the Corbyn-led Labour Party over antisemitism and how to counter attempts to shut down open debate on Israeli/Palestinian questions. I was conscious in my remarks both to explicitly discuss the IHRA working definition of antisemitism and to illuminate with as much precision as possible what is permissible in relation to the working definition and the list of possible examples appended to it.

I did not imagine that the repercussions would include:

- That I would be denounced by the *Jewish Chronicle (JC)*, which implied I had said things that were antisemitic, but did not explicitly use the term.

- Have anonymous emails sent to my new colleagues at the University of Bristol denouncing me as an antisemite.
- Be described as an antisemite by the student newspaper at Bristol in a libellous and defamatory story. This followed the earlier *JC* piece and was then removed when challenged.
- Be subject to a complaint to the Labour Party that I had breached the IHRA guidelines by describing the founding of the state of Israel as a 'racist endeavour'.
- Be subject to complaints to the University of Bristol, that I was an antisemite.
- Be part of the reason that the *JC* denounced the Corbyn-led Labour Party for failing to tackle antisemitism because I was not expelled from the Party.

This chapter tells the story of this episode including the conclusion that the IHRA, while chilling dissent, being imprecise and blurring together criticism of Israel with antisemitism, is not necessarily a panacea for pro-Israel groups.

Standing up to intimidation on campus

The talk I gave was short. I was asked to address the topic of the meeting: 'How to stand up against intimidation at campuses'. It was organised by the group, Olive, whose mission is: 'Mobilising Palestinian youth by raising awareness, enabling and empowering them on their journey towards a free and peaceful homeland.'

I discussed the impact of the Prevent agenda on freedom of speech and academic freedom on campus, and in the last part of my talk and in questions afterwards I discussed the criticisms of the Corbyn-led Labour Party.

In this latter part of the talk I discussed how the IHRA definition and the examples appended to it conflated antisemitism with criticism of Israel. I also suggested that some of the examples did not necessarily disallow appropriate criticism of Israel. The difficulty is in the manner in which the examples are interpreted by pro-Israel advocates – as the specific responses to my talk illustrated very well.

In particular I drew attention to two of the specific examples appended to the IHRA definition, one on Israel as a 'racist endeavour' and the other on double standards in the treatment of Israel.

I first of all read out the IHRA (2016) example: 'Denying the Jewish people their right to self-determination, e.g., by claiming that the existence of a State of Israel is a racist endeavor.'

I went on to explicitly discuss public debate about the meaningfulness of the distinction between 'a' state of Israel and 'the' state of Israel. I specifically cited the contribution made by Shadow Chancellor John McDonnell on this in September 2018, when he tweeted:

> IHRA says 'a state of Israel' not 'the state of Israel'. So, to claim any state for Jewish people would be a racist endeavour, would discriminate against Jewish people. But to criticise the Israeli state, as it was historically constituted or its policies and practices, does not. (McDonnell, 2018)

I used this distinction to signal that I was discussing the specific historical state of Israel and made the following points:

> The creation of the state of Israel was a settler colonial project which required the native people being dispossessed and expelled. It was by definition a racist endeavour, there's no getting away from that. I say that in the cogni-

zance that to say something that I've just said is regarded by lots of people as being antisemitic. It isn't.

The whole question of settler colonialism … is a really important concept. The settler colony in the North of Ireland resembled in many ways the settler colony in Palestine. The settler colony in Algeria the same, the settler colony in South Africa the same. The settler colonies in New Zealand, Australia, and indeed in America and Canada – they don't resemble it. Why don't they resemble it? Because they eradicated the natives …

Let's be clear, settler colonialism is not something which just the Israelis or just 'the Jews' do. It's a structural relationship in colonialism. It's different from a colonial possession like the British Raj in India or many of the other British colonies. It's a specific kind of colonialism in which the natives have to be expelled or subjugated and the settlers have to be given preferential treatment.

In discussing settler colonialism in this way I was also engaging a second example appended to the IHRA definition which states that it 'may' be antisemitic. This is: 'Applying double standards by requiring of [Israel] a behavior not expected or demanded of any other democratic nation' (IHRA, 2016).

As can be seen from my comment, I was explicitly saying that Israel was not special in that particular respect. Settler colonialism has a history.

Enter Harry's Place

As it turned out, there was a critic at the meeting who recorded my talk. The file was then posted on the Soundcloud page of *Harry's Place*. *Harry's Place* is a blog that was set up in 2002 to support the invasion of Iraq and since then has been used to attack those on the left that are antiwar, or critical of Israel

('Harry's Place', 2018). By some means, a journalist at the *JC* was alerted to this and ran a story about the meeting. This cited my comments about the attacks on the Labour Party and the 'racist endeavour'.

It failed, however, to include my discussion of the distinction between 'a' and 'the' state of Israel (Sugarman, 2018). The report excised that portion of the talk and reported that:

> He also discussed the concept of Israel 'as a racist endeavour', telling the audience that 'the creation of the state of Israel is a settler colonial project which required the native people being dispossessed and expelled. It was by definition a racist endeavour, there's no getting away from that, I say that in cognizance that to say something that I've just said is regarded by lots of people as being antisemitic. It isn't.' (Sugarman, 2018)

Following correspondence with the editor, Stephen Pollard, several passages were added to the story. These included:

> Defending his talk, Prof Miller said: 'I would say that I gave a nuanced response which accepted the evidence of actual and clumsy or mistaken antisemitism in the context of the campaign led by pro-Israel forces against Jeremy Corbyn.'
>
> Commenting on his claim that Israel is a racist endeavour, he said: 'I note ... that you have excised the portion where I discuss the intricacies of the IHRA definition in which saying "a" state of Israel is a racist endeavour "could, taking into account the overall context" be antisemitic.'
>
> 'I specifically discussed "the" actual historical state of Israel – not any more general or hypothetical state of Israel; and that second I was not making a point about "the Jews" but specifically about a form of colonialism which is not

> exceptional, but which is in fact part of a wider historical pattern.'
>
> Prof Miller insists that the idea of Israel as a settler colonial entity is well supported in the scholarly literature and that his work on Israel/Palestine is rigorously evidence based.
>
> He stated: 'I reject the smear, evidenced in this article, that critics of Israeli policies are antisemitic.' (Sugarman, 2018)

In my correspondence with the *JC* and its editor, I included a list of academic references to work on settler colonialism, which the paper did not publish.[1]

As a result of the *JC* story several of my colleagues at the University of Bristol received emails denouncing me as 'a dis-

1. These included the following: N. Abdo and N. Yuval-Davis (1995), 'Palestine, Israel and the Zionist settler project', in Daiva Stasiulis and Nira Yuval-Davis (eds), *Unsettling Settler Societies: Articulations of Gender, Race, Ethnicity and Class*, London: Sage, pp. 291–322. C. Elkins and S. Pedersen (eds) (2005), *Settler Colonialism in the Twentieth Century: Projects, Practices, Legacies*, London: Routledge. D. Lloyd (2012), 'Settler colonialism and the state of exception: The example of Palestine/Israel', *Settler Colonial Studies*, 2(1), 59–80. I. Lustick (1993), *Unsettled States, Disputed Lands: Britain and Ireland, France and Algeria, Israel and the West Bank-Gaza*, Ithaca, NY: Cornell University Press. T.G. Mitchell (2000), *Native vs. Settler: Ethnic Conflict in Israel/Palestine, Northern Ireland, and South Africa*, Westport, CT: Greenwood Publishing Group. I. Pappe (2008), 'Zionism as colonialism: A comparative view of diluted colonialism in Asia and Africa', *South Atlantic Quarterly*, *107*(4), 611–33. M. Rodinson, P. Buch and D. Thorstad (1973), *Israel: A Colonial-Settler State?* New York: Monad Press. O.J. Salamanca, M. Qato, K. Rabie and S. Samour (2012), 'Past is present: Settler colonialism in Palestine', *Settler Colonial Studies*, 2(1), 1–8. L. Veracini (2010), *Settler Colonialism*, Basingstoke: Palgrave Macmillan. P. Wolfe (2006), 'Settler colonialism and the elimination of the native', *Journal of Genocide Research*, *8*(4), 387–409.

gusting anti-Semite' who is 'supposedly educated, but when it comes to Jews he is a total disgusting lout just like the most illiterate Nazi'. The student newspaper *Epigram* also published a defamatory piece, which did not incorporate responses I had made to its reporter. The editor removed the piece and apologised when the defamatory content and the fact my responses had been ignored was pointed out to him.

Several months later the *JC* returned to the story revealing that a complaint had been made to the Labour Party that I had breached the IHRA definition in my talk in November 2018. It reported that: 'A complaint against Prof Miller was dismissed last week by Labour, which told the complainant it had "determined that this does not amount to a breach of Party rules" and would there[fore] "not be taking any further action"' (Sugarman, 2019).

The article quoted David Toube of the think tank Quilliam Foundation, who 'said Labour's rejection of the complaint against Prof Miller made it "now apparent that Labour's claim to abide by the IHRA Definition is a barefaced lie"' (Sugarman, 2019).

On Twitter, Toube posted a screen capture of a letter from the Labour Party dismissing a complaint, said to relate to me (Toube, 2019). Toube was previously, and apparently still is, closely associated with the *Harry's Place* blog, which was responsible for posting the recording of my talk in the first place ('David Toube', 2010). We can see in this case a microcosm of the way in which false allegations of antisemitism can arise and gain traction sometimes with significant negative effects for those so accused.

It is argued that since the appointment of the new general secretary Jennie Formby that the Labour Party complaints process has become more efficient and fit for purpose. One could be tempted to see my case and those of others who have rightly been found not to have breached the IHRA definition as a hopeful sign that this is the case.

To the extent that these decisions are now tending more towards an evidence-based approach this should be welcomed. In the end, an evidence-based approach will expose the overreach of those making complaints in bad faith.

Conclusion

What to do next

The first priority is to stamp out racism in the Labour Party whether it is against Jewish people, Roma or any other group. The Party cannot patrol every thought of every member, but it must always be clear in both public statements and in its procedures that there is no tolerance for any form of discrimination. It must do this, not because it is being told to, or because of the controversy in the Parliamentary Party or the media. It must be done because it is a democratic and socialist party and being utterly opposed to racism has to be at its core. It cannot speak with moral authority as a progressive movement if it is unable to resolve problems in its own house. To do this, it needs an effective, rapid and fair process as has been said above. This is needed to deal with instances of racism, but it is also needed to combat false claims. It is an unacceptable situation that hundreds of people have been wrongly accused and have suffered the consequences of this over long periods. In Jennie Formby's figures of February 2019, over 200 people were said to have no case to answer. The Party must defend members and elected representatives who are in these circumstances.

The leadership must also not be afraid to say clearly what is antisemitic and what is not. It needs a much more proactive approach towards clarifying the confusions which now exist in public debate. For example, when Richard Burgon MP was attacked for criticising Zionism, the leadership should have immediately made it clear what is acceptable commentary. It should not have been left to Geoffrey Bindman and Stephen Sedley to write to the *Guardian* pointing out that Burgon had no need to apologise. He had actually said:

> The enemy of the Palestinian people is not the Jewish people. The enemy of the Palestinian people are Zionists, and Zionism is the enemy of peace and the enemy of the Palestinian people

On this, Bindman and Sedley comment that:

> As Jewish lawyers who have been concerned for much of our lives with opposing racism in general and antisemitism in particular, we see no reason for any such apology. We are among the large number of Jews, worldwide, who regard with shame the military oppression by Israel of the Palestinian people and the ongoing appropriation, by illegal settlement, of the little land that is still theirs.
>
> The Jewish Labour Movement, a pro-Zionist group within the Labour party, has no entitlement to speak for Jews at large in seeking to stigmatise all criticism of Zionism as antisemitic. (Bindman and Sedley, 2019)

We can consider also the case of Miriam Margolyes who in a *Radio Times*' interview defended Corbyn. She is reported in the magazine as follows:

> A Labour Party member, she has firm opinions about anti-Semitism accusations directed at the party … 'Jeremy Corbyn, who is an excellent constituency representative, a serious person, is not an anti-Semite. I don't think there is the extent of anti-Semitism in the Labour Party that people seem to imply,' she says. 'I think it's to do with trying to stop Corbyn from being prime minister'.

She is also reported as being critical of Israel's treatment of the Palestinians: 'It's just a fact that the Israelis have behaved appallingly, they continue to do so, and people are dying. I am ashamed, as a Jew, of what's been done in my my name. I can't bear it' (Hodges, 2019: 21). Margolyes and the *Radio Times* were then attacked by the Campaign Against Antisemitism:

> The actor Miriam Margolyes, best known for her portrayal of Professor Sprout in the Harry Potter film series, has attempted to diminish the scale and impact of the Labour antisemitism scandal by characterising it as a plot to undermine Jeremy Corbyn ...
>
> Accusing Jews of making accusations of antisemitism in bad faith in order to aid a hidden agenda is a well-established antisemitic slur.

The CCA also called on the *Radio Times* to apologise for 'providing Ms Margolyes with a platform from which to spread her repulsive views' (Campaign Against Antisemitism, 2019).

We should see by now that such an argument collapses in its own contradictions. It seeks to suggest that Jews alone are being singled out as 'having an agenda', as 'acting in bad faith'. Even to suggest that estimates of antisemitism might be used in a political argument is supposed to be antisemitic. But actually all sorts of groups in our society have agendas, engage in public relations, use figures to their best advantage, or even produce propaganda or misinformation. To say that all Jewish people should be exempt from even the suggestion of such activity is an oddly inverted racial stereotype.

We might also ask, would it be antisemitic to suggest that some Jewish people are plotting to *support* Corbyn? The Jewish Voice for Labour have been accused of being founded to tackle allegations of antisemitism in the Labour

Party. They deny this and refute what they call the myths and misrepresentations which are made about them. As far as they are concerned, these misrepresentations suggest there is nothing to their position except an 'agenda' to support Corbyn. Those who criticise them might even think they are acting in bad faith. But would it be antisemitic to say so because they happen to be Jewish? The answer is of course not. It could only become antisemitic if it were linked to a racial stereotype. So it is acceptable to say that some people are acting in a specific way to achieve a purpose, in the same manner as other groups. But it is not acceptable to say that the behaviour is bad because it is done by people of a specific racial type and the activity is the sort of bad behaviour that characterises that 'type'. In the case of Israel, it is not racist to criticise the state for what it does, but it would be to say that Israel acts as it does because it is Jewish. Arguments about what antisemitism actually is become confused by the misuse of the term and the careless use of the label degrades the debate.

In the end, the arguments about the level of antisemitism in society and the Labour Party can only be resolved by evidence. The leadership should not be afraid to say very clearly what that evidence is. In that sense, it should not apologise for a version of the Party that does not exist. It should refute the view that there is 'an army of antisemites' and that the Party is 'riddled' with antisemitism when the evidence suggests that it is not. At the most basic level, it must correct the extraordinary level of public misunderstanding on what the number of cases actually is. The issue is how can a clear message be given on this and all the areas of policy which must be explained and promoted publicly. This is especially important in the face of intense attacks from the media and the divisions in the Party which have produced so much dissent and confusion.

Futures

It goes almost without saying that the Party needs an effective communications infrastructure for both mainstream and new media. It should have a well-resourced Rebuttal Unit to immediately counter false stories and to provide information both for key speakers and for distribution throughout local branches. It needs to train its members to use the available space in mainstream media such as phone-ins for radio, letters or any television which is open to contributions. Speakers who represent the Party need effective media training and must learn that careless talk costs elections. It cannot be a surprise that a right wing media attack the Labour Party. That is all the more reason to learn how to defuse loaded questions and give clear, well-informed answers. Most of all, the Party needs a proactive approach and to take the argument to the media. It is not just that, as our focus group members put it, the leader should 'stand up', or be forceful. The bigger issue is that Labour's responses were simply not getting through to them. To the extent that people criticised very high estimates of antisemitism in the Party, it was likely to be from their own resources – for example, based on distrust of the media, or because they had personal knowledge of Labour members.

Consider Labour's response to *The Sunday Times* headline on the 'anti-semite army' (7 April 2019a). This is a story that was simply waiting to be rejected. By this time, Labour had the figure of 0.1 per cent for reported cases and knew that a large number of accusations had turned out not to be Party members. The description of an antisemite army can thus be rejected. It is the type of story which produced in our focus group members responses such as: 'It's manipulated, political, blown out of proportion', 'It's such overkill, you think, "Oh come on!"'. These comments were not actually from Labour voters, but they were ready to accept that such an overblown claim was false.

The Sunday Times story was picked up by many news outlets. On the BBC website, it was noted that:

> The Sunday Times reported that it had seen internal documents which showed the party had failed to take disciplinary action in hundreds of cases.
>
> The newspaper reported that the documents, which have not been seen by the BBC, showed the party's system for dealing with complaints had been beset by delays, inaction and interference from the leader's office. (BBC News Online, 7 April 2019)

Labour stated that the figures were wrong and had been selectively leaked to misrepresent the content of emails. So the Labour response which should come from several major figures has to be to attack the headline. It can be said that there are cases still to be resolved, but talk of an army should be dismissed. On the BBC, the actual Labour response is reported as follows:

> Labour defended its handling of complaints, saying the figures used in the newspaper report were not accurate and had been 'selectively leaked from emails to misrepresent their overall contents'.
>
> 'The Labour Party takes all complaints of anti-Semitism extremely seriously and we are committed to rooting it out of our party,' a spokeswoman said.
>
> 'All complaints about anti-Semitism are fully investigated in line with our rules and procedures.' (BBC News Online, 7 April 2019)

It is not said who is speaking and a commentary on Labour's rules and procedures is unlikely to make an impact on public understanding. Why is Labour not able to offer a more powerful and positive response? One answer is, as we have seen, that it is internally divided and the integrity of the leader and the Party's procedures are being publicly attacked by some of its own MPs. This is a situation that cannot continue if Labour is to be electable. The issue is not simply that it needs to give a clear message. More importantly, it is not reasonable to ask the public to vote for a party which looks so disorganised, divided and confused. There has to be discipline within it which applies equally to all sections of the Party. It wishes to present itself as an organisation which is capable of implementing a major transformative programme. But how can it do so if its own MPs are bringing it into disrepute by, for example, leaking stories to a hostile media? The issue of the integrity of the Party as a whole and its credibility with the public is crucial. That integrity must be defended by the leadership. The constant traducing of the Party and its members produces a sense of disillusion both for members and potential voters. This is especially so since with the accession of Corbyn, people joined out of a sense of moral commitment and the hope that change is possible.

The rise of Corbyn and the new left wing leadership followed a period of around 30 years in which the Party had moved increasingly to the right. With the rise of New Labour and the leadership of Tony Blair, the Party had supported the war in Iraq, had embraced free markets, PFI, the securitisation of the state and globalisation. Later, under Ed Miliband, it was able to offer only minimal criticisms of the Conservative austerity programme. Left wing alternatives had been confined to the margins. But in the society as a whole, there was a growing discontent over inequality, insecurity at work, the casualisation of labour and the running down of health and other public services – in Galbraith's memorable phrase, the contrast between private wealth and public squalor.

There were very few politicians on the left who could offer an alternative, so in this sense Corbyn along with McDonnell were crucial to mobilising a more radical mass membership which could push for a new political programme. In practice, a great deal was achieved in this in a very short period. Previously marginal policies such as national ownership were pushed into the centre of public debate. In the election of June 2017, Corbyn increased Labour's share of the vote more than any other party leader since 1945. He and McDonnell began to look as if they were offering the most serious challenge to established power since the post-war Attlee government. This did not escape the attention of the right wing media. *The Sunday Times* editorial on the day of its headline on the 'anti-semite army', notes that:

> There are many concerns that should rule out a Jeremy Corbyn-led Labour Party from running this country. (*Sunday Times*, 7 April 2019b)

And indeed, this paper and the others of its stable will no doubt list them all. In the face of such hostility, the mass movement of Labour's membership is essential to defend Labour's programme. This is because activists have the capacity to engage in large-scale face-to-face contact with voters, and this is a very powerful way of countering distorted media messages. The process of knocking on doors and meeting directly with voters makes it possible to open a wider political conversation. In the Scottish Independence Referendum of 2014, support for the 'Yes' campaign had moved from around 29 per cent in 2013 to 45 per cent in the final vote. This was in the face of a mostly hostile press. A key factor in the vote was very extensive grassroots campaigning as the movement had recruited large numbers of new members. As Annie Thiec writes:

> the campaign on the ground … alongside party activists involved extra-parliamentary groups whose ambition was to engage people in a wider debate on what kind of society they wanted Scotland to be. (Thiec, 2015)

In the UK General Election of 2017, grassroots campaigning was again seen as a key factor. Emma Rees writes on what made the difference for Labour: 'In an era where many mistrust the media, face-to-face conversations that speak to the issues people care about only become more crucial' (Rees, 2017). Rachel Shabi also points to the effect of new first time canvassers recruited by Momentum: 'The group also sent scores of campaigners – some of them first-time canvassers – into the country's most marginal constituencies, helping to drive up support for Labour, house by house and street by street' (Shabi, 2017). There were other very important factors such as the use of social media and the training of activists. But what is crucial in making a movement such as this function effectively and grow is the sense of purpose and solidarity amongst the membership group. For this to be sustained, they must believe in the commitment of the candidates whose election they are seeking. Local democracy and the ability to select prospective MPs and other representatives is therefore another critical issue.

It is clear that the membership needed Corbyn and McDonnell since they offered the best hope to move the Labour Party towards a more progressive politics. At the same time, the leadership depended on the members to keep their own position in the face of attacks within the Parliamentary Party. As we have seen, the activists are also a key force in advocating a progressive alternative politics in public debate.

It is therefore central that the leadership should work to expand this mass movement and defend its integrity since it is key to Labour's future.

Last words

These are grim days for the fight against racism. Mainstream media stigmatise and spread hatred about groups such as asylum-seekers, migrants, Muslims and Roma (Philo et al., 2013). We live in times where a child can actually be taken from her parents because she looks a bit 'too white' to be with them. In this case from Ireland, the *Daily Mirror* reported:

> **Second blonde girl seized from gypsy family in Ireland 'looks nothing like siblings and speaks much better English'**
> (*Mirror*, 23 October 2013)

Her sister was reported in the *Daily Mail* as saying:

> 'We have all the documentation and we can prove that she is who we say she is ...
>
> They didn't give us a reason, but they said they had to take her,' she added. 'We think it is because she is different. She has blonde hair and blue eyes. Everybody was crying. This is all very traumatic for everybody.' (*Mail Online*, 23 October 2013)

The *Guardian* reported that the child was returned to her parents the following day after DNA tests and that a two-year-old boy had also been returned to another Roma family – he too had DNA samples taken (*Guardian*, 24 October 2013). What society can report such an event without a sense of outrage? There is little doubt that a climate of racism is being legitimised.

Antisemitism is most likely to be seen in social media, but there is strong evidence of a rise in this form of racism across Europe and elsewhere. In the US, there have been antisemitic attacks on synagogues. In October 2018, eleven people were killed in The Tree of Life synagogue in Pittsburg. Six months later, there was another shooting in San Diego, killing a woman and injuring three people. The second killer was also linked to an arson attempt on a mosque in the US. A letter which he was reported to have posted online said he was inspired by the attack on the mosque in Christchurch, New Zealand, in which 50 people had been killed (McDonald, 2019).

In Europe, the French government reported a rise of 74 per cent in antisemitic acts and threats between 2017 and 2018. On this, Frederick Potier, a French government official, responsible for combating racism and discrimination, commented that: 'What is new and what is feeding this anti-Semitic fever ... is the resurgence of a far right with really violent speech and acts' (Valadares, 2019). Potier also noted that the same figures had increased by 66 per cent in Italy the previous year and by around 50 per cent in the US (Valadares, 2019).

In France, there have also been antisemitic killings. As Pierre Tartakowsky of the French Human Rights League put it, 'People are now being killed simply because they are Jewish' (Valadares, 2019). In 2012, a rabbi and three children were shot dead at a Jewish school in Toulouse. In 2015, four people were killed at a kosher supermarket in Paris. Across Europe, there are reports of Jewish people being intimidated by the spread of antisemitism. *The Times* commented on the rise of ultra nationalist politics in Hungary. It notes that there are attempts to rehabilitate the reputation of Miklos Horthy, the Hungarian leader who oversaw the deportation of Jews to concentration camps. The report points also to the cover of a pro-government magazine:

> The image on the front page of the Hungarian pro-government magazine could easily have been propaganda from Nazi Germany: a portrait of Andras Heisler, president of the Federation of Hungarian Jewish Communities, surrounded by a shower of high-denomination banknotes. (Moody, 2019)

But as *The Times* notes, criticism was muted as 'Jews are scared to speak out' (Moody, 2019). In Holland, a survey in 2018, showed that nearly half of Dutch Jews actively tried to hide their Jewish identity or avoided situations where they thought they would be exposed to antisemitic reactions (*Ha'aretz*, 27 November 2018). *The Irish Times* reported on Poland where the nationalist Law and Justice Party has now made it illegal to speak of Polish complicity in the Holocaust. The paper notes that 'Jewish organisations in Poland have recently reported being flooded with hate mail' (*The Irish Times*, 15 February 2019).

In Germany, Petra Pau, an MP for the Die Linke Party, was reported as saying that more and more people now felt free 'to deny the Holocaust and engage in antisemitic agitation'. Pau is quoted in *The Irish Times* speaking about the violence of the far-right: 'Militant rightwing extremists are now openly calling for the desecration of Jewish institutions and attacks against Jewish people' (*The Irish Times*, 15 February 2019). The *Guardian* reported on the actions of the AfD party in Germany:

> The far-right Alternative für Deutschland (AfD) party has been widely accused of fomenting hate against refugees, Muslims and Jews.

> The party's co-leader, Alexander Gauland, described the Holocaust as a 'small bird dropping in over 1,000 years of successful German history'. (Henley, 2019)

The French politician Jean-Marie Le Pen notoriously stated that the gas chambers used to kill Jews were only a 'detail' of history. The *Guardian* notes that he had said this publicly several times, most recently in 2015 on a French television channel (*Guardian*, 6 April 2016).

In the UK, a study by the Pew Research Centre showed the population had a more favourable opinion of Jewish people than the European average (Pew Research Centre, 2014). But in 2018, the *Guardian* reported that:

> **British politics has worst record for antisemitism in Europe, poll says**
> (*Guardian*, 10 December 2018)

The headline is based on an attitudes survey of Jewish people in Europe by the EU's Agency for Fundamental Rights. The results show that antisemitism is perceived to be rising across Europe. But those for the UK were said to be peculiar because of the high level of concern expressed about the political sphere. Once again, the finger of blame is pointed at Jeremy Corbyn:

> The European commissioner for justice, Věra Jourová, told the Guardian the results were a dismal setback for the EU that should be taken up as a challenge by the heads of states and government.
>
> She urged Jeremy Corbyn, whose Labour party has battled accusations that it has allowed antisemitism to take hold within its ranks, to take heed of the results. (*Guardian*, 10 December 2018)

The issue of antisemitism in the Labour Party should not be minimised, but is it really credible to suggest that British politics is the worst in Europe citing Jeremy Corbyn? He has been criticised on issues such as not identifying the Mear One mural as antisemitic and as ignoring the charter of Hamas because the organisation was opposed to the Israeli occupation. But after his lifetime of anti-racism, can he really be classed alongside white supremacists, Holocaust deniers or the hard right parties that are now rising in Europe? Does anyone really believe that if the Battle of Cable Street was re-fought in the UK, then Corbyn and the movement he leads would be anywhere else than on the barricades with the Jews, rather than on the other side with the fascists?

Racism in the Labour Party has to be rooted out, but focusing so much on Corbyn and the Party can reduce the capacity to deal with other serious issues. The Israeli lawyer and activist, Eitay Mack, has commented on how Israel has chosen to fight 'the new anti-Semitism', rather than 'fighting anti-Semitism in eastern Europe or right-wing populist parties throughout Europe that are popular among anti-Semites, neo-nazis, anti-immigration activists, and Islamophobes' and he notes the danger:

> I am very worried about it. In Israel, you see daily articles about Jeremy Corbyn and his alleged anti-Semitism or his alleged support for it. This is ... a very dangerous game the Netanyahu government is playing. (Patel, 2018)

The Battle of Cable Street was invoked in a speech in 2018 by John McDonnell. *The Times of Israel* reported his call for unity and for a mass protest against the politics of the far-right:

> A newly-energised, well-funded network of hate is emerging ... Mr McDonnell added: 'The working class of Britain

> have a proud history of beating the far-right ... At Cable Street, the local Jewish community and socialists from across Britain stood firm against Oswald Mosley's Blackshirts.' (*Jewish News, Times of Israel*, 30 November 2018)

There are difficult times ahead for those who wish to defend progressive societies or the rights of migrants and refugees and to combat racism. The growth of inequality, insecurity in work, the effects of climate change and the mass movement of populations have all in some ways stimulated the demand for a new left wing politics. But they are also a fertile breeding ground for the rise of the far-right where the problems generated by an irrational economy can be laid at the door of minorities.

We were struck by the comments of one of the Labour activists with whom we spoke who had for many years demonstrated against the far-right on the streets. He said in the past, he had spoken with some of them and they had assured him that they weren't really fascists, they were just worried about migrants. But now, he said, they marched along with their arms in the air, doing Nazi salutes. There is a growing body of politicians and propagandists in Europe and elsewhere who are legitimising racism and pushing it into the mainstream of political life. To fight this requires a united front and the Labour Party should be a central part of it. It is a key progressive force and it must have a leadership and membership which is committed to fighting racism wherever it occurs, including within its own ranks. But the constant attacks for other purposes on its leader and the traducing of the membership as a whole is in the end counterproductive. It weakens the forces on which all minorities including Jewish people will depend for their security in the conflicts which lie ahead.

Appendix: Timeline of Events

Mike Berry and Greg Philo

This chapter charts the major controversies affecting Labour from the beginning of the Party's leadership election in 2015. The core focus of this review is the debates around antisemitism in the Party but it also references other key controversies such as the disputes over Labour's defence policy and the attempts by members of the Parliamentary Party to remove Jeremy Corbyn from the leadership. This period saw an intense focus on claims of antisemitism within Labour and the sheer volume of accusations means that this review only provides an account of a fraction of the more high-profile interventions. To give some indication of the extraordinary scale of the print media's coverage of this issue a Nexis search on national newspaper coverage mentioning Labour or Jeremy Corbyn and antisemitism produced 5497 articles between 15 June 2015 and 31 March 2019 at a rate of approximately four articles per day. A small selection (approximately 10 per cent) of headlines from a single week in 2018 gives an indication of the scale and intensity of this coverage:

'Corbyn's Labour has become a force for anti-Semitism'; Veteran MP Frank Field resigns the whip in protest over a culture of 'nastiness and intolerance' (*Telegraph*, 31 August 2018)

At Social Gatherings of British Jews All the Talk of is of Which Country to Flee to if Corbyn Becomes PM
(*Daily Mail*, 30 August 2018)

Corbyn is a Racist Say Jewish Leaders
(*Daily Mail*, 30 August 2018)

Jewish leaders condemn Corbyn over 'racist trope'
(*Telegraph*, 30 August 2018)

Corbynites will picket meeting to stop U-turn on antisemitism
(*The Times*, 30 August 2018)

Corbyn's comments most offensive since Enoch Powell, says ex-chief rabbi; Jonathan Sacks says Labour leader is antisemite who has given support to racists, terrorists and dealers of hate
(*Guardian*, 28 August 2018)

Labour 'will punish annoying antisemitism claims'
(*The Times*, 28August 2018)

JEZ MINDER FURY; Jewish MPs hire bodyguards for Labour conference amid anti-Semitism crisis
(*Sun*, 27 August 2018)

Labour MP 'agonising every day' about whether to quit over antisemitism row
(*Independent*, 26 August 2018)

Here's why this rabbi quit Unite over Len McCluskey's comments about Jews
(*Independent*, 26 August 2018)

Party Members 'Questioned Loyalty of UK Jews'
(*Mail on Sunday*, 26 August 2018)

KILLING LABOUR; Senior MP: Racism could lead to death of party
(*Sun*, 26 August 2018)

Jewish charity condemns Corbyn's 'antisemitic hate'
(*Independent*, 25 August 2018)

THE Sun SAYS Racist Corbyn
(*Sun*, Editorial, 25 August 2018)

Labour's Moral Vacuum: Corbyn's antisemitism makes Jewish MPs feel unwelcome in his party. It is time for the party to tell him he is no longer welcome as its leader
(*The Times*, Editorial, 25 August 2018)

Far right comes out for Corbyn; MP poised to quit over Labour leader's 'Zionist' slur as ex-BNP and Ku Klux Klan chiefs show support
(*The Times*, 25 August 2018)

Timeline

15 June 2015: The deadline closed for candidates to secure the nominations needed to be on the ballot for Labour's leadership election. Jeremy Corbyn secured the necessary 36 nominations shortly before the noon deadline with a number of Labour MPs reportedly giving him their vote to 'broaden the terms of debate'. Many MPs later regretted this decision with Margaret Beckett describing herself as a 'moron' for having nominated Corbyn (BBC Online, 2016). The other candidates on the ballot were Andy Burnham, Liz Kendal and Yvette Cooper.

13 July 2015: Jeremy Corbyn was questioned on *Channel 4 News* by Krishnan Guru-Murthy on his links to Hamas and Hezbollah and his description of them as 'friends'. This was followed by a series of articles in the *Mail* (McTague, 2015), *The Times* (Editorial, 17 July 2015) and the *Telegraph* (Gilligan, 2015) also criticising Corbyn for these links.

21 July 2015: A government spending bill which mandated cuts of £12 billion to the welfare budget passed the Commons with 184 Labour MPs following the Party whip and abstaining from the vote. Jeremy Corbyn was the only leadership candidate to vote against the bill and this decision was widely seen as proving a major boost to his leadership bid (Wintour and Watt, 2015).

22 July 2015: A YouGov poll of Labour Party members was published showing Corbyn having a decisive lead over the other candidates in the leadership election (Wintour and Perraudin, 2015). This led to a rash of interventions from New Labour figures urging Party members not to vote for Corbyn. Tony Blair warned that with Corbyn as leader the next election would 'mean rout, possibly annihilation' (Blair, 2015) and that 'if your heart is with Corbyn, get a transplant' (Savage and Fisher, 2015). Alan Johnson (2015) implored Labour voters to 'end the madness and elect' Yvette Cooper, while Neil Kinnock (2015) criticised the 'malign purposes' of the 'Troskyite left' and told voters that 'we are not choosing the chair of a discussion group'. Later in the month, the other candidates reportedly discussed a potential legal challenge to Corbyn's likely victory and an arrangement whereby two would drop out leaving the best placed candidate with a better opportunity to defeat Corbyn (Wintour and Watt, 2015). There were also reports from 'senior

Labour MPs' that were he to be elected Corbyn 'would never be allowed to remain in the job long enough to fight the 2020 general election' and that 'a coup could be launched within days of the result' (Ross and Gosden, 2015).

12 August 2015: The *Jewish Chronicle* (2015) published a front page editorial criticising Corbyn. The editorial stated that 'we are certain that we speak for the vast majority of British Jews in expressing deep foreboding at the prospect of Mr Corbyn's election as Labour leader. Because, although there is no direct evidence that he has an issue himself with Jews, there is overwhelming evidence of his association with, support for – and even in one case, alleged funding of – Holocaust deniers, terrorists and some outright antisemites'.

14 August 2015: Shadow Northern Ireland Secretary Ivan Lewis accused Jeremy Corbyn of 'expressing support for and failing to speak out against people who have engaged not in legitimate criticism of Israeli governments but in antisemitic rhetoric' (Mason, 2015a).

25 August 2015: Jeremy Corbyn was attacked by Yvette Cooper for 'appearing to endorse' Hamas and describing them as 'friends' in a 'fiery' leadership hustings on Radio 5 Live (Bloom, 2015).

29 August 2015: Jonathan Arkush, the president of the Board of Deputies of British Jews, stated that the 'Jewish community' were 'very angered' by his views on Israel and 'reported links to a Holocaust denier and anti-Semite' (Riley-Smith, 2015a).

31 August 2015: Corbyn was attacked from Conservative, Labour and Liberal Democrat MPs as well as parts of the press for comments he made in 2011 on Press TV that the decision to kill Bin Laden rather than arrest him was a 'tragedy' (Withnall, 2015).

12 September 2015: Corbyn was elected leader of the Labour Party in a landslide victory. He topped the poll with nearly 59.5 per cent of first-preference votes followed by Andy Burnham with 19 per cent, Yvette Cooper with 17 per cent and Liz Kendall with 4.5 per cent. Shortly afterwards, Yvette Cooper and six other shadow cabinet ministers said that they wouldn't serve under Corbyn. Jamie Reed, 'a shadow health minister, published his resignation letter on Twitter while Corbyn was still delivering his victory speech' (Mason, 2015b). When Corbyn attended his first meeting with the PLP it was reported that he was greeted with near silence which Forsyth (2015) claimed 'for a new leader ... is quite unprecedented'.

14 September 2015: Corbyn unveiled his first cabinet. Reflecting the weakness of the left within the Labour Party the cabinet was primarily composed of those from the centre and right of the Party. Key appointments included John McDonnell as Chancellor of the Exchequer, Andy Burnham as Home Secretary and Hilary Benn as Foreign Secretary.

15 September 2015: Politicians from both the Conservative and Labour Parties together with former military commanders and much of the press criticised Jeremy Corbyn for not singing the national anthem during a Battle of Britain remembrance ceremony at St Paul's Cathedral (Hope, 2015).

20 September 2015: A *Sunday Times* report featured comments from a serving general 'that there would be a direct challenge from the army and mass resignations if Corbyn became prime minister'. It was also reported that intelligence chiefs had told the newspaper that Corbyn would only be given 'restricted access' to intelligence through the police and security services (Shipman et al., 2015).

30 September 2015: Corbyn faced widespread criticism from political and media figures after telling the *Today Programme* that if he were to become prime minister he would tell the UK's defence chiefs never to use Britain's nuclear weapons (Wintour, 2015).

6 October 2015: The *Telegraph* was officially censured by IPSO, an independent press regulator, for a 'significantly misleading' front page story which had claimed that a prominent Labour MP had called Corbyn an 'anti-Semite' (Sweney, 2015).

5 November 2015: Less than two months into his leadership the *Independent* reported that Corbyn 'could be hit by a wave of resignations by moderate frontbenchers in an attempt to destabilise his leadership and pave the way for a coup aimed at ousting him' (Grice, 2015).

9 November 2015: Jeremy Corbyn was attacked by politicians and sections of the press and politicians for not bowing at the Remembrance Day service in Whitehall. When it was revealed he had bowed he was accused of not bowing low enough (Elgot, 2015).

16 November 2015: The Labour leader was subject to sustained criticism from within the PLP over an interview he gave in which he questioned the use of a 'general ... shoot to kill policy' and suggested that Britain's involvement in a series of foreign wars may have increased the terrorism threat to Britain. Following the interview

Corbyn was attacked in the Commons by his own MPs and later BBC Online (17 November 2015) reported that 'one Labour MP "savaged" Mr Corbyn during the meeting of the Parliamentary Labour Party ... while others said he was "aggressively heckled"'. The BBC Trust later found in the original interview which had created the controversy, the reporter Laura Kuenssberg had breached the Corporation's impartiality and accuracy guidelines by misrepresenting the context in which Corbyn had opposed 'shoot to kill' (Martinson, 2017).

24 November 2015: 14 Labour rebels voted to renew the Trident nuclear weapons system in defiance of the Party whip which was to abstain while Labour policy was still under review (Riley-Smith, 2015b).

2 December 2015: A vote on airstrikes against Islamic State in Syria saw Corbyn again come into conflict with parts of the PLP. He also faced calls to resign from three MPs (Smith, 2015). Corbyn had initially told his shadow cabinet that he wanted to agree a collective position and urged MPs to consult with local party members before making a decision. However, with many front bench MPs publicly siding with the government and threatening to resign unless being allowed a free vote, Corbyn backed down (Dominiczak and Riley-Smith, 2015). In the final vote a majority of the PLP voted with the leadership against airstrikes, but 66 MPs voted in favour.

17 February 2016: It was reported that the Labour Party's national student organisation had launched an inquiry into allegations of antisemitism at Oxford University (Tran, 2016). The co-chair of the club Alex Chambers had resigned claiming that 'a large proportion of both OULC and the student left in Oxford more generally have some kind of problem with Jews'. A number of Labour MPs also criticised the club's decision to support 'Israel Apartheid Week' with Louise Ellmann, the vice-chair of Labour Friends of Israel, describing the comparison to apartheid era South Africa as a 'grotesque smear'. The controversy was widely reported with the *Sun*'s Tony Parsons (2016) arguing that the controversy 'highlights the fact that Corbyn's Labour gives a very warm welcome to Jewhaters'. The two students accused of antisemitism were eventually cleared by an internal Labour Party investigation with the decision being criticised by Baroness Jan Royall, a former Labour leader in the House of

Lords, the Oxford University's Jewish society and the Jewish Labour Movement (Mairs, 2016).

20 March 2016: Lord Levy threatened to quit Labour over claims of antisemitism (Mason, 2016a).

27 April 2016: The Bradford West MP Naz Shah, and former Parliamentary Private Secretary (PPS) to John McDonnell, was suspended by Labour over a series of posts on Facebook. In one, Shah shared an image of Israel's outline superimposed over a map of the United States under the headline 'Solution for Israel-Palestine Conflict – Relocate Israel into United States', and added a comment – 'Problem solved' (Stewart, 2016a). Shah made a series of apologies over the posts and was given a formal warning that she faced expulsion from the Party for another transgression.

28 April 2016: Former London mayor Ken Livingstone was suspended by Labour following an interview on BBC Radio London. During the interview where he had defended Naz Shah's comments as 'over the top' but not antisemitic, Livingstone also claimed that Hitler had supported Zionism 'before he went mad and ended up killing 6 million Jews' and that there was a 'well-orchestrated campaign by the Israel lobby to smear anybody who criticises Israel policy as antisemitic' (Asthana and Mason, 2016) .The interview led to calls from numerous Labour MPs for Livingstone to be expelled and after the interview he was confronted by the Bassetlaw MP John Mann who shouted that Livingstone was a 'disgusting Nazi apologist' and 'a fucking disgrace' in front of a watching television crew (Withnall, 2016).

29 April 2016: Jeremy Corbyn announced the setting up of an independent inquiry into antisemitism in the Labour Party to be led by human rights lawyer and former director of Liberty Shami Chakrabarti (Stewart and Asthana, 2016).

2 May 2016: It was reported in *The Times* that 'Labour front-benchers were threatening to resign within weeks over Jeremy Corbyn's handling of the antisemitism row, amid claims that Jewish donors have abandoned the party' (Savage, 2016).

4 May 2016: Britain's Chief Rabbi Ephraim Mirvis (2016) launched an attack on Jeremy Corbyn for what he alleged was Labour's 'severe' problem with antisemitism and also criticised figures in the Party who 'claim that Zionism is separate from Judaism as a faith; that it is purely political; that it is expansionist, colonialist and imperialist'. Corbyn was also criticised by MPs from Israel's Labour Party with one Itzik Shmuli calling on him to resign (Dominiczak, 2016).

5 May 2016: The May local elections provided a mixed picture for Labour. The Party lost ground in Scotland and Wales but its vote share held up in England and it won the London mayoral contest. The day after the election two Labour MPs blamed the results in part on Corbyn's 'weak leadership, poor judgment and a mistaken sense of priorities' (Cox and Coyle, 2016).

28 May 2016: Jackie Walker, the vice-chair of Momentum, was readmitted after her suspension over a Facebook comment about Jews being 'the chief financiers of the sugar and slave trade' was lifted. It was also announced that Ken Livingstone had been fired from his job at LBC (Mortimer, 2016).

13 June 2016: The *Telegraph* reported that rebel Labour MPs were considering an attempt to force Jeremy Corbyn to resign. The newspaper reported that some MPs 'believe they can topple Jeremy Corbyn after the EU referendum in a 24-hour blitz by jumping on a media storm of his own making'. One MP explained how it could happen: 'Things go wrong, people have had enough, you start to see resignations, and it spirals from there' (Riley-Smith, 2016).

16 June 2016: Jo Cox, the Labour MP for Batley and Spen, was murdered by a far-right extremist outside Birstall library in West Yorkshire.

23 June 2016: Britain voted to leave the EU in the European Membership referendum.

24 June 2016: Two Labour MPs, Margaret Hodge and Ann Coffey, submitted a motion of no confidence in the leadership of Jeremy Corbyn. The motion, which was scheduled to be debated at the next meeting of the PLP, accused Corbyn of running a lacklustre campaign to remain in the EU. Within hours, Labour MPs began to publicly back the no confidence motion (Mason and Asthana, 2016).

25 June 2016: A report in the *Observer* claimed that Hilary Benn was coordinating a 'coup' attempt against Jeremy Corbyn (Boffey, 2016). Shortly afterwards, Corbyn sacked Benn triggering the resignation of over 20 shadow cabinet ministers. Corbyn refused to resign and began to assemble a new shadow cabinet.

28 June 2016: Labour MPs backed a no confidence vote in Corbyn by a margin of 172 to 40. However, the vote was non-binding and

Corbyn refused to resign citing the support of the Party's membership: 'I was democratically elected leader of our party for a new kind of politics by 60% of Labour members and supporters, and I will not betray them by resigning. Today's vote by MPs has no constitutional legitimacy' (Asthana et al., 2016).

30 June 2016: The Chakrabarti Report (2016) was released at a press conference in London. The report found that Labour was 'not overrun by antisemitism ... However, as with wider society, there is too much clear evidence (going back some years) of minority hateful or ignorant attitudes and behaviours festering within a sometimes bitter incivility of discourse' (2016: 1). The report made a series of recommendations about improving the Party's complaints and disciplinary procedures and urged 'members resist the use of Hitler, Nazi and Holocaust metaphors, distortions and comparisons in debates about Israel-Palestine in particular' (Chakrabarti, 2016: 11). Professor David Feldman, director of the Pears Institute for the Study of Antisemitism, described the report as 'an important document ... [that] marks a positive step towards ensuring that the Labour Party is a welcoming place for all minority groups' (Pears Institute for the Study of Antisemitism, 2016). However, Jonathan Sacerdoti, director of Communications at the Campaign Against Antisemitism, took a very different position arguing that the report 'did not examine the disgraceful cases of anti-Semitism in the party, or their even more disgraceful mishandling by the party leadership, including Jeremy Corbyn, who presides over a regime of the lightest slaps on wrists for even the most offensive and deliberate anti-Semites ... this inquiry is a vague, meaningless whitewash that will do nothing to rid Labour of anti-Semitism' (Hughes, 2016). The launch of the report was marred by a row at the event between the Labour MP Ruth Smeeth and the Momentum activist, Marc Wadsworth. Smeeth had walked out of the event after Wadsworth accused her of working 'hand in hand' with the *Telegraph*. Smeeth accused Wadsworth of spreading 'vile conspiracy theories about Jewish people' and argued that the fact that Jeremy Corbyn 'failed to intervene is final proof for me that he is unfit to lead, and that a Labour Party under his stewardship cannot be a safe space for British Jews' (Marshall, 2016).

5 July 2016: Naz Shah's suspension from Labour was lifted with the chair of the Jewish Labour Movement, Jeremy Newmark, praising her as 'a bold and courageous agent of change' (Elgot, 2016a).

8 July 2016: A report in the *Guardian* revealed that Labour membership had risen to half a million with more than 100,000 people joining following the referendum and challenge to Corbyn's leadership (Stewart, 2016b).

9 July 2016: Angela Eagle announced her intention to stand against Jeremy Corbyn in a leadership election. Four days later, Owen Smith also declared that he would stand in the contest.

12 July 2016: Labour's National Executive Committee (NEC) met to finalise the arrangements for the leadership election. In a secret ballot NEC members voted by 18 to 14 that the incumbent should automatically be on the ballot paper. The NEC also decided that new members who had joined in the previous six months would not be permitted to vote in the election and that registered supporters[1] who wanted to vote were to be given two days to register for a fee of £25.

18 July 2016: Jeremy Corbyn once again found himself at odds with the PLP, this time over the parliamentary vote to renew the Trident nuclear weapons system. Only 46 Labour MPs voted with Corbyn to oppose retention of Trident while 140 voted in favour of its renewal. A number of Labour MPs condemned Corbyn's stance with Jamie Reed describing it as 'juvenile and narcissistic' (Kuenssberg, 2016).

20 July 2016: Nominations closed for the Labour Party leadership election. With Angela Eagle having withdrawn the previous day the election was a two-way contest between Jeremy Corbyn and Owen Smith.

5 August 2016: The decision by the Labour Party to give Shami Chakrabarti a peerage after she conducted the inquiry into antisemitism in the Party was heavily criticised by Jewish leaders and Labour MPs. The Chief Rabbi, Ephraim Mirvis, said that after accepting the peerage the 'credibility of her report lies in tatters' (Hope and Hughes, 2016).

2 September 2016: A report in the *Guardian* alleged that the MP Ruth Smeeth had received more than 25,000 abusive messages, mostly on social media after the launch of the Chakrabarti Report

1. In the 2015 leadership election Labour allowed people to register as Labour supporters and have a vote in the contest for a payment of £3. In the 2016 election registered supporters were again allowed to vote but the registration fee was increased to £25.

into antisemitism. It was reported that the police were investigating one threatening message that Smeeth had received. Smeeth argued that Corbyn 'should be naming and shaming some of the worst perpetrators who are doing it in his name, and making it clear publicly that they do not speak for him, that this is unacceptable' (Mason, 2016b).

20 September 2016: Labour's NEC passed a motion promising to toughen up their rules on online abuse. It was reported that new and existing members would be required to sign a pledge about online behaviour or face expulsion from the Party (Asthana, 2016).

24 September 2016: Jeremy Corbyn was re-elected leader of the Labour Party winning 61.8 per cent of the votes cast. Corbyn also won a majority amongst all three categories of voters – Party members, registered supporters and affiliated supporters.

28 September 2016: It was reported that Jackie Walker had been suspended from the Labour Party for a second time following comments made at a Labour Party training event. Walker was criticised over statements on three subjects. It was alleged that she had downplayed the security issues facing Jewish schools, questioned why Holocaust Memorial Day did not commemorate other genocides and challenged the legitimacy of the antisemitism definition being taught by the Jewish Labour Movement. Walker didn't deny that she disagreed with the Jewish Labour Movement's definition of antisemitism – which she argued restricted criticism of Zionism – but disputed the claim that she had downplayed security fears face by Jewish schools: 'I did not raise a question on security in Jewish schools. The trainer raised this issue and I asked for clarification, in particular as all London primary schools, to my knowledge, have security and I did not understand the particular point the trainer was making' (Elgot, 2016b). On the subject of Holocaust Memorial Day, Walker later clarified her position by saying that she wasn't downplaying the Shoah but just questioning why the event only commemorated genocides from the 1940s onwards and didn't include the African genocide during the slave trade (*Channel 4 News*, 2016). The Labour MP John Mann called for her to be expelled claiming that she had 'inspired waves of anti-Semitic and racist backlash including Holocaust denial' (Press Association, 2016). Four days later, it was reported that she had also been removed from her position as vice-chair of Momentum.

13 October 2016: The House of Commons Home Affairs Committee's report *Antisemitism in the UK* was published. The report found that 'there exists no reliable, empirical evidence to support the notion that there is a higher prevalence of antisemitic attitudes within the Labour Party than any other political party' (House of Commons Home Affairs Committee, 2016: 44). However, the report argued that Corbyn's 'lack of consistent leadership on this issue, and his reluctance to separate antisemitism from other forms of racism ... [have] created what some have referred to as a "safe space" for those with vile attitudes towards Jewish people' (p. 44). Furthermore, it argued, the 'failure of the Labour Party to deal consistently and effectively with antisemitic incidents in recent years risks lending force to allegations that elements of the Labour movement are institutionally antisemitic' (p. 45). Jeremy Corbyn rejected those conclusions and argued that 'the report's political framing and disproportionate emphasis on Labour indicated that the report had become "politicized"' (Boffey and Sherwood, 2016).

30 November 2016: 158 Labour MPs rebelled against the leadership by voting against an SNP motion to carry out a new investigation into whether Tony Blair misled Parliament in the run-up to the Iraq war.

7 January 2017: The *Guardian* reported on an undercover investigation by Al Jazeera on the pro-Israel Lobby in Britain (MacAskill and Cobain, 2017). The documentary revealed the activities of an Israeli Embassy employee, Shai Masot, who was secretly filmed plotting to 'take down' MPs supportive of a Palestinian state. The documentary series also showed Masot discussing setting up a new pro-Israel youth group within the Labour Party while warning that nobody should discuss the fact that the Israeli Embassy has established the group. 'LFI (Labour Friends of Israel) is an independent organisation. No one likes that someone is managing his organization. That really is the first rule in politics.' The documentary sparked angry protests. Emily Thornberry described the revelations as 'deeply disturbing' and argued that the 'government should launch an immediate inquiry into the extent of this improper interference and demand from the Israeli government that it be brought to an end'.

2 February 2017: 47 Labour MPs rebelled against a three line whip and voted against triggering Article 50 to begin the process of leaving the EU. The leadership was also hit by a number of front bench resignations over the issue (Stewart and Mason, 2017).

5 April 2017: The Board of Deputies of British Jews, the Chief Rabbi, Tom Watson, Sadiq Khan and other Labour MPs condemned the decision by a disciplinary panel to extend Ken Livingstone's suspension by another year rather than expel him from the Party (Mason and Weaver, 2017).

18 April 2017: Theresa May announced a snap General Election on 8 June to 'make a success of Brexit' (Boyle and Maidment, 2017).

29 May 2017: Reports in the *Sun* and *Telegraph* accused Jeremy Corbyn of laying a wreath at the grave of Palestinians who were allegedly involved in the killing of Israeli athletes at the 1972 Munich Olympics. Jennifer Gerber, director of the Labour Friends of Israel, said 'It is almost unbelievable that any Labour MP would participate in a ceremony honouring a man involved in the vicious murder of innocent Israeli athletes.' A spokesperson for Corbyn said the Labour leader attended the ceremony because it was 'commemorating the bombing of the PLO headquarters in Tunis in 1985' and he did not personally lay a wreath (Hope, 2017). David Hearst (2018) argued that the media framing of the two PLO men who Corbyn had allegedly commemorated was misleading: 'Who were these two terrorists, anyway? Both were PLO men, the Palestinian faction that went on to negotiate Oslo and recognise Israel. One was Salah Khalaf, who met with the US ambassador in Tunis as part of the dialogue with the PLO authorised by the then US Secretary of State James Baker. Khalaf was identified by the Americans as a pragmatist who was shifting PLO policy. The second one was Atef Bseiso, the PLO's liaison officer with the CIA. Are we saying that two PLO men who created backchannels that would lead to the Madrid Conference and thence to Oslo should now be considered terrorists decades after the State department had got over that hurdle?'

8 June 2017: The General Election produced a major shock with the Conservative government losing its majority but remaining the largest party. Theresa May then moved to form a coalition government with the Democratic Unionist Party. Despite being predicted to lose up to a hundred seats, Labour won 30 seats with the Party increasing its share of the vote by the largest margin (9.6 per cent) since the end of the Second World War (Agerholm and Dore, 2017).

20 August 2017: The *Independent* reported a YouGov poll commissioned by the Campaign Against Antisemitism which found that 83 per cent of British Jews thought that the Labour Party was too tolerant of antisemitism amongst its MPs, members and supporters (Cowburn, 2017). The author of the report concluded that Labour voters 'are less likely to be antisemitic than other voters, so the cause of British Jews' discontentment with the party must be the way that it has very publicly failed to robustly deal with the anti-Semites in its ranks' (Campaign Against Antisemitism, 2017). However, Full Fact (2018) argued that although that explanation was 'plausible', it overlooked another possibility which was that since 'British Jewish people are more likely to vote for the Conservatives ... [they] might have a less favourable view of Labour as a result'. Full Fact also noted that the validity of the survey was questionable since it was based on a self-selected group rather than a random probability sample.

17 September 2017: Corbyn backed a Party rule change put forward by the Jewish Labour Movement which strengthened sanctions against antisemitic abuse (Elgot, 2017).

29 October 2017: Jeremy Corbyn opted not to attend an official dinner with Theresa May and Benjamin Netanyahu to celebrate the hundredth anniversary of the Balfour Declaration. Instead, Emily Thornberry went in his place. *The Sunday Times* reported that Mark Regev, Israel's ambassador to the UK, told the newspaper that 'those who oppose the historic declaration are "extremists" who reject Israel's right to exist and could be viewed on a par with terrorist groups such as Hamas' (Gadher, 2017).

6 November 2017: Three leading authors, Simon Schama, Howard Jacobson and Simon Sebag Montefiore, published a joint letter in *The Times* which was highly critical of Labour's approach to Zionism and antisemitism (Jacobson et al., 2017). In it the authors argued that they were 'alarmed' that 'constructive criticism of Israeli governments has morphed into something closer to antisemitism under the cloak of so-called anti-Zionism'. 'Anti-Zionism', they argued, 'frequently borrows the libels of classical Jewhating' which 'have become widespread in Jeremy Corbyn's Labour Party'. 'Anti-Zionism', the authors wrote, 'with its antisemitic characteristics, has no place in a civil society'.

6 December 2017: A leading minster in Benjamin Netanyahu's government, Gilad Erdan, publicly accused the Labour leadership of being antisemitic (Boffey, 2017).

1 March 2018: Ken Livingstone's suspension from Labour was extended by a further year while the Party opened another formal internal investigation into antisemitism (Elgot, 2018a).

9 March 2018: It was reported that Jeremy Corbyn used to be a member of a Facebook group – Palestine Live – where antisemitic messages had been posted. Corbyn said he had 'never trawled through the whole group. I have never read all the messages on it. I have removed myself from it ... obviously, any anti-Semitic comment is wrong.' The Campaign Against Antisemitism were reported as saying that there was 'no conceivable justification' for Corbyn's involvement in the group and that it would be filing a disciplinary complaint against him to the Labour Party (McGuinness and Heffer, 2018).

23 March 2018: Jeremy Corbyn apologised for having defended a mural by the grafitti artist Mear One in a Facebook post from 2012. The mural which had since been removed from a wall in London's East End featured caricatures of Rothschild and others on the backs of oppressed people. Corbyn stated that 'I sincerely regret that I did not look more closely at the image I was commenting on, the contents of which are deeply disturbing and anti-Semitic ... The defence of free speech cannot be used as a justification for the promotion of antisemitism in any form. That is a view I've always held' (Stewart, 2018).

25 March 2018: The Jewish Leadership Council and the Board of Deputies of British Jews issued a joint open letter criticising Jeremy Corbyn and the Labour Party. In the letter they accused the Labour Party of 'repeated institutional failure to properly address Jewish concerns and to tackle antisemitism.' The letter also accused Corbyn of 'repeatedly siding with antisemites rather than Jews', an attitude derived from the 'far left's obsessive hatred of Zionism, Zionists and Israel' and a 'conspiratorial worldview in which mainstream Jewish communities are believed to be a hostile entity, a class enemy' (Jewish Leadership Council, 2018). Shortly afterwards, Corbyn issued a statement which said he was 'sincerely sorry for the pain which has been caused' by 'pockets of antisemitism' and pledged that 'we must stamp this out from our party and movement.' Corbyn also extended an offer to meet the Board of Deputies of British Jews to hear their concerns (Coulter, 2018).

26 March 2018: Hundreds of people attended a rally in Parliament Square to protest against antisemitism in the Labour Party. The protest called by the Jewish Leadership Council and the Board of Deputies of British Jews was attended by MPs from different parties, including Labour, a number of whom gave speeches. Wes Streeting described the Chakrabarti Report as a 'whitewash' and pledged 'to drain the cesspit of antisemitism in the Labour Party' while Luciana Berger claimed 'that antisemitism within the Labour Party is now more conspicuous, it's now more commonplace and it's now more corrosive' (Cowburn and Kentish, 2018). Parliament Square also saw a counter-demonstration by the Jewish Voice for Labour group who put out a statement questioning the motives of those demonstrating against Labour: 'The Board of Deputies and the JLC and those supporting them must be aware that this is an attempt to influence local elections and has nothing to do with the real and necessary task of challenging racism and anti-Semitism at all levels of political life. We call on them to stop playing party politics and start representing what our community needs' (Brand, 2018).

28 March 2018: Christine Shawcroft resigned from her post as chair of Labour's internal disputes panel after leaked emails revealed that she had argued for a Labour councillor – who had been suspended for sharing an antisemitic image on Facebook – to be reinstated so he could stand in the local elections. Alan Bull, a council candidate in Peterborough had shared a photograph of the gates of the Auschwitz concentration camp headlined by the caption the 'International Red Cross report confirms the Holocaust of 6m Jews is a hoax'. In the leaked email Shawcroft had claimed that 'elements of Peterborough Labour party' had 'political reasons' for wanting Bull suspended and the Facebook post had been 'taken completely out of context' (Stewart and Perkins, 2018).

3 April 2018: Corbyn was criticised for attending a Passover Seder with members of the left wing Jewish group, Jewdas. The MP John Woodcock condemned the meeting as 'deliberately baiting the mainstream Jewish community days after they pleaded with him to tackle anti-Semitism', while the fertility expert Robert Winston said that Corbyn had made 'a humiliating insult to virtually the entire Jewish community' (Craig, 2018; Swinford and Maidment, 2018).

5 April 2018: A group of peers wrote to the Metropolitan police to report antisemitic behaviour on Facebook pages which backed Jeremy Corbyn. The letter drafted by Lord Polak, the honorary president of the Conservative Friends of Israel, stated that the social media messages 'go well beyond what can reasonably be considered as free speech, and we believe those which incite violence should urgently be investigated to establish whether they were made with serious intent' (Elgot, 2018c).

8 April 2018: A protest organised by the Campaign Against Antisemitism took place outside the Labour headquarters in Westminster. At the protest the actress Maureen Lipman accused Jeremy Corbyn of being an 'antisemite' while Gideon Falter, chairman of the Campaign Against Antisemitism, said that 'under Jeremy Corbyn, Labour has become a safe haven for racists. He is at home among them, having spent his political career seeking out and giving succour to Holocaust deniers, genocidal anti-Semitic terrorist groups and a litany of Jew-haters' (Haywood and Stevens, 2018).

10 April 2018: Avi Gabbay, the leader of the Israeli Labor Party, announced that the party was going to suspend links with Jeremy Cobyn and his office over antisemitism but would maintain contacts with the rest of the Labour Party. In a letter sent to the Labour leader Gabbay said that Corbyn had expressed 'very public hatred of the policies of the government of the state of Israel, many of which regard the security of our citizens and actions of our soldiers' (Elgot, 2018b).

17 April 2018: Labour MPs including Luciana Berger, Ruth Smeeth, Ian Austin, Joan Ryan, Margaret Hodge, Louise Ellman and John Mann made speeches denouncing their party during a Commons' debate on antisemitism (Crerar and Perkins, 2018). The same day a poll conducted for the *Independent* found that 61 per cent of respondents thought that Labour had a problem with religious or racial prejudice and that half of those polled thought that Jeremy Corbyn had handled the accusations of antisemitism 'badly'. However, 32 per cent also agreed to some extent with the statement that 'the problem of antisemitism is exaggerated to damage Jeremy Corbyn and the Labour leadership' (Watts, 2018).

18 April 2018: During Prime Minister's Questions Theresa May accused Jeremy Corbyn of allowing antisemitism to 'run rife' in the Labour Party.

24 April 2018: Jeremy Corbyn and Labour officials held a two-hour meeting with the leaders of the British Board of Deputies of British Jews and the Jewish Leadership Council. Corbyn described the meeting as 'positive and constructive' and re-emphasised his commitment to 'rooting out antisemitism from our party and our society'. However, the leaders of the two Jewish groups said that the meeting had been a 'missed opportunity' in that Corbyn hadn't agreed to implement any of their recommendations such as adopting the International Holocaust Remembrance Alliance (IHRA) definition of antisemitism (Walker and Elgot, 2018).

25 April 2018: Len McCluskey of Unite accused 'Corbyn-hater Labour MPs' of collaborating with the 'Tory press' to undermine their leader by presenting the 'Labour party as a morass of misogyny, antisemitism and bullying'. McCluskey named five MPs: Chris Leslie, Neil Coyle, John Woodcock, Wes Streeting and Ian Austin as being among 'a dismal chorus whose every dirge makes winning a Labour government more difficult' (Merrick, 2018a).

27 April 2018: Marc Wadsworth who accused the MP Ruth Smeeth of working 'hand in hand' with the *Telegraph* at the launch of the Chakrabarti Report was expelled by Labour for bringing the Party into disrepute (Hughes and Lister, 2018).

21 May 2018: Ken Livingstone resigned from the Labour Party saying the controversy around his suspension had become a distraction.

23 June 2018: Julia Neuberger, one of Britain's most senior rabbis, called on Jews to leave Labour because antisemitism in the Party was a 'disgrace' (Ellicott, 2018a).

6 July 2018: Labour's decision to adopt the IHRA definition of antisemitism in full – but without four of the eleven examples that accompanied it – proved controversial. The new definition was welcomed by some groups. Jewish Voice for Labour supported the decision as did Jon Lansman, the founder of Momentum, who argued that the new definition 'should be seen as the new gold standard' for defining antisemitism. In particular, Lansman (2018) argued the new code 'provides additional examples of antisemitism while giving context and detailed explanations to ensure it can be practically applied to disciplinary cases within the party'. Lansman also noted that 'three of the four examples that the party has been falsely accused of omitting are explicitly discussed in the code'. Ultimately Lansman argued the new code would take a robust approach to antisemitism while protecting free speech for critics of Israel particularly those 'oppressed groups, who have suffered at the hands of discriminatory Israeli state policies' (Lansman, 2018). However, the new definition was heavily criticised by Jewish groups. The Chief Rabbi Ephraim Mirvis stated that applying the new code would 'send an unprecedented message of contempt to the Jewish community'. The Board of Deputies, Jewish Leadership Council and the Community Security Trust issued a joint statement which said: 'They have distorted and diluted the IHRA definition of anti-Semitism that is widely accepted and used by the Jewish community, the UK Government, the Scottish Parliament, the Welsh Assembly, the Crown Prosecution Service, the police, and dozens of local authorities, to create their own weaker, flawed definition whose main purpose seems to be to protect those who are part of the problem.' It was also attacked by some of Jeremy Corbyn's most vociferous critics within the PLP (ITV News, 2018). Ian Austin described the decision to adopt the new definition as 'utterly shameful' and claimed that Labour had 'adopted a position on antisemitism that allows members to be antisemitic', while Wes Streeting (2018) dubbed it an 'utterly contemptible' move which would inflict 'devastating damage ... on Labour's relationship with the Jewish community' (ITV News, 2018).

16 July 2018: 68 rabbis sent a joint letter to the *Guardian* criticising the decision by the Labour Party not to adopt all the examples in the IHRA definition of antisemitism. In the letter the rabbis argued that by ignoring 'those who understand antisemitism the best, the Jewish community', the Labour leadership had chosen 'to act in the most insulting and arrogant way' (Belovski et al., 2018).

17 July 2018: Labour's NEC endorsed its new guidelines on the definition of antisemitism after a three-hour meeting though a decision was taken to consult again with Jewish groups on the definition. Afterwards the decision was criticised by Joan Ryan, chair of Labour Friends of Israel, who argued that the 'NEC has decided to prioritise the rights of those who wish to demonise and delegitimise the state of Israel over the struggle against anti-Semitism. This shameful action is antithetical to Labour's values and its history' (Schofield, 2018). Following the move to endorse the new definition of antisemitism Jeremy Corbyn was confronted over the issue by Margaret Hodge in the Commons. According to an MP, Hodge said to Corbyn 'You're a fucking anti-Semite and a racist ... you have proved you don't want people like me in the party' – though friends of Hodge later denied she swore. One MP who witnessed the altercation described Hodge's behaviour as 'shocking, bullying, intimidating and grossly offensive' (Crerar and Stewart, 2018). It was reported that Corbyn's response was 'calm' and he said 'I'm sorry you feel like that.' It was also reported that Corbyn was 'expected to want to invite Hodge to discuss the issue more calmly in a meeting, where he will explain the latest move to consult the Jewish community' (Waugh, 2018).

18 July 2018: Labour launched an investigation into Margaret Hodge's conduct after her attack on Jeremy Corbyn in the Commons the previous day (Bates, 2018).

23 July 2018: In an interview with Sky News, John McDonnell called for the investigation into Margaret Hodge to be dropped. McDonnell said that 'sometimes you can express anger – I'm one of these people who has in the past – and basically you have to accept that sometimes people can be quite heated in their expressions. Let's understand that and just move on' (Sparrow, 2018). Later that day, Labour MPs and peers used an emergency meeting to vote to force all MPs to abide by the IHRA definition with all examples. The motion tabled by Louise Ellman, vice-chair of Labour Friends of Israel, and Ruth Smeeth would have needed to be put to a vote of the full PLP to be binding but carried symbolic weight (Kentish, 2018a).

26 July 2018: Joint front page editorials published by Britain's three most prominent Jewish newspapers declared that the election of a Jeremy Corbyn government would pose an 'existential threat to Jewish life' in Britain. Under the heading 'United We Stand', the *Jewish Chronicle*, *Jewish News* and *Jewish Telegraph* argued that the 'stain and shame of antisemitism has coursed through her majesty's opposition since Jeremy Corbyn became leader in 2015' as the Party has 'seen its values and integrity eroded by Corbynite contempt for Jews and Israel'. A Labour spokesperson responded by saying that the Party posed 'no threat of any kind whatsoever to Jewish people' and their safety was a priority (Rawlinson and Crerar, 2018).

28 July 2018: It was reported that Ian Austin was under investigation by the Labour Party for 'abusive conduct' over a dispute in Parliament with fellow MP Ian Lavery over the IHRA definition of antisemitism (Doward et al., 2018).

30 July 2018: The *Jewish Chronicle* reported on a leaked secret recording of a NEC meeting on 17 July in which Pete Willsman questioned some of the accusations of antisemitism made against the Labour Party (Harpin, 2018a). In the recording Willsman said 'we should ask the 70 rabbis "where is your evidence of severe and widespread antisemitism in this Party?"' because 'what the rabbis have said about antisemitism in the Labour Party is simply false'. Willsman also said that 'some of these people in the Jewish community support Trump, are Trump fanatics and all the rest of it so I am not going to be lectured to by Trump fanatics making up duff information without any evidence at all'. After the recording was made public Willsman apologised for his comments and the Labour Party opted not to open a formal disciplinary hearing although he was warned that 'repetition of similar conduct is likely to result in formal disciplinary action' (Harpin, 2018b). However, the Board of Deputies of British Jews called for his expulsion from the Party and Momentum removed him from their slate of candidates for the NEC elections – though this didn't stop him later being elected to the governing body (BBC Online, 2018).

1 August 2018: Jeremy Corbyn apologised for attending an event featuring speakers 'whose views I completely reject' when he hosted a Holocaust Memorial Day event in 2010. At the event 'Never Again for Anyone – Auschwitz to Gaza', a speech was delivered by Hajo Meyer, a Jewish survivor of the Auschwitz concentration camp which repeatedly compared Israel's actions in Gaza to the Holocaust. It was reported that the Campaign Against Antisemitism had reported Labour to the Equality and Human Rights Commission over Corbyn's hosting of the event and over comments he made on Press TV where he suggested Israel could have been involved in the killing of Egyptian policemen. Gideon Falter, the chair of the Campaign Against Antisemitism, said: 'The evidence shows beyond all doubt that Jeremy Corbyn is an antisemite and the Labour party has become institutionally antisemitic. The problem is not one man but an entire movement which has hijacked the anti-racist Labour party of old and corrupted it with a racist rot' (Marsh, 2018).

6 August 2018: Labour dropped the investigation into Margaret Hodge. A Labour source claimed that Hodge had 'expressed regrets' for her comments but this was denied by Hodge who said neither she nor the Party had apologised (Elgot, 2018d).

11 August 2018: Jeremy Corbyn was accused of comparing Israel to Nazi Germany while speaking to the Palestinian Return Centre in 2013. In his speech Corbyn said the 'West Bank is under occupation of the very sort that is recognisable by many people in Europe who suffered occupation during the Second World War with the endless roadblocks, imprisonment, irrational behaviour by the military and the police.' Jennifer Gerber, the director of Labour Friends of Israel, said the statement was 'appalling' (Zeffman, 2018). It was also reported that the former Labour MP Jim Murphy had taken out a full page advert in the *Jewish Telegraph* where he accused the Labour leadership of being 'intellectually arrogant, emotionally inept and politically maladroit' in its handling of accusations of antisemitism (Zeffman, 2018). The controversy over Corbyn's visit to a Palestinian cemetery (see entry for 29 May 2017) was also reignited after the *Daily Mail* featured the story in its Saturday edition (Sinmaz, 2018). Accusations over what happened in Tunis dominated headlines for a week following the initial *Daily Mail* article with Corbyn denying repeated claims that he commemorated Palestinians allegedly linked to the killing of Israeli athletes at the 1972 Munich Olympics. The controversy was particularly unusual as at one point the Labour leader became involved in a war of words on Twitter with the Israeli Prime Minister who had stated: 'The laying of a wreath by Jeremy Corbyn on the graves of the terrorist who perpetrated the Munich massacre and his comparison of Israel to the Nazis deserves unequivocal condemnation' (Kentish, 2018b).

16 August 2018: The leaders of three major unions – Unite, UNISON and GMB – were reported to be calling on Labour to adopt the IHRA definition with all examples in an attempt to end the controversy. However, Len McCluskey, the head of UNITE, also accused the leadership of the Jewish community of 'truculent hostility' and 'refusing to take 'yes for an answer', while pointing to a series of commitments made by Labour to tackle antisemitism (Stewart and Elgot, 2018). On the same day in a Sky News interview, Margaret Hodge accused Jeremy Corbyn of being an antisemite and compared Labour's disciplinary process to Nazi Germany. She said: 'On the day that I heard they were going to discipline me and possibly suspend me, I kept thinking: what did it feel like to be a Jew in Germany in the 30s? It felt almost as if they were coming for me' (Kentish, 2018c). A Labour source described Hodge's comments as 'extreme and disconnected from reality'.

23 August 2018: *The Mail Online* posted a video of a speech Corbyn had given at a conference in Parliament in 2013. In the speech Corbyn had praised a talk made by the Palestinian ambassador, Manuel Hassassian, about the history of Palestine. He then directed criticism at pro-Israel activists including Richard Millett, who had confronted Hassassian after his speech. According to Corbyn, he had 'defended the Palestinian ambassador in the face of what I thought were deliberate misrepresentations by people for whom English was a first language, when it isn't for the ambassador'. The excerpt from his speech which caused the controversy was as follows: 'This [Hassassian's speech] was dutifully recorded by the, thankfully silent, Zionists who were in the audience on that occasion, and then came up and berated him afterwards for what he had said. They clearly have two problems. One is that they don't want to study history, and secondly, having lived in this country for a very long time, probably all their lives, don't understand English irony either. Manuel does understand English irony, and uses it very effectively. So I think they needed two lessons, which we can perhaps help them with.' Corbyn later said that he had used the term Zionist 'in the accurate political sense and not as a euphemism for Jewish people' but also that 'I am now more careful with how I might use the term "Zionist" because a once self-identifying political term has been increasingly hijacked by antisemites as code for Jews' (Stewart and Sparrow, 2018). However, Corbyn's speech was heavily criticised. Gideon Falter, chair of the Campaign Against Antisemitism, said: 'The fact that Jeremy Corbyn knew Richard Millett makes this incident even worse. From his privileged platform as an MP, he was using antisemitism to bully and abuse a Jewish member of the public. This rank antisemitic bullying would be the end of any other politician. Jeremy Corbyn must go'. The MP Mike Gapes branded Corbyn a 'racist anti-Semite' and pledged to quit the Party while Luciana Berger said the video contained 'inexcusable comments' which made her 'as a proud British Jew feel unwelcome in my own party' (Simons and Stickings, 2018).

25 August 2018: A number of newspapers reported that Jewish Labour MPs were to be offered bodyguards because of 'fears of attacks from Jeremy Corbyn's hardline supporters' (Owen, 2018).

28 August 2018: The former chief Rabbi Jonathan Sacks claimed the speech in which Corbyn described Richard Millett and fellow pro-Israel activists as not understanding English irony was 'the most offensive statement made by a senior British politician since Enoch Powell's 1968 "Rivers of Blood" speech'. Sacks said that the speech was 'divisive, hateful and, like Powell's speech, it undermines the existence of an entire group of British citizens by depicting them as essentially alien' (Merrick, 2018b).

30 August 2018: The Birkenhead MP Frank Field quit the Labour Party and accused Jeremy Corbyn of being 'a force for antisemitism in British politics'. Field had also lost a no confidence vote by his local party the previous month. Field declined to call a by-election so he could stand as an independent (Kentish, 2018d).

2 September 2018: During an appearance on the *Andrew Marr Show* the former chief Rabbi Jonathan Sacks reiterated his claim that Jeremy Corbyn was as great a threat to race relations as Enoch Powell. Sacks claimed that a majority of British Jews now feared bringing up their children and that the Labour leader was 'in danger of engulfing Britain in the kind of flames of hatred that have reappeared throughout Europe' (Embury-Dennis, 2018). On the same day, an alliance of four Arab-dominated parties in Israel's Parliament issued a letter which both defended Jeremy Corbyn and rejected the view that Labour should adopt the IHRA definition of antisemitism with all examples. The letter said: 'when some try to force the Labour party into using as its litmus test a definition of antisemitism that goes far beyond anti-Jewish animus to include anti-Zionism, we must raise our voices and decry these efforts. We commend Jeremy Corbyn for his decades of public service to the British people, and for his longstanding solidarity with all oppressed peoples around the world, including his unflinching support for the Palestinian people. We stand in solidarity with Jeremy Corbyn and we recognise him as a principled leftist leader who aspires for peace and justice and is opposed to all forms of racism, whether directed at Jews, Palestinians, or any other group' (Tibi et al., 2018).

4 September 2018: Labour's NEC agreed to adopt the IHRA definition of antisemitism with all examples. Jeremy Corbyn had attempted to add a page and half clarification to protect free speech on Israel but this was not endorsed by the NEC. Part of Corbyn's rejected statement dealt with criticism of discrimination in the Israeli state: 'It cannot be considered racist to treat Israel like any other state or assess its conduct against the standards of international law. Nor should it be regarded as antisemitic to describe Israel, its policies or the circumstances around its foundation as racist because of their discriminatory impact, or to support another settlement of the Israel-Palestine conflict' (Sabbagh, 2018).

6 September 2018: A number of national newspapers reported on a poll commissioned by the *Jewish Chronicle* which found that nearly 40 per cent of British Jews would seriously consider leaving the UK if Jeremy Corbyn became prime minister (Drury, 2018).

7 September 2018: Joan Ryan, the chair of Labour Friends of Israel and one of Jeremy Corbyn's most persistent critics, lost a vote of confidence called by her local constituency party. Ryan denounced the constituency members who voted against her as 'Trots, Stalinists Communists and assorted hard left' (Kentish, 2018e).

9 September 2018: During an interview on Sky News the Labour MP Chuka Umunna claimed that Labour had failed to adequately deal with cases of antisemitism, which meant that the Party now fitted 'the definition of institutional racism as outlined by Sir William Macpherson in the Macpherson report'. Labour's Dawn Butler said that Umunna's comments were 'disappointing', and tweeted 'I have literally spent all of my life fighting racism. And today is a sad day. UK Labour is NOT institutionally racist' (Walker, 2018). In the Sky News interview Umunna also called on Jeremy Corbyn to 'call off the dogs' – a reference to constituency Labour Party members who had recently passed votes of no confidence in Labour MPs such as Joan Ryan and Frank Field.

11 September 2018: During a fringe event at the annual TUC Conference Mark Serwotka, head of the Public and Commercial Services Union, suggested that Israel could have been behind the accusations of antisemitism against Labour to distract from its killing of unarmed civilians. Serwotka had said 'in a year when dozens of Palestinians including children were gunned down – unarmed innocent civilians – by the Israeli military, in a year when the Americans are cutting off aid ... isn't it a vile world when, instead of being on the front foot, denouncing these atrocities, demanding an independent and sovereign state for the Palestinian people, we have had a summer of asking ourselves whether leading Labour movement people are in any way antisemitic?'. Serwotka continued: 'I'm not a conspiracy theorist, but I'll tell you what – one of the best forms of trying to hide from the atrocities that you are committing is to go on the offensive and actually create a story that does not exist for people on this platform, the trade union movement or, I have to say, for the leader of the Labour Party.' The comments were denounced by Euan Philipps, a spokesperson for Labour against Antisemitism, who said: 'Mark Serwotka's speech is a stark illustration of how deeply embedded antisemitism is within the Labour movement. To intimate that the Israeli government is somehow responsible for the antisemitism crisis that has torn across the Labour Party this summer is a baseless lie' which 'callously dismisses the serious and legitimate concerns of the Jewish community, while also drawing on antisemitic tropes (including dual loyalty and conspiracy theory) to draw attention from what is a recognised issue of discrimination against Jews across the political left. The suggestion that there is a malevolent power manipulating British politics is as absurd as it is offensive.' Jennifer Gerber, director of Labour Friends of Israel, said: 'Mr Serwotka's comments are despicable ... for a general secretary of a major trade union to allude to conspiracy theories and blame Jews for their own persecution shows the extent of the problem we now see on the left' (Kentish, 2018f).

12 September 2018: In an interview on ITV's *Good Morning Britain* Labour's deputy leader, Tom Watson, suggested that the Labour general secretary should step down if the problems in the Labour Party over antisemitism hadn't been resolved by Christmas (Cowburn, 2018).

23 September 2018: The Labour Party was heavily criticised by some of its own MPs at a fringe meeting at the Labour Party Conference. Speaking at a rally organised by the Jewish Labour Movement, Wes Streeting said that antisemitism could cost Labour the next election and condemned as 'sickening' the 'double standards of Labour MPs and Labour members who attacked Boris Johnson [over his comments about the Muslim niqab] but stay silent on antisemitism in our party'. Stella Creasy went even further and said: 'Nazism doesn't turn up fully formed, wearing shiny black boots and black shirts and goose-stepping. It appears every single day, slowly but surely, as the debate is turned. It builds bit by bit, it gains little by little. It paints itself as the victim punching up, it paints its victims as enemies, as traitors, as the other, with dual loyalties. It rejects those norms and the conventions on antisemitism that we have worked so hard to defend. To many it looks like it's moral but weak, until we are too late and it becomes evil and powerful. That is the threat we face if we do not confront this' (Kentish, 2018g).

24 September 2018: During a speech at the annual Labour Party Conference, Len McCluskey, the leader of the Unite union, hit out at those who had criticised Jeremy Corbyn over claims of antisemitism. McCluskey said that 'anyone has a right to disagree and a right to criticise – we are a democratic party – but I am talking about some MPs turning into an echo chamber for whatever line of attack the Tories and the press are deploying against us'. He continued: 'anyone with a point of view should be heard, but anyone screaming: "You are a racist" at Jeremy Corbyn, has lost every sense of moral proportion, and I might add, comrades, that they've lost every shred of decency as well ... It's time for all of us – each and every one of us – to speak up for our leader: the most decent and principled man in politics today. He should not have to face these attacks alone, and while Unite is here and good comrades like you, he never will have to' (Kentish, 2018h).

1 November 2018: A poll commissioned by the pro-Israel advocacy group, the British Israel Communications and Research Centre (BICOM), on public perceptions of Jeremy Corbyn was published in the national press. The poll found that 38 per cent agreed with the statement: 'Whatever Jeremy Corbyn claims, his actions and past history point to him being anti-Semitic' (Ellicott, 2018b).

2 November 2018: It was reported that Scotland Yard had begun an investigation into antisemitic hate crime by Labour members. A file of paperwork produced by Labour Party staff on alleged cases of antisemitism was leaked to the LBC radio station who then handed it the Metropolitan Commissioner Cressida Dick. Dick told the *Today Programme* that the Met were 'not going to investigate the Labour Party' but 'if somebody passes us material which they say amounts to a crime we have a duty to look at that and not just dismiss it' (Wyatt, 2018).

27 November 2018: Labour dropped its disciplinary investigation into the MP Ian Austin over alleged abusive conduct (Elgot, 2018e).

28 December 2018: It was reported in the national press that Jeremy Corbyn had been 'ranked fourth in a list of the world's biggest threats to Jews last year by a human rights group', the Simon Wiesenthal Center (Ellicott, 2018c). Corbyn was ranked below the Tree of Life Synagogue Attack and the desecration of US campuses with Swastikas but above AirBNB who were listed at number six for delisting 200 rental units in Israeli settlements in the occupied territories (Israel, 2018).

27 January 2019: *The Times* and a number of other national titles reported that the *Countdown* host Rachel Riley was being given extra security on the programme after online abuse and threats from people who claimed to be supporters of Jeremy Corbyn (Sylvester, 2019). Riley (2019) said she had been motivated to act against antisemitism in the Labour Party after seeing posters at London bus stops saying 'Israel is a racist endeavour' and that after speaking out the abuse and threats had started.

28 January 2019: The former Archbishop of Canterbury George Carey criticised Jeremy Corbyn over his handling of accusations of antisemitism in the Labour Party and said that the 'weakness of his statements can give the impression that he is, deep-down, somebody who doesn't like Jewish people' (Spillett, 2019).

7 February 2019: A report by the Community Security Trust found that nearly one in ten incidents of 'verbal or physical abuse or damage' were linked to disputes over antisemitism in the Labour Party (Hymas, 2019).

8 February 2019: A no confidence motion in Luciana Berger MP by Liverpool Waverly constituency branch was withdrawn, reportedly 'after considerable pressure from the central party and Corbyn's office'. Tom Watson, the deputy leader, had written to the Party's general secretary asking her to suspend the branch because of allegations that Berger was being subject to antisemitic bullying. Local party members who supported Berger pointed to the actions of Kenneth Campbell, a local critic who had written on Facebook that Berger should be 'exposed for the disruptive Zionist she is'. However, others said that the vote of no confidence was motivated by other considerations including the view that Berger was continually trying to undermine the Labour leadership together with the belief that she was preparing to leave the Party (Parveen and Walker, 2019).

11 February 2019: In an email to Labour MPs the Party's general secretary Jenny Formby revealed that since April 2018, 673 Labour members had been investigated for antisemitism and twelve expelled. The Party also stated that no prior data could be compiled because there was 'no consistent and comprehensive system for recording and processing cases of antisemitism' – a claim disputed by the previous general secretary Iain McNicol. Of the 673, Formby revealed that 220 did not have sufficient evidence to proceed while 146 were given a preliminary warning. Of the 307 members who were investigated or suspended, decisions had been made by the NEC in approximately a third of them and more than 40 members left voluntarily and 42 members were referred to Labour's highest disciplinary body the National Constitutional Committee (NCC), the only body with the ability to expel members. The NCC had expelled twelve members, six had received other sanctions, five had left of their own accord and there were 19 cases outstanding. Formby also reported that more than 400 complaints had been made against people who had turned out not to be Labour members. Formby denied that the accusation that antisemitism existed in the Labour Party was just a smear and said: 'I have seen hard evidence of it and that is why I have been so determined to do whatever is possible to eliminate it from the party. It is also the reason why I made it a priority to implement robust procedures to deal with it whenever it is identified.' However, at the weekly meeting of the PLP some MPs questioned the data and demanded more details of the criteria for different sanctions. Margaret Hodge queried the figures pointing out she had personally submitted more than 200 cases of 'vile antisemitism'. Formby later reported that just 20 of those related to Labour Party members. It was also reported that MPs felt 'deflated' leaving the meeting with one commenting, the 'bigger issue in all this is a lack of solidarity for Jewish MPs and an expectation of needing to prove everything with the party, rather than support for victims of racism' (Elgot, 2019a).

17 February 2019: Former Labour vice-chairman Michael Dugher announced he was leaving the Party stating that the organisation he joined 'no longer exists' and is 'institutionally anti-Semitic' (Telegraph reporters, 2019).

18 February 2019: Seven Labour MPs declared they were leaving the Party to form the Independent Group. In explaining their decision to leave, the seven – all of whom were long-term and persistent critics of the Labour leadership – pointed to policy differences and concerns over antisemitism in the Party. One MP, Luciana Berger, said she could not remain in a party that was 'institutionally antisemitic' and that she was leaving behind 'a culture of bullying, bigotry and intimidation'. The Shadow Chancellor John McDonnell called on the seven MPs to face by-elections since they were no longer sitting as Labour MPs – the basis on which they had been elected – but all seven refused. It was also reported that the Independent Group had set itself up as a private company which meant that details of its funding structure didn't have to be disclosed. After the resignations the deputy leader Tom Watson warned that more MPs would leave Labour unless it changed its policy on Brexit and antisemitism (Perraudin and Rawlinson, 2019).

19 February 2019: The Jewish Labour Movement were reportedly planning to hold an extraordinary general meeting to consider disaffiliating from Labour amid claims that the Party could see a 'mass walkout' of Jewish members (Kentish, 2019a). It was also reported that a Labour MP had apologised after criticism of comments she had made on social media about the funding of the Independent Group. Ruth George, the MP for High Peak, had written on Facebook: 'Support from the State of Israel, which supports both Conservative and Labour Friends of Israel, of which Luciana [Berger] was chair, is possible and I would not condemn those who suggest it, especially when the group's financial backers are not being revealed. It's important for democracy to know the financial backers for any political group or policy.' The comments were condemned by the Board of Deputies of British Jews who tweeted: 'What on earth does Ruth George MP think she is saying? That the departure of seven previously Labour MPs could be funded by Israel? Jews are rightly concerned when elected representatives start indulging conspiracy theories and tropes' (Sugarman, 2019).

20 February 2019: An eighth Labour MP Joan Ryan, the chair of Labour Friends of Israel, quit the Labour Party to join the Independent Group. In resigning, Ryan accused Corbyn and the 'Stalinist clique that surrounds him' of 'presiding over a culture of anti-Jewish racism and hatred of Israel' (Kirby, 2019).

21 February 2019: Over 200 Jewish members and supporters of the Labour Party wrote a joint letter to the *Guardian* reaffirming their commitment to the Labour Party and Jeremy Corbyn who they described as 'a crucial ally in the fight against bigotry and reaction' with a 'lifetime record of campaigning for equality and human rights, including consistent support for initiatives against antisemitism' (Dore et al., 2019).

22 February 2019: Ian Austin became the ninth MP to quit Labour inside a week. Austin said he had resigned because of a 'culture of extremism, antisemitism and intolerance' in the Party and said he didn't want to see Jeremy Corbyn become prime minister (Sabbagh, 2019).

24 February 2019: In an interview on the *Andrew Marr Show* Tom Watson urged Jeremy Corbyn to address what he described as a 'a crisis for the soul of the Labour party'. Watson claimed that he had been given a dossier of 50 instances of antisemitism perpetrated by Labour members and challenged Corbyn to take a personal lead in reviewing each case. Watson also said that the Labour general secretary's reforms 'have not been adequate. They have not succeeded' (Stewart, 2019a).

25 February 2019: On the *Today Programme* on Radio Four, Jon Lansman said that the problem of antisemitism was widespread in the Labour Party and that he felt 'regret, sadness and some shame' over Luciana Berger's decision to quit the Party. Lansman said Labour was not 'institutionally antisemitic' and Jeremy Corbyn was an 'anti-racist' but the Party now contained 'perhaps a few hundred ... hardcore antisemites' who could be 'kicked out ... if we improve our processes' (Jacobson, 2019). Later that day, Tom Watson was reported as claiming he was going to take personal charge of antisemitism and bullying complaints made by MPs to bring them to the attention of the Labour leadership, 'effectively creating' what one MP described as a 'a parallel disciplinary process' (Elgot, 2019b). Also on the same day, the *Guardian* published a joint letter from 561 Jewish people challenging those who had written the letter supporting Corbyn the previous week (see entry for 21 February 2019). In the letter the signatories said that Labour was no longer 'a force for good in promoting anti-racism' because 'it could not root out antisemitism from its midst' and 'tolerated those accusing Jews of manufacturing antisemitism' (Aaron et al., 2019).

27 February 2019: The Derby MP Chris Williamson was suspended from the Party after comments he made to a Sheffield Momentum group that Labour had not been robust enough in pushing back against claims that it was a racist party. In footage posted online, Williamson said: 'The party that has done more to stand up to racism is now being demonised as a racist bigoted party. I've got to say I think our party's response has been partly responsible for that because in my opinion – I never have I would say – we've backed off far too much we've given too much ground, we've been too apologetic. What have we got to apologise for? For being an anti-racist party? And we've done more to actually address the scourge of anti-semitism than any other political party. Any other political party and yet we're being traduced.' Williamson's speech drew fierce condemnation with Tom Watson, the GMB leader Tim Roche and the charity Hope Not Hate calling for the whip to be removed from Williamson (Stewart and Walker, 2019).

28 February 2019: Nearly 500 Corbyn supporters signed a joint letter to the *Guardian* apologising to the Jewish community for the Party's handling of antisemitism. In the letter which was backed by Momentum the signatories said: 'We are Labour members who support Jeremy Corbyn in his leadership and the progressive, socialist programme and anti-racist principles of the Labour Party. We have seen antisemitism from Labour members and supporters, online or offline. We recognise that as a movement we have been too slow to acknowledge this problem, too tolerant of the existence of antisemitic views within our ranks, too defensive and too eager to downplay it. We sincerely apologise to the Jewish community, and our Jewish comrades in the party, for our collective failure on this issue to date' (Walker and Mason, 2019).

2 March 2019: A controversy erupted over leaked emails detailing how the Labour Party disciplinary unit handled accusations of antisemitism in 2018. The leaked email showed that staff from the leader's office and officials acting on behalf of the general secretary, Jennie Formby, were involved in adjudicating on cases – sometimes recommending more severe punishments and sometimes less stringent penalties than those suggested by Party staff. Tom Watson claimed the leaked emails suggested 'unacceptable political interference in dealing with antisemitism cases' and that the processes for dealing with 'racism and abuse had failed'. However, this was contested. A Party source said that 'seeking advice on cases was a hangover from the previous process, which Jennie Formby overhauled when she took up her post' so that the leader's office and her team were cut out of the procedure. The source also claimed that Watson's criticisms represented 'a deeply unfair attack on staff working in good faith to apply the party rule book to individual cases and get through the backlog of unresolved complaints Formby inherited' (Savage and Helm, 2019).

4 March 2019: It was reported that the Labour Party was looking into bringing in Lord Falconer to carry out an independent review of how the Party investigated antisemitism cases (Stewart, 2019b).

6 March 2019: It was reported that the Equalities and Human Rights Commission (EHRC) were close to making a decision on whether to launch an investigation into whether the Labour Party complied with equalities law in its handling of complaints of antisemitism. The EHRC were responding to separate dossiers compiled by the Campaign Against Antisemitism and the Jewish Labour Movement (Sabbagh and Pidd, 2019). Later in the day, it was reported that at an emergency meeting of the Jewish Labour Movement, the organisation had decided to 'stay and fight' rather than cut ties with the Labour Party (Kentish, 2019n).

8 March 2019: Margaret Hodge called for Labour branches which had supported Chris Williamson or had rejected the IHRA definition of antisemitism to be shut down. Hodge also argued that antisemitism had got much worse in the Party since her argument with Corbyn in July 2018: 'What has happened under Corbyn is that antisemitism, which was always completely stamped on at the fringes, has been given permission to come into the mainstream and, like a cancer, is infecting and growing through the party ... One of my real concerns is: what started off as absolutely the exception became the familiar and is now becoming systemic … Anyone who is really serious about zero-tolerance of antisemitism would close down constituencies where it happens' (Mason, 2019a).

27 March 2019: Jackie Walker was expelled from the Labour Party for a pattern of behaviour which demonstrated 'prejudicial and grossly detrimental behaviour against the party' following a two-year suspension (Elgot, 2019c).

2 April 2019: In a video produced by the charity Hope Not Hate the former prime minister Gordon Brown said that Labour had 'let the Jewish community down' over its handling of the anti-Semitism scandal and he had joined the Jewish Labour Movement (Milne, 2019).

7 April 2019: The Jewish Labour Movement passed a motion of no confidence in Jeremy Corbyn and claimed that he was 'unfit to be prime minister' (Maidment, 2019).

14 April 2019: A secret recording made by Margaret Hodge of a conversation between the MP and Jeremy Corbyn was reported in *The Sunday Times*. In the recording Corbyn expressed concern that evidence of antisemitism in the Party may have been 'mislaid or ignored' (Kerbaj et al., 2019). Corbyn was then criticised by David Lammy who told the BBC's Andrew Marr that 'there has been a failure of leadership, it's a stain on Jeremy Corbyn's leadership of this party'.

19 April 2019: The Shadow Justice Secretary Richard Burgon apologised after video footage came to light of him saying that: 'The enemy of the Palestinian people is not the Jewish people, the enemy of the Palestinian people are Zionists and Zionism is the enemy of peace and the enemy of the Palestinian people. We need to be loud, we need to be proud in support of a free Palestine'. Burgon had previously denied saying that 'Zionism was the enemy of peace' and when the footage came to light he stated that he regretted making the statement and didn't agree with it. Mike Katz, chair of the Jewish Labour Movement, said that a majority of Jews identified as Zionists and 'insulting a core part of their identity and then dissembling about it is shameful behaviour from a senior frontbencher in our party' (Mason, 2019b). However, Burgon was defended in a letter to the *Guardian* by two Jewish lawyers Geoffrey Bindman and Stephen Sedley. In their letter the lawyers said that they saw 'no reason' for Burgon to apologise and declared themselves to be 'among the large number of Jews, worldwide, who regard with shame the military oppression by Israel of the Palestinian people and the ongoing appropriation, by illegal settlement, of the little land that is still theirs' (Bindman and Sedley, 2019).

1 May 2019: Jeremy Corbyn was criticised by Jewish groups for having written a forward in 2011 for an updated edition of J.A. Hobson's 1902 book, *Imperialism: A Study*. The book had contained a short section which featured antisemitic theories about Jewish bankers and Corbyn hadn't criticised this in the forward. The

Jewish Labour Movement called for Corbyn to resign and the Board of Deputies of British Jews demanded a 'full explanation' (Martin, 2019). However, Donald Sassoon (2019), Emeritus Professor of Comparative European History at Queen Mary University of London denounced the criticism as 'ridiculous'. Sassoon stated the book 'has been taught for years in universities up and down the country and 'no one has ever felt the need to highlight the 10 lines or so, in a book of 400 pages, which are antisemitic'. Furthermore, Sasson argued that the antisemitic passage was 'completely marginal to the text' which he could never recall being discussed in any scholarly journals.

5 May 2019: The *Mail on Sunday* reported that the group Labour Against Antisemitism had compiled a dossier involving over 15,000 screenshots detailing instances of antisemitism in the Labour Party (Carlin, 2019). A spokesman for the organization, Euan Phillips, said that it had presented the evidence to Labour's compliance unit but the Party's response had been 'shocking and alarming' with reports ignored and members who had exhibited the 'most appalling levels of racism ... given only the lightest reprimand'.

28 May 2019: The Equalities and Human Rights Commission announced that it was launching a formal investigation into Labour's handling of antisemitism complaints following submissions made by the Campaign Against Antisemitism and the Jewish Labour Movement. The Labour Party rejected claims it had not handled antisemitism complaints fully and fairly or that it had acted unlawfully. It also pledged to cooperate fully with the EHRC investigation (Mason, 2019c).

Bibliography

Aaron, S., Aarons-Richardson, B., Abendstern, S., et al. (2019) 'Labour is no longer a force for good in promoting anti-racism' [Letter to the editor], *Guardian*, 25 February. Available from: www.theguardian.com/news/2019/feb/25/labour-is-no-longer-a-force-for-good-in-promoting-anti-racism, accessed 1 July 2019.

ADR (2009) CST, *Antisemitic Discourse Report 2009*. Available from: https://cst.org.uk/publications/cst-publications/antisemitic-discourse-reports, accessed 11 May 2019.

Agerholm, H. and Dore, L. (2017) 'Jeremy Corbyn increased Labour's vote share more than any of the party's leaders since 1945', *Independent*, 9 June. Available from: www.independent.co.uk/news/uk/politics/jeremy-corbyn-election-result-vote-share-increased-1945-clement-attlee-a7781706.html, accessed 1 July 2019.

Alderman, G. (2016) 'Expel Labour's enemy within', *Jewish Chronicle*, 24 March. Available from: www.thejc.com/comment/columnists/expel-labour-s-enemy-within-1.62310, accessed 28 March 2019.

Appeal (2018) 'Labour must reject biased IHRA definition that stifles advocacy for Palestinian rights', Appeal by Palestinian civil society to the British Labour Party and affiliated trade unions, *openDemocracy*, 28 August. Available from: www.opendemocracy.net/uk/palestinian-civil-society-groups/labour-must-reject-biased-ihra-definition-that-stifles-advocacy-, accessed 27 June 2019.

Asthana, A. (2016) 'Labour introduces tougher policy to tackle "tsunami of online abuse"', *Guardian*, 21 September. Available from: www.theguardian.com/media/2016/sep/20/labour-launches-tougher-policy-on-tsunami-of-online-abuse, accessed 1 July 2019.

Asthana, A. and Mason, R. (2016) 'Ken Livingstone suspended from Labour after Hitler remarks', *Guardian*, 28 April. Available from: www.theguardian.com/politics/2016/apr/28/ken-livingstone-suspended-from-labour-after-hitler-remarks, accessed 1 July 2019.

Asthana, A., Syal, R. and Elgot, J. (2016) 'Labour MPs prepare for leadership contest after Corbyn loses confidence vote', *Guardian*, 28 June. Available from: www.theguardian.com/politics/2016/jun/28/

jeremy-corbyn-loses-labour-mps-confidence-vote, accessed 1 July 2019.

Baldwin, T. (2018) *Ctrl Alt Delete*, London: Hurst & Company.

Bates, L. (2018) 'Margaret Hodge launches legal challenge to Labour attempt to discipline her in anti-Semitism row', *PoliticsHome*, 23 July. Available from: www.politicshome.com/news/uk/political-parties/labour-party/jeremy-corbyn/news/97077/margaret-hodge-launches-legal, accessed 1 July 2019.

BBC Online (2015) 'Jeremy Corbyn backtracks on "shoot-to-kill" policy', 17 November. Available from: www.bbc.co.uk/news/uk-34106214, accessed 1 July 2019.

BBC Online (2016) 'Margaret Beckett: I was moron to nominate Jeremy Corbyn', 22 July. Available from: www.bbc.co.uk/news/uk-politics-33625612, accessed 1 July 2019.

BBC News Online (2018) 'Ken Livingstone "cannot stay in Labour", says Chakrabarti', *Daily Politics*, 13 May. Available from: www.bbc.co.uk/news/amp/uk-politics-44099540, accessed 8 April 2019.

BBC Online (2018) 'Labour action urged over Peter Willsman's anti-Semitism remarks', 31 July. Available from: www.bbc.co.uk/news/uk-politics-45014771, accessed 1 July 2019.

BBC News Online (2018) 'Anti-Semitism: Labour suspends member over Tom Watson "Jewish donors" post', 6 August. Available from: www.bbc.co.uk/news/amp/uk-politics-45086365, accessed 13 March 2019.

BBC News Online (2018) 'Jeremy Corbyn "wreath laying"' attacked by Israeli PM', 14 August. Available from: www.bbc.co.uk/news/amp/uk-politics-45170622, accessed 18 April 2019.

BBC News Online (2019) 'Labour anti-Semitism row: Falconer under pressure to reject job', 5 March. Available from: www.bbc.co.uk/news/uk-politics-47458111, accessed 12 May 2019.

BBC News Online (2019) 'Corbyn criticised over handling of anti-Semitism cases', 7 April. Available from: www.bbc.co.uk/news/amp/uk-politics-47845390, accessed 26 April 2019.

BBC One, Andrew Marr Show (2018) 'Thornberry: Home Secretary "should quit' over Windrush failures', 22 April. Available from: https://www.bbc.co.uk/programmes/p0651kq9, accessed 27 June 2019.

BBC Radio 4 (2018) PM at 5pm: Interviews, context and analysis, 30 October. Available from: www.bbc.co.uk/programmes/m0000y9c, accessed 27 March 2019.

BDS (2019) 'What is BDS?' Available from: https://bdsmovement.net/what-is-bds, accessed 28 April 2019.

Beinart, P. (2019) 'Debunking the myth that anti-Zionism is antisemitic', *Guardian*, 7 March. Available from: www.theguardian.com/news/2019/mar/07/debunking-myth-that-anti-zionism-is-antisemitic, accessed 28 March 2019.

Belovski, H., Dweck, J., Janner-Klausner, L. et al. (2018) 'Labour party must listen to the Jewish community on defining antisemitism' [Letter to the editor], *Guardian*, 16 July. Available from: www.theguardian.com/politics/2018/jul/16/labour-party-must-listen-to-the-jewish-community-on-defining-antisemitism, accessed 1 July 2019.

Bennett, W.L. and Livingston, S. (2018) 'The disinformation order: Disruptive communication and the decline of democratic institutions', *European Journal of Communication*, 33(2), 122–39.

Bindman, G. (2018) 'How should antisemitism be defined'. Available from: www.theguardian.com/commentisfree/2018/jul/27/antisemitism-ihra-definition-jewish-writers, accessed 12 May 2019.

Bindman, G. and Sedley, S. (2019) 'Richard Burgon and criticism of Zionism' [Letter to the editor], *Guardian*, 23 April. Available from: www.theguardian.com/politics/2019/apr/23/richard-burgon-and-criticism-of-zionism?CMP=Share_AndroidApp_Facebook, accessed 25 April 2019.

Bisharat, O. (2017) 'Start by fighting anti-Arab racism in Israel', *Ha'aretz*, 12 June. Available from: www.haaretz.com/opinion/.premium-start-by-fighting-anti-arab-racism-in-israel-1.5483158, accessed 26 June 2019.

Blair, T. (2015) 'Tony Blair: Even if you hate me, please don't take Labour over the cliff edge', *Guardian*, 13 August. Available from: www.theguardian.com/commentisfree/2015/aug/12/even-if-hate-me-dont-take-labour-over-cliff-edge-tony-blair, accessed 1 July 2019.

Bloom, D. (2015) 'Yvette Cooper accuses Jeremy Corbyn of legitimising homophobic and anti-Semitic extremists in fiery radio hustings', *Mirror*, 25 August. Available from: www.mirror.co.uk/news/uk-news/yvette-cooper-accuses-jeremy-corbyn-6315098, accessed 1 July 2019.

Boffey, D. (2016) 'Hilary Benn seeks shadow cabinet backing to oust Corbyn', *Observer*, 25 June. Available from: www.theguardian.com/politics/2016/jun/25/hilary-benn-jeremy-corbyn-labour-leadership-eu-referendum-brexit, accessed 1 July 2019.

BoD (2014) 'Jews in numbers'. Available from: www.bod.org.uk/jewish-facts-info/jews-in-numbers/, accessed 12 May 2019.

BoD (2018) 'Board of Deputies and Jewish Leadership Council react to Labour's refusal to adopt antisemitism definition in full', 5 July.

Available from: www.bod.org.uk/board-of-deputies-and-jewish-leadership-council-react-to-labours-refusal-to-adopt-antisemitism-definition-in-full/, accessed 27 June 2019

Boffey, D. (2017). 'Labour leadership in UK has antisemitic views, says Israeli minister', *Guardian*, 6 December, Available from: www.theguardian.com/politics/2017/dec/06/labour-leadership-in-uk-has-antisemitic-views-says-israeli-minister-gilad-erdan, accessed 1 July 2019.

Boffey, D. and Sherwood, H. (2016) 'Jeremy Corbyn accused of incompetence by MPs over antisemitic abuse', *Guardian*, 16 October. Available from: www.theguardian.com/politics/2016/oct/16/jeremy-corbyn-antisemitism-chakrabarti-inquiry, accessed 1 July 2019.

Boyle, D. and Maidment, J. (2017) 'Theresa May announces snap general election on June 8 to "make a success of Brexit"', *Telegraph*, 18 April. Available from: www.telegraph.co.uk/news/2017/04/18/breaking-theresa-may-make-statement-downing-street-1115am1/, accessed 1 July 2019.

Brand, P. (2018) 'Jeremy Corbyn sorry for "pain and hurt" caused by anti-Semitism in Labour Party', ITV News, 25 March. Available from: www.itv.com/news/2018-03-25/corbyn-labour-anti-semitism-apology/, accessed 1 July 2019.

Brennan, S. (2019) '"Hitler had the right idea" claim posted from Labour councillor's Facebook on thread about travellers', *North Wales Live*, 8 April. Available from: www.dailypost.co.uk/news/north-wales-news/hitler-right-idea-claim-posted-16094361, accessed 9 April 2019.

BuzzFeed News (2019) 'Leaked emails reveal Labour's Compliance Unit took months to act over its most serious anti-semitism cases', 11 May. Available from: www.buzzfeed.com/alexwickham/leaked-emails-reveal-labours-compliance-unit-took-months-to, accessed 20 May 2019.

Cammaerts, B., DeCillia, B., Viera Magalhães, J. and Jimenez-Martínez, C. (2016) *Journalistic Representations of Jeremy Corbyn in the British Press: From 'Watchdog' to 'Attackdog'*, Media@LSE Report. Available from: http://eprints.lse.ac.uk/67211/1/CAmmaerts_Journalistic%20representations%20of%20Jeremy%20Corbyn_Author_2016.pdf, accessed 1 June 2019.

Campaign Against Antisemitism (2017) 'Antisemitism Barometer 2017'. Available from: https://antisemitism.uk/wp-content/uploads/2017/08/Antisemitism-Barometer-2017.pdf, accessed 1 July 2019.

Campaign Against Antisemitism (2019) 'Radio Times publishes Miriam Margolyes' vile claims that antisemitism in Labour is exaggerated "to stop Corbyn from being Prime Minister"', 19 April. Available from: https://antisemitism.uk/radio-times-publishes-miriam-margolyes-claims-that-antisemitism-in-labour-is-exaggerated-to-stop-corbyn-from-being-prime-minister/?mc_cid=730e5a4035&mc_eid=2229d5091f&fbclid=IwAR2a1Bj6nDXHm1edlEBbl9m4kfRaAcJnoop9zoZPMOuTXibd2BP4ZXDoQDQ, accessed 25 April 2019.

Carlin, B. (2019) 'Now Labour is facing 15,000 page dossier of racism claims', *Mail on Sunday*, 5 May.

Cartwright, A. (2016) 'Corbyn's first week: Negative agenda setting in the press', Media Reform Coalition. Available from: www.mediareform.org.uk/wp-content/uploads/2015/11/CorbynCoverageUPDATED.pdf, accessed 1 June 2019.

Chakrabarti, S. (2016) 'The Shami Chakrabarti Enquiry'. Available from: https://labour.org.uk/wp-content/uploads/2017/10/Chakrabarti-Inquiry-Report-30June16.pdf, accessed 1 July 2019.

Channel 4 News (2016) Twitter, 4 October. Available from:https://twitter.com/Channel4News/status/783356543752216577, accessed 1 July 2019.

Cohen, B. (2019) 'The Lawrence Inquiry 20 years on', February. Available from: www.runnymedetrust.org/uploads/StephenLawrence20briefing.pdf, accessed 12 May 2019.

Cohen, N. (2018) 'Why has Labour run the risk of alienating progressive Jews?', 7 July. Available from: www.theguardian.com/commentisfree/2018/jul/07/labour-antisemitism-jeremy-corbyn, accessed 27 June 2019.

Cohen, R. (2017) 'Artists for Palestine UK', 5 March. Available from: https://artistsforpalestine.org.uk/2017/03/05/dear-rabbi-sacks-stop-your-lies-about-bds/, accessed 27 March 2019.

Compaine, B.M. (2005) 'The media monopoly myth: How new competition is expanding our sources of information and entertainment', New Millennium Research Council. Available from: http://cloudfront-assets.techliberation.com/wp-content/uploads/2008/02/Final_Compaine_Paper_050205.pdf, accessed 1 June 2019.

Cotler, I. (2010) 'Defining the new antisemitism', *National Post*, 9 November. Available from: https://nationalpost.com/full-comment/irwin-cotler-defining-the-new-anti-semitism, accessed 11 May 2019.

Coulter, M. (2018) 'Jeremy Corbyn anti-Semitic mural row: Party leader sorry for pain caused by "pockets"' of anti-semitism within Labour', *Evening Standard*, 25 March. Available from: www.standard.co.uk/news/politics/jeremy-corbyn-apologises-for-pain-and-hurt-caused-by-antisemitism-in-the-labour-party-a3798716.html, accessed 1 July 2019.

Cowburn, A. (2017) 'Over 80 per cent of British Jews believe Labour is too tolerant of anti-Semitism within its ranks, poll finds; The poll also found that a further 65 per cent of respondents believe the Government does not do enough to protect British Jews, while 52 per cent said the Crown Prosecution Service could do more', *Independent*, 20 August.

Cowburn, A. (2018) 'Tom Watson suggests Labour's general secretary should quit if antisemitism row not dealt with by Christmas', *Independent*, 12 September. Available from: www.independent.co.uk/news/uk/politics/labour-antisemitism-row-corbyn-tom-watson-general-secretary-quit-christmas-a8534546.html, accessed 1 July 2019.

Cowburn, A. and Kentish, B. (2018) 'Hundreds of people protest outside Parliament against antisemitism in the Labour Party', *Independent*, 26 March. Available from: www.independent.co.uk/news/uk/politics/labour-party-antisemitism-jeremy-corbyn-protest-parliament-square-israel-palestine-jewish-a8274996.html, accessed 1 July 2019.

Cox, J. and Coyle, N. (2016) 'We nominated Jeremy Corbyn for the leadership. Now we regret it', *Guardian*, 6 May. Available from: www.theguardian.com/commentisfree/2016/may/06/jeremy-corbyn-leadership-labour-mps-elections, accessed 1 July 2019.

Craig, J. (2018) 'Jeremy Corbyn criticised for meeting radical group Jewdas amid anti-Semitism row', Sky News, 4 April. Available from: https://news.sky.com/story/jeremy-corbyn-criticised-for-meeting-radical-group-jewdas-amid-anti-semitism-row-11314813, accessed 1 July 2019.

Crerar, P. and Perkins, A. (2018) 'Jeremy Corbyn accused of lacking moral clarity on antisemitism', *Guardian*, 17 April. Available from: www.theguardian.com/world/2018/apr/17/jeremy-corbyn-accused-of-lacking-moral-clarity-on-antisemitism, accessed 1 July 2019.

Crerar, P. and Stewart, H. (2018) 'Labour acts against Margaret Hodge for calling Corbyn racist', *Guardian*, 18 July. Available from: www.theguardian.com/politics/2018/jul/18/labour-party-to-take-action-against-mp-who-called-corbyn-a-racist, accessed 1 July 2019.

Daily Mail, PressReader (2019) '15,000 incidents on anti-Semitism dossier', 6 May. Available from: www.pressreader.com/uk/daily-mail/20190506/281655371504357, accessed 26 May 2019.

Dana, J. (2019) 'This election has nailed once and for all the myth that Israeli voters want peace', *The National*, 10 April. Available from: www.thenational.ae/opinion/comment/this-election-has-nailed-once-and-for-all-the-myth-that-israeli-voters-want-peace-1.847446, accessed 21 April 2019.

'David Toube' (2010) *Powerbase*. Last modified 21 July 2010. Available from: http://powerbase.info/index.php/David_Toube, accessed 6 June 2019.

Dearden, L. (2019) 'Two-thirds of Tory members believe UK areas "under sharia law", as poll reveals scale of Islamophobia in party', *Independent*, 24 June. Available from: www.independent.co.uk/news/uk/politics/tory-islamophobia-sharia-law-poll-conservative-party-members-leadership-a8971731.html, accessed 26 June 2019.

Dhrodia, A. (2017) 'Unsocial media: Tracking Twitter abuse against women MPs', *Amnesty Global Insights*, 3 September. Available from: https://medium.com/@AmnestyInsights/unsocial-media-tracking-twitter-abuse-against-women-mps-fc28aeca498a, accessed 26 June 2019.

Dominiczak, P. (2016) 'Chief Rabbi: Labour has a "severe" problem with anti-Semitism', *Telegraph*, 4 May. Available from: www.telegraph.co.uk/news/2016/05/03/chief-rabbi-labour-has-a-severe-problem-with-anti-semitism/, accessed 1 July 2019.

Dominiczak, P. and Riley-Smith, B. (2015) 'Labour civil war: How Jeremy Corbyn failed to make his party oppose Syrian air strikes', *Telegraph*, 30 November. Available from: www.telegraph.co.uk/news/politics/Jeremy_Corbyn/12026058/Labour-civil-war-How-Jeremy-Corbyn-failed-to-make-his-party-oppose-Syrian-air-strikes.html, accessed 1 July 2019.

Dore, E., Epstein, D., Feder, G. et al. (2019) 'Jeremy Corbyn's Labour is a crucial ally in the fight against antisemitism' [Letter to the editor], *Guardian*, 21 February. Available from: www.theguardian.com/politics/2019/feb/20/jeremy-corbyn-labour-party-crucial-ally-in-fight-against-antisemitism, accessed 1 July 2019.

Doward, J., Helm, T. and Ramchandan, J. (2018) 'Second MP investigated in row over Labour's antisemitism code', *Guardian*, 28 July. Available from: www.theguardian.com/politics/2018/jul/28/labour-anti-semitism-code-ian-austin-mp-faces-suspension, accessed 1 July 2019.

Drury, I. (2018) 'Four in 10 Jews may leave the country if Corbyn becomes PM', *Daily Mail*, 6 September.

Edwards, C. (2016) 'Ruth Smeeth: "I've never seen anti-Semitism in Labour like this, it's normal now"', *Evening Standard*, 20 September. Available from: www.standard.co.uk/lifestyle/london-life/ruth-smeeth-ive-never-seen-antisemitism-in-labour-like-this-its-normal-now-a3349201.html, accessed 23 March 2019.

EHRC (7 March 2019) 'Antisemitism in the Labour Party: Our response to complaints', 7 March. Available from: www.equalityhumanrights.com/en/our-work/news/antisemitism-labour-Party-our-response-complaints, accessed 27 June 2019.

Elgot, J. (2015) 'Jeremy Corbyn's bow: What really happened', *Guardian*, 9 November. Available from: www.theguardian.com/politics/2015/nov/09/jeremy-corbyns-bow-remembrance-day-what-really-happened, accessed 1 July 2019.

Elgot, J. (2016a) 'Labour antisemitism row: Naz Shah's suspension lifted', *Guardian*, 5 July. Available from: www.theguardian.com/politics/2016/jul/05/labour-antisemitism-row-naz-shahs-suspension-lifted, accessed 1 July 2019.

Elgot, J. (2016b) 'Momentum vice-chair under pressure to resign over antisemitism row', *Guardian*, 28 September. Available from: www.theguardian.com/politics/2016/sep/28/momentum-vice-chair-jackie-walker-pressure-resign-antisemitism-row-jewish-labour-movement, accessed 1 July 2019.

Elgot, J. (2017) 'Jeremy Corbyn will back change to allow tough line on antisemitism', *Guardian*, 17 September. Available from: www.theguardian.com/politics/2017/sep/17/jeremy-corbyn-will-back-change-to-allow-tough-line-on-antisemitism, accessed 1 July 2019.

Elgot, J. (2018a) 'Labour extends Ken Livingstone's suspension over antisemitism claims', *Guardian*, 1 March. Available from: www.theguardian.com/politics/2018/mar/01/labour-extends-ken-livingstones-suspension-over-antisemitism-claims, accessed 1 July 2019.

Elgot, J. (2018b) 'Antisemitism: Israeli Labor leader cuts ties with Jeremy Corbyn', *Guardian*, 10 April. Available from: www.theguardian.com/politics/2018/apr/10/israeli-labor-leader-cuts-ties-jeremy-corbyn-antisemitism, accessed 1 July 2019.

Elgot, J. (2018c) 'Peers report pro-Corbyn Facebook pages to police for antisemitism', *Guardian*, 5 April. Available from: www.theguardian.

com/world/2018/apr/05/peers-ask-met-police-to-investigate-pro-corbyn-bloggers-antisemitism, accessed 1 July 2019.

Elgot, J. (2018d) 'Labour ends action against Margaret Hodge in antisemitism row', *Guardian*, 6 August. Available from: www.theguardian.com/politics/2018/aug/06/labour-ends-action-against-margaret-hodge-in-antisemitism-row, accessed 1 July 2019.

Elgot, J. (2018e) 'Labour drops abusive conduct investigation into MP Ian Austin', *Guardian*, 27 November. Available from: www.theguardian.com/politics/2018/nov/27/labour-drops-disciplinary-investigation-mp-ian-austin, accessed 1 July 2019.

Elgot, J. (2019a) 'Labour says it has looked into 673 cases of alleged antisemitism', *Guardian*, 11 February. Available from: www.theguardian.com/politics/2019/feb/11/labour-has-looked-into-673-cases-of-alleged-antisemitism-figures-show, accessed 1 July 2019.

Elgot, J. (2019b) 'Tom Watson says he will personally monitor antisemitism cases', *Guardian*, 25 February. Available from: www.theguardian.com/politics/2019/feb/25/tom-watson-says-he-will-monitor-labour-antisemitism-cases, accessed 1 July 2019.

Elgot, J. (2019c) 'Labour expels Jackie Walker for leaked antisemitism remarks', *Guardian*, 27 March. Available from: www.theguardian.com/politics/2019/mar/27/labour-expels-jackie-walker-for-leaked-antisemitism-comments, accessed 1 July 2019.

Ellicott, C. (2018a) 'Rabbi: It's time for Jews to leave Labour', *Daily Mail*, 23 June.

Ellicott, C. (2018b) 'Four in ten say Corbyn is an anti-semite', *Daily Mail*, 1 November.

Ellicott, C. (2018c) 'Jeremy Corbyn's handling of Labour's anti-Semitism crisis ranked fourth in a list of the world's biggest threats to Jews last year by a human rights group', *Daily Mail*, 27 December. Available from: www.dailymail.co.uk/news/article-6533341/Jeremy-Corbyn-ranked-forth-list-worlds-biggest-threats-Jews-human-rights-group.html, accessed 1 July 2019.

Embury-Dennis, T. (2018) 'Labour antisemitism causing British Jews to consider leaving country, says leading rabbi', *Independent*, 2 September. Available from: www.independent.co.uk/news/uk/politics/jeremy-corbyn-labour-antisemitism-lord-jonathan-sacks-zionist-enoch-powell-a8519221.html, accessed 1 July 2019.

EUMC wd (2005) 'In praise of the EUMC Working Definition of Anti-Semitism'. Available from: http://honestreporting.com/in-praise-of-the-eumc-working-definition-of-anti-semitism/, accessed 11 May 2019.

Evening Standard (2019) 'Momentum founder and Corbyn ally Jon Lansman: Labour has "major problem" with anti-Semitism', 25 February. Available from: www.standard.co.uk/news/politics/momentum-founder-jon-lansman-labour-has-major-problem-with-antisemitism-a4075736.html, accessed 4 April 2019.

Evening Standard (2019) 'Chuka Umunna condemns "nasty, bullying and racist" Labour Party', 19 March. Available from: www.standard.co.uk/news/politics/chuka-umunna-condemns-nasty-bullying-and-racist-labour-party-a4095291.html, accessed 18 April 2019.

Express (2019) 'Corbyn has brought anti-Semitism "into the MAINSTREAM" – author lists out over RACISM', 19 April. Available from: www.express.co.uk/news/uk/1115738/Jeremy-Corbyn-news-Labour-Party-anti-Semitism-racism-British-Jews, accessed 18 April 2019.

Feldman (2015) *Sub-Report Commissioned to Assist the All-Party Parliamentary Inquiry into Antisemitism*, 1 January. Available from: www.pearsinstitute.bbk.ac.uk/home/SearchForm?Search=Feldman+parliamentary+sub-committee&action_results=Go, accessed 11 May 2019.

Feldman, D. (2016) 'Will Britain's new definition of antisemitism help Jewish people? I'm sceptical', *Guardian*, 28 December. Available from: www.theguardian.com/commentisfree/2016/dec/28/britain-definition-antisemitism-british-jews-jewish-people, accessed 13 May 2019.

Forsyth, J. (2015) 'No enthusiasm for Corbyn as he addresses Labour MPs', *Spectator*, 14 September. Available from: https://blogs.spectator.co.uk/2015/09/no-enthusiasm-for-corbyn-as-he-addresses-labour-mps/, accessed 1 July 2019.

FRA Survey (2014) Discrimination and hate crime against Jews in EU member states: experiences and perceptions of antisemitism. Available from: https://fra.europa.eu/en/publication/2013/discrimination-and-hate-crime-against-jews-eu-member-states-experiences-and, accessed 3 June 2019.

Full Fact (2018) 'Beware cherry-picked stats on Labour and antisemitism'. Available from: www.channel4.com/news/factcheck/factcheck-anti-semitism-political-parties, accessed 1 July 2019.

Gadher, D. (2017) 'Jeremy Corbyn snubs Benjamin Netanyahu dinner', *Sunday Times*, 29 October. Available from: www.thetimes.co.uk/

edition/news/jeremy-corbyn-snubs-benjamin-netanyahu-dinner-fwf72mz02, accessed 1 July 2019.

Gelblum, B. (2019) 'Guardian defends not publishing 205 Jewish women's complaints over Margaret Hodge antisemitism claims', *London Economic*, 20 March. Available from: www.thelondoneconomic.com/news/guardian-defends-not-publishing-205-jewish-womens-complaint-over-margaret-hodge-antisemitism-claims/20/03/, accessed 26 March 2019.

Gilligan, A. (2015) 'Jeremy Corbyn, friend to Hamas, Iran and extremists', *Telegraph*, 18 July. Available from: www.telegraph.co.uk/news/politics/labour/11749043/Andrew-Gilligan-Jeremy-Corbyn-friend-to-Hamas-Iran-and-extremists.html, accessed 1 July 2019.

Glick, C. (2018) 'Corbyn to use his power to harm Israel – be ready', *Jerusalem Post*, 13 December. Available from: www.jpost.com/Opinion/Column-One-Corbyns-threat-to-Israel-574287, accessed 4 May 2019.

Goldstein, H. (2019) 'Where is the Antisemitism?', *Jewish Voice for Labour*, 20 February. Available from: www.jewishvoiceforlabour.org.uk/blog/ther-is-no-sound-evidence-to-back-the-claims-of-labours-antisemitism/, accessed 9 April 2019.

Gordon, N. (2018) 'The new Antisemitism', *London Review of Books*. Available from: www.lrb.co.uk/v40/n01/neve-gordon/the-new-anti-semitism, accessed 27 June 2019.

Gould, Rebecca Ruth (2018) 'Legal form and legal legitimacy: The IHRA definition of antisemitism as a case study in censored speech', *Law Culture and the Humanities*, 19 June. Available from: https://ssrn.com/abstract=3178109, accessed 12 May 2019.

Grice, A. (2015) 'Jeremy Corbyn could be hit by a wave of resignations in attempt to pave way for coup', *Independent*, 5 November. Available from: www.independent.co.uk/news/uk/politics/jeremy-corbyn-could-be-hit-by-wave-of-resignations-in-attempt-to-pave-way-for-a-coup-a6723186.html, accessed 1 July 2019.

Guardian (2013) 'Irish police return blonde girl to Roma family', 24 October. Available from: www.theguardian.com/world/2013/oct/24/blonde-girl-roma-parents-returned-dna, accessed 1 May 2019.

Guardian (2016) 'Jean-Marie Le Pen fined again for dismissing Holocaust as "detail"', 6 April. Available from: www.theguardian.com/world/2016/apr/06/jean-marie-le-pen-fined-again-dismissing-holocaust-detail, accessed 27 June 2019.

Guardian (2016) 'Jeremy Corbyn says he regrets calling Hamas and Hezbollah "friends"', 4 July. Available from: www.theguardian.com/politics/2016/jul/04/jeremy-corbyn-says-he-regrets-calling-hamas-and-hezbollah-friends, accessed 2 April 2019.

Guardian (2016) 'Jeremy Corbyn accused of incompetence by MPs over antisemitism abuse', 16 October. Available from: www.theguardian.com/politics/2016/oct/16/jeremy-corbyn-antisemitism-chakrabarti-inquiry, accessed 27 June 2019.

Guardian (2017) 'Equalities body accused of targeting BAME staff for redundancies', 5 March. Available from: www.theguardian.com/society/2017/mar/05/equalities-body-accused-of-targeting-bame-staff-for-redundancies-letter-ehrc-black-asian-communities, accessed 27 June 2019.

Guardian (2017) 'Does the Tory attack ad take Corbyn's remarks out of context?', 2 June. Available from: www.theguardian.com/politics/2017/jun/02/tory-attack-ad-corbyn-remarks-context, accessed 3 April 2019.

Guardian (2018) 'Jewdas: Political activists who make fun of establishment Judaism', 3 April. Available from: www.theguardian.com/politics/2018/apr/03/jewdas-political-activists-make-fun-communal-bodies-jeremy-corbyn, accessed 5 May 2019.

Guardian (2018) 'Labour Jewish affiliate in row with Party over anti-semitism code', 11 July. Available from: www.theguardian.com/world/2018/jul/11/labour-jewish-affiliate-in-row-with-Party-over-anti-semitism-code, accessed 11 May 2019.

Guardian (2018) 'Labour antisemitism code could breach Equality Act', 16 July. Available from: www.theguardian.com/politics/2018/jul/16/labour-antisemitism-code-could-breach-equality-act, accessed 11 May 2019.

Guardian (2018) 'Jewish newspapers claim Corbyn poses "existential threat"', 26 July. Available from: www.theguardian.com/politics/2018/jul/25/jewish-newspapers-claim-corbyn-poses-existential-threat, accessed 5 April 2019.

Guardian (2018) 'How should antisemitism be defined?', 27 July. Available from: www.theguardian.com/commentisfree/2018/jul/27/antisemitism-ihra-definition-jewish-writers, accessed 27 June 2019

Guardian (2018) 'Corbyn "sorry" for hurt inflicted on Jewish people by antisemitism row', 6 August. Available from: www.theguardian.com/politics/2018/aug/05/corbyn-sorry-for-hurt-inflicted-on-jewish-people-by-antisemitism-row-labour, accessed 18 April 2019.

Guardian (2018) 'British politics has worst record for antisemitism in Europe, poll says', 10 December. Available from: www.theguardian.com/news/2018/dec/10/britain-has-worst-record-for-antisemitism-in-europe-says-report, accessed 2 May 2019.

Guardian (2019) 'Formby denies Labour leadership is ignoring MPs on antisemitism', 12 February. Available from: www.theguardian.com/politics/2019/feb/12/formby-denies-labour-leadership-is-ignoring-mps-on-antisemitism, accessed 8 May 2019.

Guardian (2019) 'In their own words: Why seven MPs are quitting Labour', 18 February. Available from: www.theguardian.com/politics/2019/feb/18/in-their-own-words-why-seven-mps-are-quitting-labour-independent-group, accessed 12 May 2019.

Guardian (2019) '"Institutional racism": 20 years since Stephen Lawrence inquiry', 22 February. Available from: www.theguardian.com/uk-news/2019/feb/22/institutional-racism-britain-stephen-lawrence-inquiry-20-years, accessed 12 May 2019.

Guardian (2019) 'Labour faces new row over efforts to curb antisemitism', 2 March. Available from: www.theguardian.com/politics/2019/mar/02/new-labour-Party-row-over-antisemitism-jeremy-corbyn, accessed 12 May 2019.

Guardian (2019) 'Jewish Labour affiliate threatens campaigning "work to rule"', 9 April. Available from: www.theguardian.com/politics/2019/apr/09/jewish-labour-movement-radical-steps-antisemitism, accessed 12 May 2019.

Ha'aretz (2018) 'Jeremy Corbyn is patron of blacklisted pro-BDS group whose senior members will be barred from Israel', 7 January. Available from: www.haaretz.com/israel-news/.premium-corbyn-is-patron-of-bds-group-whose-members-will-be-barred-from-israel-1.5729796, accessed 5 May 2019.

Ha'aretz (2018) 'Almost half of Dutch Jews say they're afraid of identifying as Jewish', 27 November. Available from: www.haaretz.com/world-news/europe/almost-half-of-dutch-jews-say-they-re-afraid-of-identifying-as-jewish-1.6696177, accessed 2 May 2019.

Hall, S. (1982) 'The rediscovery of ideology: Return of the repressed in media studies', in M. Gurevitch, T. Bennet, J. Curran and J. Woollacott (eds), *Culture, Society and the Media*, London: Methuen, pp. 56–90.

Hanley, D. (2005) 'Israel washes away the sins of former Army Chief of Staff Rafael Eitan', *Washington Report on Middle East Affairs*, January/February. Available from: www.wrmea.org/005-january-february/

special-report-israel-washes-away-the-sins-of-former-army-chief-of-staff-rafael-eitan.html, accessed 21 April 2019.

'Harry's Place' (2018) *Powerbase*. Last modified 13 March 2018. Available from: http://powerbase.info/index.php/Harry's_Place, accessed 6 June 2019.

Harry's Place (2018) David Miller Lecture. Available from: https://soundcloud.com/harrys-place-399676902/david-miller-lecture, accessed 6 June 2019.

Harpin, L. (2018a) 'Bombshell tape shows Jeremy Corbyn ally blamed "Jewish Trump fanatics"' for inventing Labour antisemitism', *Jewish Chronicle*, 30 July. Available from: www.thejc.com/news/uk-news/bombshell-recording-proves-corbyn-ally-blamed-jewish-trump-fantatics-for-false-antisemitism-clai-1.467802, accessed 1 July 2019.

Harpin, L. (2018b) 'Labour NEC member dodges formal investigation for inflammatory antisemitism remarks', *Jewish Chronicle*, 27 July. Available from: www.thejc.com/news/uk-news/pete-willsman-apologises-jennie-formby-jlm-antisemitism-nec-meeting-1.467755, accessed 1 July 2019.

Haywood, E. and Stevens, J. (2018) 'Lipmann: There's an antisemite at the head of Labour', *Daily Mail*, 9 April.

Hearst, D. (2018) 'Fascist tactics: How Jeremy Corbyn's detractors are plotting to remove him', *Middle East Eye*, 14 August. Available from: www.middleeasteye.net/opinion/fascist-tactics-how-jeremy-corbyns-detractors-are-plotting-remove-him, accessed 1 July 2019.

Henley, J. (2019) 'Antisemitism rising sharply across Europe, latest figures show', *Guardian*, 15 February. Available from: www.theguardian.com/news/2019/feb/15/antisemitism-rising-sharply-across-europe-latest-figures-show, accessed 2 May 2019.

Hilsenrath (2017) Twitter, 26 September. Available from: https://twitter.com/ehrc/status/912611809613553665?lang=en, accessed 27 June 2019.

Hodge, M. (2019) 'Labour has gone backwards in the fight against antisemitism. Enough is enough', *Labour List*, 17 May. Available from: https://labourlist.org/2019/05/labour-has-gone-backwards-in-the-fight-against-antisemitism-enough-is-enough/, accessed 22 May 2019.

Hodges, D. (2014) 'Labour's first Jewish leader is losing the Jewish vote', *Telegraph*, 30 October. Available from: www.telegraph.co.uk/news/politics/ed-miliband/11198691/Labours-first-Jewish-leader-is-losing-the-Jewish-vote.html, accessed 26 June 2019.

Hodges, M. (2019) 'I've carved a Miriam-shaped niche in showbusiness', *Radio Times*, 20–26 April, p. 21.

Home Affairs Committee report (2016) *Antisemitism in the UK*, October. Available from: www.parliament.uk/business/committees/committees-a-z/commons-select/home-affairs-committee/inquiries/parliament-2015/inquiry2/, accessed 12 May 2019.

Home Affairs Select Committee on Antisemitism in the UK (2016) *Political Discourse and Leadership*. Available from: https://publications.parliament.uk/pa/cm201617/cmselect/cmhaff/136/13609.htm, accessed 29 March 2019.

Hope, C. (2015) 'Jeremy Corbyn branded "disloyal"' after refusing to sing national anthem on day of shambles for new Labour leader', *Telegraph*, 15 September. Available from: www.telegraph.co.uk/news/politics/Jeremy_Corbyn/11867337/Jeremy-Corbyn-disloyal-national-anthem-Labour-leader.html, accessed 1 July 2019.

Hope, C. (2017) 'Corbyn condemned by his own party for attending wreath-laying ceremony for Palestinian terror chief', *Telegraph*, 28 May. Available from: www.telegraph.co.uk/news/2017/05/28/jeremy-corbyn-criticised-labour-election-candidates-wreath-laying/, accessed 1 July 2019.

Hope, C. and Hughes, L. (2016) 'Shami Chakrabarti handed peerage weeks after suppressing Jeremy Corbyn interview from "whitewash" anti-Semitism report', *Telegraph*, 5 August. Available from: www.telegraph.co.uk/news/2016/08/05/shami-chakrabarti-handed-peerage-weeks-after-suppressing-jeremy/, accessed 1 July 2019.

House of Commons Home Affairs Committee (2016) *Antisemitism in the UK Tenth Report of Session 2016–17*, HC 136. Available from: https://publications.parliament.uk/pa/cm201617/cmselect/cmhaff/136/136.pdf, accessed 1 July 2019.

Hughes, D. and Lister, S. (2018) 'Labour expels member who heckled Jewish MP at launch of antisemitism report', *Independent*, 27 April. Available from: www.independent.co.uk/news/uk/politics/labour-marc-wadsworth-expelled-heckler-jewish-mp-antisemitism-report-ruth-smeeth-jeremy-corbyn-a8325261.html, accessed 1 July 2019.

Hughes, L. (2016) 'MP calls on Jeremy Corbyn to resign and "make way for someone with the backbone to confront antisemitism" after he appears to compare Israel to "various self-styled Islamic states and organisations"', *Telegraph*, 1 July. Available from: www.telegraph.co.uk/news/2016/06/30/angela-eagle-to-launch-labour-leadership-bid-in-battle-for-the-s/, accessed 1 July 2019.

Hymas, C. (2019) 'Labour anti-semitic rows help push hate incidents against Jewish community to high', *Telegraph*, 7 February. Available from: www.telegraph.co.uk/politics/2019/02/07/labour-anti-semitic-rows-help-push-hate-incidents-against-jewish/, accessed 1 July 2019.

IHRA (2016) 'Working definition of Antisemitism'. Available from: www.holocaustremembrance.com/working-definition-antisemitism, accessed 6 June 2019.

Independent (2018) 'Labour MPs who criticise Corbyn should quit party and "go and do something else", Len McCluskey says', 10 September. Available from: www.independent.co.uk/news/uk/politics/jeremy-corbyn-labour-party-len-mccluskey-unite-tuc-chuka-umunna-anti-semitism-left-wing-a8531471.html, accessed 14 May 2019.

Independent (2019) 'Labour MPs criticise party leaders over response to antisemitism: "Platitudinous, dismissive and far from acceptable"', 4 February. Available from: www.independent.co.uk/news/uk/politics/labour-party-antisemitism-mps-jeremy-corbyn-jewish-abuse-a8763171.html, accessed 14 May 2019.

Independent (2019) 'Labour MPs condemn party leaders after admission that just 12 members have been expelled over antisemitism', 11 February. Available from: www.independent.co.uk/news/uk/politics/labour-party-antisemitism-jeremy-corbyn-jewish-members-abuse-jennie-formby-plp-margaret-hodge-a8774586.html, accessed 13 April 2019.

iNews (2018) 'Labour campaign staff deceived Jeremy Corbyn by "targeting Facebook ads during general election"', 15 July. Available from: https://inews.co.uk/news/labour-staff-deceived-corbyn-facebook/, accessed 29 March 2019.

iNews (2018) 'Momentum founder Jon Lansman calls on Labour chiefs to attend anti-anti-Semitic prejudice course', 3 April. Available from: https://inews.co.uk/news/politics/momentum-founder-jon-lansman-calls-on-jeremy-corbyn-to-attend-anti-semitic-prejudice-course/, accessed 4 April 2019.

Israel, D. (2018) '2018 Simon Wiesenthal Center's Top Ten Worst Global Anti-Semitic Incidents', 30 December. Available from: www.jewishpress.com/news/jewish-news/antisemitism-news/2018-simon-wiesenthal-centers-top-ten-worst-global-anti-semitic-incidents/2018/12/30/, accessed 1 July 2019.

Israel National News (2018) 'A UK Corbyn government will be a major existential threat to Israel', 20 November. Available from: www.

israelnationalnews.com/Articles/Article.aspx/23028, accessed 4 May 2019.

ITV (2019) 'Jewish Labour Movement backs no confidence vote in Jeremy Corbyn as party defends handling of anti-Semitism complaints', 7 April. Available from: www.itv.com/news/2019-04-07/leaked-emails-show-labour-inaction-over-anti-semitism-complaints/, accessed 6 April 2019.

ITV News (2018) 'Labour adopts new anti-Semitism code in face of opposition from Jewish leaders', 17 July. Available from: www.itv.com/news/2018-07-17/labour-adopts-new-anti-semitism-code-in-face-of-opposition-from-jewish-leaders/, accessed 1 July 2019.

Jacobson, H., Montefiore, S.S. and Schama, S. (2017) 'The Labour Party and its approach to Zionism' [Letter to the editor], *The Times*, 6 November, p. 20.

Jacobson, S. (2019) 'Labour has widespread problem with antisemitism – Momentum founder', *Guardian*, 25 February. Available from: www.theguardian.com/politics/2019/feb/25/labour-has-widespread-problem-with-antisemitism-momentum-founder-jon-lansman, accessed 1 July 2019.

Jewish Chronicle (2015) 'The key questions Jeremy Corbyn must answer', [Editorial], 12 August. Available from: www.thejc.com/news/uk-news/the-key-questions-jeremy-corbyn-must-answer-1.68097, accessed 1 July 2019.

Jewish Chronicle (2018) 'Jonathan Arkush accused of "undermining fight against antisemitism" with Jeremy Corbyn comments', 1 June. Available from: www.thejc.com/news/uk-news/jonathan-arkush-jeremy-corbyn-rhea-wolfson-response-1.464883, accessed 5 May 2019.

Jewish Chronicle (2018) 'Read Labour's new definition of antisemitism that has caused so much anger', 5 July. Available from: www.thejc.com/comment/analysis/jeremy-corbyn-labour-definition-anti-semitism-1.466626, accessed 11 May 2019.

Jewish Chronicle (2018) 'Tom Watson: I am proud to defend Israel and we have moral obligation to rid Labour of antisemitism', 26 September. Available from: www.thejc.com/news/uk-news/tom-watson-i-am-proud-to-defend-israel-and-labour-has-moral-obligation-to-rid-itself-of-antisemit-1.470198, accessed 13 March 2019.

Jewish Chronicle (2019) 'Exclusive: Fewer than half of British adults know what "antisemitism" means, poll reveals', 14 March. Available from: www.thejc.com/news/uk-news/fewer-than-half-of-British-adults-know-what-antisemitism-means-poll-reveals-1.481476, accessed 3 June 2019.

Jewish Chronicle (2019) 'Whistleblowers "collect 100,000 Labour e-mails" to expose party's attempts to protect alleged antisemites', 15 May. Available from: www.thejc.com/news/uk-news/100000-e-mails-collected-by-ex-labour-staffers-showing-corbynite-attempts-to-protect-antisemites-1.484164, accessed 16 May 2019.

Jewish News, Times of Israel (2018) 'John McDonnell evokes Cable Street in call to oppose Tommy Robinson', 30 November. Available from: https://jewishnews.timesofisrael.com/john-mcdonnell-evokes-cable-street-in-call-to-oppose-tommy-robinson/, accessed 1 May 2019.

Jewish News, Times of Israel (2018) 'Thornberry: Corbyn hasn't tackled antisemitism because he was upset by claims', 27 December. Available from: https://jewishnews.timesofisrael.com/thornberry-corbyn-hasnt-tackled-antisemitism-because-he-was-upset-by-claims/, accessed 14 April 2019.

Jewish News, Times of Israel (2019) 'Labour MPs attack Jennie Formby over antisemitism data report', 11 February. Available from: https://jewishnews.timesofisrael.com/labour-mps-attack-jennie-formby-over-antisemitism-data-report/, accessed 13 April 2019.

Jewish Leadership Council (2018) 'Letter to Jeremy Corbyn. Available from: www.thejlc.org/letter_to_jeremy_corbyn, accessed 1 July 2019.

Jewish Voice for Labour (2018) 'Geoffrey Robertson: legal opinion of the IHRA definition', 2 September. Available from: www.jewishvoiceforlabour.org.uk/blog/geoffrey-robertson-legal-opinion-of-the-ihra-definition/, accessed 27 June 2019.

JLC (2018) 'The JLC, Board of Deputies and CST have responded to Jennie Formby's letter on the 3rd July which included documents relating to the Labour Party's diluted definition of antisemitism', 10 July. Available from: www.thejlc.org/the_jlc_boardofdeputies_and_cst_uk_have_responded_to_jennie_formby_s_letter_on_the_3rd_july_which_included_documents_relating_to_the_labour_Party_s_diluted_definition_of_antisemitism, accessed 11 May 2019.

Johnson, A. (2015) 'Why Labour should end the madness and elect Yvette Cooper', *Guardian*, 4 August. Available from: www.theguardian.com/commentisfree/2015/aug/04/labour-yvette-cooper-jeremy-corbyn-alan-johnson, accessed 1 July 2019.

Johnson, A. (2019a) *Institutionally Antisemitic: Contemporary Left Antisemitism and the Crisis in the British Labour Party*, Fathom Report. Available from: http://fathomjournal.org/fathom-report-institutionally-antisemitic-contemporary-left-antisemitism-and-the-crisis-in-the-british-labour-party/, accessed 9 April 2019.

Johnson, A. (2019b) 'My report on 130 cases of Labour antisemitism shows the importance of Gordon Brown's unequivocal stand', *Independent*, 1 April. Available from: www.independent.co.uk/voices/labour-antisemitism-gordon-brown-report-corbyn-jewish-a8849306.html, accessed 9 April 2019.

Johnson, A. and Rosenhead, J. (2016) 'The Duel: Is it anti-Semitic to boycott Israel?', *Prospect*, 16 June. Available from: www.prospectmagazine.co.uk/magazine/the-duel-is-it-anti-semitic-to-boycott-israel, accessed 21 April 2019.

JPR (2017) 'Antisemitism in contemporary Great Britain: A study of attitudes towards Jews and Israel', September. Available from: www.jpr.org.uk/publication?id=9993, accessed 12 May 2019.

JTA (2017) Ron Kampeas, 'It's Jew vs. Jew as Congress weighs a new definition for anti-Semitism', 8 November. Available from: www.jta.org/2017/11/08/news-opinion/politics/barbs-fly-in-congress-as-proponents-opponents-of-law-codifying-anti-semitism-definition-face-off, accessed 12 May 2019.

Jullian, P.M. (2011). 'Appraising through someone else's words: The evaluative power of quotations in news reports'. *Discourse & Society*, 22(6), 766–80.

JVL (2019) 'The PLP meeting on 4th Feb – a scurrilous attack on Jennie Formby', 6 February. Available from: www.jewishvoiceforlabour.org.uk/blog/the-plp-meeting-on-4th-feb-a-scurrilous-attack-on-jennie-formby/, accessed 14 April 2019.

Kentish, B. (2018a) 'Labour MPs and peers back internationally recognised definition of antisemitism as party row deepens', *Independent*, 23 July. Available from: www.independent.co.uk/news/uk/politics/antisemitism-definition-labour-party-jeremy-corbyn-jewish-holocaust-uk-parliament-a8460796.html, accessed 1 July 2019.

Kentish, B. (2018b) 'Benjamin Netanyahu says Jeremy Corbyn deserves "unequivocal condemnation" for attending memorial to Munich terrorists', *Independent*, 13 August. Available from: www.independent.co.uk/news/uk/politics/jeremy-corbyn-benjamin-netanyahu-munich-massacre-terrorists-wreath-twitter-antisemitism-a8490431.html, accessed 1 July 2019.

Kentish, B. (2018c) 'Labour says Margaret Hodge comments "disconnected from reality" after she calls Corbyn antisemitic and compares party to Nazi Germany', *Independent*, 16 August. Available from: www.independent.co.uk/news/uk/politics/labour-party-anti-semitism-jeremy-corbyn-margaret-hodge-nazi-germany-a8495351.html, accessed 1 July 2019.

Kentish, B. (2018d) 'Frank Field resigns Labour whip, saying Jeremy Corbyn has become "force for antisemitism in British politics"', *Independent*, 30 August. Available from: www.independent.co.uk/news/uk/politics/frank-field-resigns-labour-whip-jeremy-corbyn-antisemitism-racism-row-a8515036.html, accessed 1 July 2019.

Kentish, B. (2018e) 'Labour MP hits out at "Trots, Stalinists and communist" party members after losing vote of no confidence', *Independent*, 7 September. Available from: www.independent.co.uk/news/uk/politics/labour-mp-vote-no-confidence-joan-ryan-enfield-north-trots-stalinists-communists-a8527326.html, accessed 1 July 2019.

Kentish, B. (2018f) 'Labour antisemitism row was created by Israel to distract from "atrocities", trade union boss suggests', *Independent*, 13 September. Available from: www.independent.co.uk/news/uk/politics/labour-antisemitism-israel-corbyn-mark-serwotka-tuc-trade-union-pcs-a8535986.html, accessed 1 July 2019.

Kentish, B. (2018g) 'Labour antisemitism row could cost party the next election, MP warns', *Independent*, 23 September. Available from: www.independent.co.uk/news/uk/politics/labour-antisemitism-election-jeremy-corbyn-conference-mp-wes-streeting-a8551521.html, accessed 1 July 2019.

Kentish, B. (2018h) 'People accusing Jeremy Corbyn of antisemitism "have lost every shred of decency", Len McCluskey says', *Independent*, 24 September 2018. Available from: www.independent.co.uk/news/uk/politics/jeremy-corbyn-antisemitism-row-labour-conference-len-mccluskey-a8552476.html, accessed 1 July 2019.

Kentish, B. (2019a). 'Jeremy Corbyn warned of "mass walkout" of Jewish members as Labour's official Jewish group calls meeting about quitting', *Independent*, 19 February. Available from: www.independent.co.uk/news/uk/politics/jeremy-corbyn-labour-jewish-members-quit-antisemitism-independent-group-split-luciana-berger-a8786496.html, accessed 1 July 2019.

Kentish, B. (2019b) 'Labour's affiliate Jewish group remains with party amid threats of a split over antisemitism allegations', *Independent*, 6 March. Available from: www.independent.co.uk/news/uk/politics/

labour-antisemitism-jewish-group-movement-a8811286.html, accessed 1 July 2019.

Kerbaj, R., Pogrund, G. and Shipman, M. (2019) 'Jeremy Corbyn admits: Labour "ignored" anti-semitism', *Sunday Times*, 14 April 2019. Available from: www.thetimes.co.uk/edition/news/jeremy-corbyn-admits-labour-ignored-anti-semitism-rtqjzldpo, accessed 1 July 2019.

Kinnock, N. (2015) 'Labour needs a prime minister, not a debate. It needs Andy Burnham', *Guardian*, 1 August. Available from: www.theguardian.com/commentisfree/2015/aug/01/neil-kinnock-labour-leader-andy-burnham, accessed 1 July 2019.

Kirby, W. (2019) 'Joan Ryan: Labour MP quits party to join Independent Group in protest at Corbyn's Brexit stance', *Independent*, 20 February. Available from: www.independent.co.uk/news/uk/politics/joan-ryan-independent-group-labour-party-jeremy-corbyn-brexit-mp-a8787496.html, accessed 1 July 2019.

Klug, B. (2004) 'The myth of the new anti-Semitism', *The Nation*, 15 January. Available from: www.thenation.com/article/myth-new-anti-semitism/, accessed 12 May 2019.

Klug, B. (2018) 'The Code of Conduct for Antisemitism: A tale of two texts', *openDemocracy*, 17 July. Available from: www.opendemocracy.net/uk/brian-klug/code-of-conduct-for-antisemitism-tale-of-two-texts, accessed 11 May 2019.

Kuenssberg, L. (2016) 'MPs vote to renew Trident weapons system', BBC Online, 19 July. Available from: www.bbc.co.uk/news/uk-politics-36830923, accessed 1 July 2019.

Labour Briefing (2019) 'In summary: The truth behind the stats', March. Available from: www.jewishvoiceforlabour.org.uk/blog/in-summary-the-truth-behind-the-stats/, accessed 12 May 2019.

Labour List (2016) 'Chuka Umunna: Clause IV tells us to live in "solidarity, tolerance and respect" but Labour has failed on anti-Semitism', October. Available from: https://labourlist.org/2016/10/chuka-umunna-clause-iv-tells-us-to-live-in-solidarity-tolerance-and-respect-but-labour-has-failed-to-deliver/, accessed 12 May 2019.

Labour List (2019) '"Eliminate the evil of antisemitism from our movement. That is my mission," says Jennie Formby', 4 February. Available from: https://labourlist.org/2019/02/eliminate-the-evil-of-antisemitism-from-our-movement-that-is-my-mission-says-jennie-formby/, accessed 28 March 2019.

Labour List (2019) 'Jeremy Corbyn pushed for action on antisemitism – but was held back by bureaucracy', 14 May. Available from: https://

labourlist.org/2019/05/jeremy-corbyn-pushed-for-action-on-antisemitism-but-was-held-back-by-bureaucracy/, accessed 23 May 2019.

Labourbame (n.d.) https://twitter.com/labourbame?lang=en, accessed 12 May 2019.

Landis, R.J. and Koch, G.G. (1977) 'The measurement of observer agreements for categorical data', *Biometrics*, 33, 159–74.

Lansman, J. (2018) 'Labour's antisemitism code is the gold standard for political parties', *Guardian*, 12 July. Available from: www.theguardian.com/commentisfree/2018/jul/12/labour-antisemitism-code-gold-standard-political-parties, accessed 1 July 2019.

LBC (2019) 'Labour Party is anti-semitic and racist: Mike Gapes', 18 February. Available from: www.lbc.co.uk/news/uk/mike-gapes-labour-party-anti-semitic-racist/, accessed 18 April 2019.

Lerman, A. (2010) 'Undefined Anthony Julius's *Trials of the Diaspora* and the myth of the new anti-Semitism', *The Nation*, 9 June. Available from: www.thenation.com/article/undefined/, accessed 12 May 2019.

Lerman, A. (2011) 'The farcical attack on the UCU for voting against use of the EUMC "working definition" of antisemitism'. Available from: https://antonylerman.com/2011/06/02/the-farcical-attack-on-the-ucu-for-voting-against-use-of-the-eumc-working-definition-of-antisemitism/, accessed 11 May 2019.

Lerman, A. (2011) '"Racism" or "racist incident", what's the difference? UCU and the EUMC "working definition" of antisemitism', June. Available from: www.opendemocracy.net/antony-lerman/racism-or-racist-incident-whats-difference-ucu-and-eumc-%E2%80%98working-definition%E2%80%99-of-antise, accessed 11 May 2019.

MacAskill, E. and Cobain, I. (2017) 'Israeli diplomat who plotted against MPs also set up political groups', *Guardian*, 8 January. Available from: www.theguardian.com/world/2017/jan/08/israeli-diplomat-shai-masot-plotted-against-mps-set-up-political-groups-labour, accessed 1 July 2019.

Macpherson, W. (1999) Independent report. *The Stephen Lawrence Inquiry*. www.gov.uk/government/publications/the-stephen-lawrence-inquiry, accessed 27 June 2019.

Maguire, P. (2018) 'Exclusive: John McDonnell appeals to Labour MPs not to split – "I'm worried and saddened"', *New Statesman*, 1 September. Available from: www.newstatesman.com/politics/uk/2018/09/exclusive-john-mcdonnell-appeals-labour-mps-not-split-im-worried-and-saddened, accessed 26 June 2019.

Maidment, J. (2019) 'Jeremy Corbyn is "unfit to be PM", says Jewish Labour Movement as it passes no confidence motion in him', *Telegraph*, 7 April. Available from: www.telegraph.co.uk/politics/2019/04/07/jeremy-corbyn-unfit-pm-says-jewish-labour-movement-passes-no/, accessed 1 July 2019.

Mail on Sunday (2017) 'Israel plot to "take down" Tory minister: Astonishing undercover video captures diplomat conspiring with rival MP's aide to smear Deputy Foreign Secretary', 7 January. Available from: www.dailymail.co.uk/news/article-4098082/Astonishing-undercover-video-captures-diplomat-conspiring-rival-MP-s-aide-smear-Deputy-Foreign-Secretary.html, accessed 30 May 2019.

Mail Online (2013) 'Now blonde girl found at a Roma home in Ireland: Blue-eyed child of seven is led away by police and social workers', 23 October. Available from: www.dailymail.co.uk/news/article-2471521/Blonde-girl-Roma-gypsy-home-Ireland.html, accessed 1 May 2019.

Mail Online (2018) 'Villagers threaten vigilante action as 200 travellers descend on leafy Surrey common stealing boules sets and lawn tennis kits and defecating in gardens of £2m houses', 6 August. Available from: www.dailymail.co.uk/news/article-6020543/Rich-locals-arms-travellers-set-camp-Cobhams-leafy-common.html, accessed 16 April 2019.

Mail Online (2018) 'Dominic Lawson: No wonder Corbyn's Labour is riddled with anti-Semites. His idol Karl Marx was one of the worst of the lot', 3 September. Available from: www.dailymail.co.uk/debate/article-6125057/DOMINIC-LAWSON-No-wonder-Corbyns-Labour-riddled-anti-Semites-idol-Karl-Marx-one.html, accessed 18 April 2019.

Mail Online (2019) 'A credit to the nation! British traveller family hang around shirtless and swigging Red Bull outside New Zealand hotel as they say they will SUE mayor who declared them "worse than pigs"', 25 January. Available from: www.dailymail.co.uk/news/article-6632339/British-traveller-family-say-SUE-mayor-declared-worse-pigs.html, accessed 16 April 2019.

Mail Online (2019) 'British gypsies are banned from every Burger King in New Zealand for scamming free meals by taking customers' leftovers to the counter and claiming they'd been served cold food', 14 February. Available from: www.dailymail.co.uk/news/article-6704895/British-gypsy-tourists-banned-Burger-Kings-New-Zealand.html, accessed 16 April 2019.

Mail Online (2019) 'Corbyn hoped wreath trip would be cheap to avoid declaring it: Emails show Labour leader wanted his visit to tribute event for the Munich Olympics terrorists to stay under the £660 limit', 5 April. Available from: www.dailymail.co.uk/news/article-6888731/Corbyn-hoped-Tunisia-wreath-trip-cheap-avoid-declaring-leaked-email-shows.html, accessed 7 April 2019.

Mairs, M. (2016) 'Anger as Oxford University Labour students cleared of anti-Semitism', *PoliticsHome*. Available from: www.politicshome.com/news/uk/political-parties/labour-party/news/82471/anger-oxford-university-labour-students-cleared, accessed 1 July 2019.

Manning, P. (2001) *News and News Sources: A Critical Introduction*, London: Sage.

Manson, J. and Levane, L. (2018) 'Jewish Voice for Labour: We weren't founded to "tackle antisemitism allegations in Labour"', *Labour List*, 26 October. Available from: https://labourlist.org/2018/10/jewish-voice-for-labour-we-werent-founded-to-tackle-antisemitism-allegations-in-labour/, accessed 30 May 2019.

Marcetic, B. (2017) 'A history of sabotaging Jeremy Corbyn', *Jacobin*, 15 June. Available from: www.jacobinmag.com/2017/06/jeremy-corbyn-attacks-media-labour-election-prime-minister, accessed 27 June 2019.

Marsh, S. (2018) 'Corbyn apologises over event where Israel was compared to Nazis', *Guardian*, 1 August. Available from: www.theguardian.com/politics/2018/aug/01/jeremy-corbyn-issues-apology-in-labour-antisemitism-row, accessed 1 July 2019.

Marshall, T. (2016) 'Labour MP Ruth Smeeth storms out of anti-Semitism report launch "in tears"', *Evening Standard*, 30 June. Available from: www.standard.co.uk/news/politics/labour-mp-ruth-smeeth-storms-out-of-antisemitism-report-launch-a3285106.html, accessed 1 July 2019.

Martin, D. (2019) 'Calls grow for Jeremy Corbyn to quit as Labour Party leader in row over "anti-Semitic" book which he praised as a "brilliant" analysis of imperialism', *Daily Mail*, 1 May. Available from: www.dailymail.co.uk/news/article-6982453/Calls-grow-Corbyn-quit-row-anti-Semitic-book-praised-brilliant.html, accessed 1 July 2019.

Martinson, J. (2017) 'BBC Trust says Laura Kuenssberg report on Corbyn was inaccurate', *Guardian*, 18 January. Available from: www.theguardian.com/media/2017/jan/18/bbc-trust-says-laura-kuenssberg-report-on-jeremy-corbyn-was-inaccurate-labour, accessed 1 July 2019.

Mason, R. (2015a) 'Jewish Labour MP hits out at Jeremy Corbyn's record on antisemitism', *Guardian*, 14 August. Available from: www.theguardian.com/politics/2015/aug/14/jewish-labour-mp-jeremy-corbyn-antisemitism-record-ivan-lewis, accessed 1 July 2019.

Mason, R. (2015b) 'Labour leadership: Jeremy Corbyn elected with huge mandate', *Guardian*, 12 September. Available from: www.theguardian.com/politics/2015/sep/12/jeremy-corbyn-wins-labour-party-leadership-election, accessed 1 July 2019.

Mason, R. (2016a) 'Lord Levy warns he could quit Labour over antisemitism', *Guardian*, 20 March. Available from: www.theguardian.com/politics/2016/mar/20/labour-peer-lord-levy-warns-he-could-quit-party-over-antisemitism, accessed 1 July 2019.

Mason, R. (2016b) 'Jewish Labour MP: Corbyn must name and shame online abusers', *Guardian*, 2 September. Available from: www.theguardian.com/politics/2016/sep/02/jewish-labour-mp-corbyn-must-name-and-shame-online-abusers, accessed 1 July 2019.

Mason, R. (2019a) '"Just close them down": Margaret Hodge on antisemitism in Labour branches', *Guardian*, 8 March. Available from: www.theguardian.com/politics/2019/mar/08/just-close-them-down-margaret-hodge-on-antisemitism-in-labour-branches, accessed 5 May 2019.

Mason, R. (2019b) 'Labour MP expresses regret over anti-Zionist comment in 2014 video', *Guardian*, 16 April 2019. Available from: www.theguardian.com/politics/2019/apr/16/jewish-groups-condemn-labour-mps-anti-zionist-comment, accessed 1 July 2019.

Mason, R. (2019c) 'Equality body launches investigation of Labour antisemitism claims', *Guardian*, 28 May. Available from: www.theguardian.com/politics/2019/may/28/equality-body-launches-investigation-of-labour-antisemitism-claims, accessed 1 July 2019.

Mason, R and Asthana, A. (2016) 'Labour crisis: How the coup against Jeremy Corbyn gathered pace', *Guardian*, 26 June. Available from: www.theguardian.com/politics/2016/jun/26/labour-crisis-how-coup-plot-jeremy-corbyn-gathered-pace, accessed 1 July 2019.

Mason, R. and Weaver, M. (2017) 'Labour "failing Jewish community" with Livingstone ruling, says Tom Watson', *Guardian*, 5 April. Available from: www.theguardian.com/politics/2017/apr/05/ken-livingstone-pressure-mounts-on-labour-to-review-decision, accessed 1 July 2019.

McDonald, S. (2019) 'Who is John T. Earnest? Male suspect in deadly Poway Synagogue shooting', Newsweek, 27 April. Available from:

www.newsweek.com/who-john-t-earnest-male-suspect-deadly-poway-synagogue-shooting-1407693, accessed 27 June 2019.

McDonnell, J. (2018) John McDonnell MP Twitter, 6 September. Available from: https://twitter.com/johnmcdonnellMP/status/1037793832388255746, accessed 6 June 2019.

McGuinnes, A. and Heffer, G. (2018) 'Labour suspends party members over "anti-Semitic" Facebook group', Sky News, 9 March. Available from: https://news.sky.com/story/jeremy-corbyn-admits-being-member-of-controversial-facebook-group-11281462, accessed 1 July 2019.

McLean, I. (1978) 'Labour since 1945', in Chris Cook and John Ramsden (eds), *Trends in British Politics since 1945*, London: Macmillan, p. 47.

McNair, B. (2012) 'WikiLeaks, journalism and the consequences of chaos', *Media International Australia*, *144*(1), 77–86.

McTague, T. (2015) 'Labour leadership contender Jeremy Corbyn flies into a rage on live TV over questions about his terrorist "friends"', *Daily Mail*, 14 July. Available from: www.dailymail.co.uk/news/article-3160530/Labour-leadership-contender-Jeremy-Corbyn-flies-rage-live-TV-questions-terrorist-friends.html, accessed 1 July 2019.

Merrick, R. (2018a) 'Len McCluskey accuses "Corbyn-hater" Labour MPs of working in cahoots with Tory newspapers to undermine leader', *Independent*, 25 April. Available from: www.independent.co.uk/news/uk/politics/jeremy-corbyn-labour-party-newspapers-len-mcclunskey-a8322111.html, accessed 1 July 2019.

Merrick, R. (2018b) 'Jeremy Corbyn's "Zionist" comments are most offensive by a senior politician "since Enoch Powell", says leading rabbi', *Independent*. Available from: www.independent.co.uk/news/uk/politics/jeremy-corbyn-zionist-enoch-powell-antisemitism-rabbi-jonathan-sacks-labour-jewish-leadership-a8511391.html, accessed 1 July 2019.

Metro (2018) 'Labour MP turns on Jeremy Corbyn calling him a "f***ing anti-Semite and a racist"', 18 July. Available from: https://metro.co.uk/2018/07/18/labour-mp-turns-jeremy-corbyn-calling-fing-anti-semite-racist-7729431/, accessed 26 June 2019.

Miller, D. and Reilly, J. (1994) *Food 'Scares' in the Media*, Glasgow: Glasgow University Media Group (in association with the MRC Medical Sociology Unit, Glasgow University).

Milne, O. (2019) 'Labour has "let the Jewish community down" over anti-Semitism says Gordon Brown', *Mirror*, 1 April. Available from:

www.mirror.co.uk/news/politics/labour-let-jewish-community-down-14219534, accessed 1 July 2019.

Mirror (2013) 'Second blonde girl seized from gypsy family in Ireland "looks nothing like siblings and speaks much better English"', 23 October. Available from: www.mirror.co.uk/news/world-news/greece-girl-maria-found-second-2481967, accessed 1 May 2019.

Mirvis, E. (2016) 'Ken Livingstone and the hard Left are spreading the insidious virus of anti-Semitism', *Telegraph*, 3 May. Available from: www.telegraph.co.uk/news/2016/05/03/ken-livingstone-and-the-hard-left-are-spreading-the-insidious-vi/, accessed 1 July 2019.

Moody, O. (2019) 'Jews scared to speak out as antisemitism spreads in Orban's Hungary', *The Times*, 30 March. Available from: www.thetimes.co.uk/article/jews-remain-silent-as-antisemitism-spreads-in-orban-s-hungary-s29vsmdrs, accessed 2 May 2019.

Mortimer, C. (2016) 'Livingstone fired from LBC as Labour reinstates Momentum organiser', *Independent*, 29 May.

Newman, N., Fletcher, R., Kalogeropoulos, A., Levy, D.A. and Nielsen, R.K. (2018) *Reuters Institute Digital News Report 2018*. Reuters Institute for the Study of Journalism. Available from: http://media.digitalnewsreport.org/wp-content/uploads/2018/06/digital-news-report-2018.pdf, accessed 1 June 2019.

Observer (2016) '"There's nothing dodgy": Questions over Jeremy Corbyn donation', 6 August. Available from: www.theguardian.com/politics/2016/aug/06/jeremy-corbyn-campaign-donation-palestine, accessed 5 May 2019.

Owen, G. (2018), 'Jewish Labour MPs will be offered bodyguards at party conference over fears of attack by Jeremy Corbyn's hardline supporters amid anti-Semitism row', 25 August. Available from: www.dailymail.co.uk/news/article-6098375/Bodyguards-Jewish-delegates-Labour-conference.html, accessed 1 July 2019.

Parson, T. (2016) 'No place for antisemitism', *Sun*, 21 February.

Parveen, N. and Walker, P. (2019) 'No-confidence vote in Labour MP Luciana Berger withdrawn', *Guardian*, 8 February. Available from: www.theguardian.com/politics/2019/feb/08/labour-withdraws-luciana-berger-mp-no-confidence-motion, accessed 1 July 2019.

Patel, Y. (2018) 'Israeli attorney files FOIA request to determine govt role in anti-Corby campaign', *Mondoweiss*, 24 August. Available from: https://mondoweiss.net/2018/08/attorney-determine-campaign/, accessed 26 June 2019.

Pears Institute for the Study of Antisemitism (2016) 'The Shami Chakrabarti Inquiry – Report Published'. Available from: www.pearsinstitute.bbk.ac.uk/home/chakrabarti-inquiry-report-published/, accessed 1 July 2019.

Perkins, T. (2019) 'Pro-Israel donors spent over $22m on lobbying and contributions in 2018', *Guardian*, 15 February. Available from: www.theguardian.com/us-news/2019/feb/15/pro-israel-donors-spent-over-22m-on-lobbying-and-contributions-in-2018, accessed 27 May 2019.

Perraudin, F. and Rawlinson, K. (2019) 'Labour MPs applaud colleagues who quit at party meeting – as it happened', *Guardian*, 18 February. Available from: www.theguardian.com/politics/live/2019/feb/18/several-labour-mps-set-to-quit-the-party-politics-live, accessed 1 July 2019.

Pew Research Centre (2014) 'Global attitudes & trends', 12 May. Available from: www.pewglobal.org/2014/05/12/chapter-4-views-of-roma-muslims-jews/, accessed 27 June 2019.

Philo, G. and Berry, M. (2004) *Bad News from Israel*, London: Pluto Press.

Philo, G., Briant, E. and Donald, P. (2013) *Bad News for Refugees*, London: Pluto Press.

Philpot, R. (2019) 'Jewish MP Smeeth says she's staying in Labour to fight UK party's anti-Semitism', *Times of Israel*, 1 March. Available from: www.timesofisrael.com/jewish-mp-smeeth-says-shes-staying-in-labour-to-fight-uk-partys-anti-semitism/, accessed 26 June 2019.

Piazza, R. and Lashmar, P. (2017) 'Jeremy Corbyn according to the BBC: Ideological representation and identity construction of the Labour Party leader', *Critical Approaches to Discourse Analysis Across Disciplines*, 9(2), 120–41.

Pitt, B. (2019) 'Has the Labour left subjected Luciana Berger to hatespeak and death threats?', 20 March, medium.com, accessed 27 June 2019.

Plosker, S. (2014) 'Sharon and the wrong "drugged cockroach"', *Honest Reporting*, 13 January. Available from: https://honestreporting.com/sharon-and-the-wrong-drugged-cockroach/, accessed 21 April 2019.

PoliticsHome (2018) 'WATCH Shami Chakrabarti: Ken Livingstone should be expelled from the Labour party', 13 May. Available from: www.politicshome.com/news/uk/political-parties/labour-party/news/95134/watch-shami-chakrabarti-ken-livingstone-should-be, accessed 8 April 2019.

Pollard, S. (2018) 'Labour's new guidelines show it is institutionally antisemitic', *Jewish Chronicle*, 5 July. Available from: www.thejc.com/

comment/comment/labour-s-new-guidelines-show-it-is-institutionally-antisemitic-1.466685, accessed 11 May 2019.

Press Association (2016) 'Momentum chief Jackie Walker suspended from Labour over Holocaust Memorial Day comments', *Telegraph*, 30 September. Available from: www.telegraph.co.uk/news/2016/09/30/momentum-chief-jackie-walker-suspended-from-labour-over-holocaus/, accessed 1 July 2019.

Private Eye (2019) 'Corbyn cornered', 17–30 May, p. 11.

Rawlinson, K. and Crerar, P. (2018) 'Jewish newspapers claim Corbyn poses "existential threat"', *Guardian*, 26 July. Available from: www.theguardian.com/politics/2018/jul/25/jewish-newspapers-claim-corbyn-poses-existential-threat, accessed 1 July 2019.

Rees, E. (2017) 'What made the difference for Labour? Ordinary people knocking on doors', *Guardian*, 12 June. Available from: www.theguardian.com/commentisfree/2017/jun/12/labour-knocking-on-doors-jeremy-corbyn-momentum, accessed 30 April 2019.

Report (2016) 'The Shami Chakrabarti Inquiry – report published', 30 June. Available from: www.pearsinstitute.bbk.ac.uk/home/chakrabarti-inquiry-report-published/, accessed 27 June 2019.

Riley, R. (2019) 'Why I spoke out about Labour's anti-Semitism shame', *Spectator*, 23 January. Available from: https://blogs.spectator.co.uk/2019/01/why-i-spoke-out-about-labours-anti-semitism-shame/, accessed 1 July 2019.

Riley-Smith B. (2015a) 'Jewish leaders urge Corbyn to renounce extremists; Board of Deputies warns Labour front-runner he must address concerns about links to anti-Semites', *Telegraph*, 29 August.

Riley-Smith, B. (2015b) 'Twenty Labour MPs rebel against Jeremy Corbyn and vote on Trident', *Telegraph*, 24 November. Available from: www.telegraph.co.uk/news/politics/Jeremy_Corbyn/12014722/Twenty-Labour-MPs-rebel-against-Jeremy-Corbyn-and-vote-on-Trident.html, accessed 1 July 2019.

Riley-Smith, B. (2016) 'Labour rebels hope to topple Jeremy Corbyn in 24-hour blitz after EU referendum', *Telegraph*, 13 June. Available from: www.telegraph.co.uk/news/2016/06/13/labour-rebels-hope-to-topple-jeremy-corbyn-in-24-hour-blitz-afte/, accessed 1 July 2019.

Robertson, G. (2018) 'Geoffrey Robertson: Legal opinion of the IHRA definition'. Available from: www.jewishvoiceforlabour.org.uk/blog/geoffrey-robertson-legal-opinion-of-the-ihra-definition/, accessed 27 June 2019.

Rosenberg, D. (2019) 'Liverpool Wavertree and Luciana Berger: The facts', *Labour Briefing*, 10 February. Available from: http://labourbriefing.squarespace.com/home/2019/2/10/liverpool-and-luciana-berger-mp, accessed 11 April 2019.

Ross, T. and Gosden, E. (2015) 'Jeremy Corbyn faces coup plot if he wins Labour leadership', *Telegraph*, 27 July. Available from: www.telegraph.co.uk/news/politics/labour/11764159/Jeremy-Corbyn-faces-coup-plot-if-he-wins-Labour-leadership.html, accessed 1 July 2019.

Sabbagh, D. (2018) 'Labour adopts IHRA antisemitism definition in full', *Guardian*, 4 September. Available from: www.theguardian.com/politics/2018/sep/04/labour-adopts-ihra-antisemitism-definition-in-full, accessed 1 July 2019.

Sabbagh, D. (2019) 'Labour MP Ian Austin quits the party over "culture of antisemitism"', *Guardian*, 22 February. Available from: www.theguardian.com/politics/2019/feb/22/labour-mp-ian-austin-quits-the-party, accessed 1 July 2019.

Sabbagh, D. and Pidd, H. (2019) 'Equality watchdog to decide if Labour broke law over antisemitism', *Guardian*, 6 March. Available from: www.theguardian.com/news/2019/mar/06/equality-watchdog-could-rule-on-whether-labour-broke-law, accessed 1 July 2019.

Sassoon, D. (2019) 'Jeremy Corbyn, Hobson's Imperialism, and antisemitism' [Letter to the Editor], *Guardian*, 2 May. Available from: www.theguardian.com/news/2019/may/02/jeremy-corbyn-hobsons-imperialism-and-antisemitism, accessed 1 July 2019.

Savage, M. (2016) 'Corbyn faces frontbench exodus over antisemitism; election wipeout could trigger resignations; frontbenchers poised to quit', *The Times*, 2 May.

Savage, M and Fisher, L. (2015) 'If your heart is with Corbyn get a transplant, says Blair', *The Times*, 23 July. Available from: www.thetimes.co.uk/article/if-your-heart-is-with-corbyn-get-a-transplant-says-blair-wpgfon8dh03, accessed 1 July 2019.

Savage, M. and Helm, T. (2019) 'Labour faces new row over efforts to curb antisemitism', *Guardian*, 2 March. Available from: www.theguardian.com/politics/2019/mar/02/new-labour-party-row-over-antisemitism-jeremy-corbyn, accessed 1 July 2019.

Schlesinger, P. (1987) *Putting 'Reality' Together: BBC News*, London: Methuen.

Schlosberg, J. (2016) 'Should he stay or should he go: Television and online news coverage of the Labour Party in crisis', Media Reform

Coalition. Available from: www.mediareform.org.uk/wp-content/uploads/2016/07/Corbynresearch.pdf, accessed 1 June 2019.

Schlosberg, J. and Laker, L. (2018) ‚Labour, antisemitism and the news: A disinformation paradigm', Media Reform Coalition. Available from: www.mediareform.org.uk/wp-content/uploads/2018/09/Labour-antisemitism-and-the-news-FINAL-PROOFED.pdf, accessed 1 June 2019.

Schofield, K. (2018) 'Jeremy Corbyn criticised by Labour group for demanding Palestinian "right to return"', *PoliticsHome*, 27 June. Available from: www.politicshome.com/news/world/middle-east/news/96360/jeremy-corbyn-criticised-labour-group-demanding-palestinian-right, accessed 5 May 2019.

Schofield, K. (2018) 'Jewish Labour MP calls Jeremy Corbyn an "anti-Semitic racist"' in furious Commons tirade', *PoliticsHome*, 17 July. Available from: www.politicshome.com/news/uk/political-parties/labour-party/jeremy-corbyn/news/96941/jewish-labour-mp-calls-jeremy-corbyn, accessed 1 July 2019.

Sedley, S. (2017) 'Defining anti-Semitism', 4 May, *London Review of Books*. Available from: www.lrb.co.uk/v39/no9/stephen-sedley/defining-anti-semitism, accessed 27 June 2019.

Shabi, R. (2017) 'Momentum's grassroots democracy can make Labour an unstoppable force', *Guardian*, 14 June. Available from: www.theguardian.com/commentisfree/2017/jun/14/momentum-grassroots-democracy-labour-unstoppable, accessed 30 April 2017.

Shipman, T., Rayment, S., Kerbaj, R. and Lyons, J. (2015) 'Corbyn hit by mutiny on airstrikes', *Sunday Times*, 20 September. Available from: www.thetimes.co.uk/article/corbyn-hit-by-mutiny-on-airstrikes-wgrvzpt3old, accessed 1 July 2019.

Shlaim, A. (2017) 'Anti-Zionism and anti-Semitism in British politics', *Al Jazeera*, 12 January. Available from: www.aljazeera.com/indepth/opinion/2017/01/170111143904887.html, accessed 27 March 2019.

Silkoff, A. (2018) Twitter. Available from: https://twitter.com/silkoff/status/979283532261609473?lang=en, accessed 24 April 2019.

Simons, J.W. and Stickings, T. (2018) 'Corbyn is hit by official anti-Semitism complaint as blogger he said lacked "English irony" reveals they knew each other and the Labour leader was aware he was Jewish', *MailOnline*, 26 August. Available from: www.dailymail.co.uk/news/article-6099279/Labour-Against-Anti-Semitism-group-official-complaint-Jeremy-Corbyn-Zionists-comments.html, accessed 1 July 2019.

Sinmaz, E. (2018) 'Corbyn's wreath at graves of Munich terrorists', *Daily Mail*, 11 August.

Smith, M. (2015) 'Why are people calling for Jeremy Corbyn to resign? Here's what you need to know', *Mirror*, 27 November. Available from: www.mirror.co.uk/news/uk-news/people-calling-jeremy-corbyn-resign-6913143, accessed 1 July 2019.

Skwawkbox (2019) 'Excl: What really happened in Monday's PLP – no vote, but a scurrilous attack on Formby', 5 February. Available from: https://skwawkbox.org/2019/02/05/excl-what-really-happened-in-mondays-plp-no-vote-but-a-scurrilous-attack-on-formby/, accessed 25 June 2019.

Skwawkbox (2019) 'Gardiner perfectly quantifies antisemitism in Labour – and party's actions to deal with it', 25 February. Available from: https://skwawkbox.org/2019/02/25/video-gardiner-perfectly-quantifies-antisemitism-in-labour-and-Partys-actions-to-deal-with-it/, accessed 12 May 2019.

Sky News (2017) 'Labour PLP meeting erupts in fury with shouting at Jeremy Corbyn', 21 March. Available from: https://news.sky.com/story/labour-plp-meeting-erupts-in-fury-with-shouting-at-corbyn-10809203, accessed 25 June 2019.

Sky News (2018) 'Wreath-laying row: Jeremy Corbyn hits back at Israeli leader Benjamin Netanyahu', 14 August. Available from: https://news.sky.com/story/benjamin-netanyahu-attacks-jeremy-corbyn-over-wreath-laying-memorial-11471988, accessed 18 April 2019.

Sky News (2019) 'Labour to be investigated by EHRC over alleged discrimination against Jews', 28 May. Available from: https://news.sky.com, accessed 3 June 2019.

Sloan, A. (2017) 'Corbyn's pro-Palestine stance may prove to be costly', *Middle East Monitor*, 4 May. Available from: www.middleeastmonitor.com/20170504-corbyns-pro-palestine-stance-may-prove-to-be-costly/, accessed 2 April 2019.

Sparrow, A. (2018) 'Labour should drop action against Margaret Hodge, McDonnell says', *Guardian*, 23 July. Available from: www.theguardian.com/politics/2018/jul/22/labour-should-drop-action-against-margaret-hodge-mcdonnell, accessed 1 July 2019.

Spillett, R. (2019) 'Jeremy Corbyn gives the impression "he is, deep-down, somebody who doesn't like Jewish people", says former Archbishop of Canterbury', *MailOnline*, 28 January. Available from: www.dailymail.co.uk/news/article-6640115/Jeremy-Corbyn-gives-impression-doesnt-like-Jewish-people-says-former-Archbishop.html, accessed 1 July 2019.

Stewart, H. (2016a) 'Naz Shah suspended by Labour party amid antisemitism row', *Guardian*, 27 April. Available from: www.theguardian.com/politics/2016/apr/27/naz-shah-suspended-labour-party-antisemitism-row, accessed 1 July 2019.

Stewart, H. (2016b) 'Jeremy Corbyn stands defiant after Labour membership surge', *Guardian*, 8 July. Available from: www.theguardian.com/politics/2016/jul/08/jeremy-corbyn-stands-defiant-after-labour-membership-surge, accessed 1 July 2019.

Stewart, H. (2018) 'Corbyn in antisemitism row after backing artist behind "offensive" mural', *Guardian*, 23 March. Available from: www.theguardian.com/politics/2018/mar/23/corbyn-criticised-after-backing-artist-behind-antisemitic-mural, accessed 1 July 2019.

Stewart, H. (2019a) 'Tom Watson urges Corbyn to get a grip on Labour "crisis"', *Guardian*, 24 February. Available from: www.theguardian.com/politics/2019/feb/24/tom-watson-corbyn-needs-to-understand-labour-must-change-antisemitism-crisis, accessed 1 July 2019.

Stewart, H. (2019b) 'Labour general secretary fails to placate angry MPs over antisemitism', *Guardian*, 4 March. Available from: www.theguardian.com/politics/2019/mar/04/labour-general-secretary-fails-to-placate-mps-over-antisemitism, accessed 1 July 2019.

Stewart, H and Asthana, A. (2016) 'Jeremy Corbyn sets up inquiry into Labour antisemitism claims', *Guardian*, 29 April. Available from: www.theguardian.com/politics/2016/apr/29/jeremy-corbyn-sets-up-inquiry-into-labour-antisemitism-claims, accessed 1 July 2019.

Stewart, H. and Elgot, J. (2018) 'Labour antisemitism row: Unite boss accuses Jewish leaders of "truculent hostility"', *Guardian*, 16 August. Available from: www.theguardian.com/politics/2018/aug/16/labour-antisemitism-row-unite-boss-accuses-jewish-leaders-of-truculent-hostility, accessed 1 July 2019.

Stewart, H. and Mason, R. (2017) 'Brexit: Fifth of Labour MPs defy three line whip to vote against article 50 bill', *Guardian*, 2 February. Available from: www.theguardian.com/politics/2017/feb/01/a-fifth-of-labour-mps-defy-three-line-whip-to-vote-against-article-50-bill, accessed 1 July 2019.

Stewart, H. and Perkins, A. (2018) 'Labour's disputes panel chair resigns over antisemitism case', *Guardian*, 28 March. Available from: www.theguardian.com/politics/2018/mar/28/christine-shawcroft-labour-disputes-panel-chair-resigns-antisemitism-case, accessed 1 July 2019.

Stewart, H. and Sparrow, A. (2018) 'Jeremy Corbyn: I used the term "Zionist" in accurate political sense', *Guardian*, 24 August. Available from: www.theguardian.com/politics/2018/aug/24/corbyn-english-irony-video-reignites-antisemitism-row-labour, accessed 1 July 2019.

Stewart, H. and Walker, P. (2019) 'Labour splits exposed as MP is suspended over antisemitism remarks', *Guardian*, 27 February. Available from: owww.theguardian.com/politics/2019/feb/27/labour-suspends-chris-williamson-over-antisemitism-remarks, accessed 1 July 2019.

Streeting, W. (2018) Twitter, 17 July. Available from: https://twitter.com/wesstreeting/status/1019263595157352448, accessed 1 July 2019.

Sugarman, D. (2018) 'Academic tells university event Jewish students' campus fears are "propaganda"', *Jewish Chronicle*, 20 November. Available from: www.thejc.com/news/uk-news/shocking-comments-of-uk-academic-on-israel-and-antisemitism-at-a-palestinian-event-hosted-by-ucl-stu-1.472789, accessed 6 June 2019.

Sugarman, D. (2019) 'Labour accused of ignoring IHRA antisemitism definition after dismissing two complaints with identical responses', *Jewish Chronicle*, 4 February. Available from: www.thejc.com/news/uk-news/labour-accused-of-ignoring-ihra-antisemitism-definition-after-dismissing-two-complaints-1.479556, accessed 6 June 2019.

Sugarman, D. (2019) 'Labour MP suggests breakaway MPs may be "financially backed" by Israel', *Jewish Chronicle*, 19 February 2019. Available from: www.thejc.com/news/uk-news/labour-mp-ruth-george-suggests-breakaway-mps-financially-backed-by-israel-1.480301, accessed 1 July 2019.

Sun (2018) 'Radical voices: What is Jewdas and why did Jeremy Corbyn attend a Passover seder hosted by the left-wing Jewish group?', 3 April. Available from: www.thesun.co.uk/news/5959115/jewdas-jeremy-corbyn-pesach-passover-seder/, accessed 5 May 2019.

Sun (2018) 'Labour's Emily Thornberry admits anti-Semitic party supporters have stopped her in the street and made "appalling" comments', 22 April. Available from: www.thesun.co.uk/news/6115357/labours-emily-thornberry-admits-anti-semitic-party-supporters-have-stopped-her-in-the-street-and-made-appalling-comments/, accessed 4 April 2019.

Sun (2018) 'Jeremy Corbyn, the anti-racist who turned Labour into the party of anti-Semitism', 18 July. Available from: www.thesun.co.uk/news/6813834/corbyn-turned-labour-into-anti-semitic-party/, accessed 18 April 2019.

Sunday Times (2019a) 'Labour's hate files expose Jeremy Corbyn's anti-semite army', 7 April. Available from: www.thetimes.co.uk/article/labour-s-hate-files-expose-corbyn-s-anti-semite-army-9zzlogxpv, accessed 26 April 2019.

Sunday Times (2019b) 'Labour can't sweep this anti-semitism under the carpet', 7 April. Available from: www.thetimes.co.uk/edition/comment/labour-can-t-sweep-this-anti-semitism-under-the-carpet-rxwnfod3c, accessed 26 April 2019.

Sweney, M. (2015) 'Daily Telegraph censured over Jeremy Corbyn "anti-Semite" story', *Guardian*, 6 October. Available from: www.theguardian.com/media/2015/oct/06/daily-telegraph-jeremy-corbyn-antisemite-ipso, accessed 1 July 2019.

Swinford, S. and Maidment, J. (2018) 'Chief Rabbi "has grave concerns" about Jeremy Corbyn's handling of anti-Semitism', *Telegraph*, 3 April. Available from: www.telegraph.co.uk/politics/2018/04/03/chief-rabbi-has-grave-concerns-jeremy-corbyns-handling-anti/, accessed 1 July 2019.

Sylvester, R. (2019) 'Rachel Riley of Countdown finds her Jewish roots to take on the Corbynistas', *The Times*, 26 January. Available from: www.thetimes.co.uk/article/rachel-riley-of-countdown-finds-her-jewish-roots-to-take-on-the-corbynistas-7hdmshx7f, accessed 1 July 2019.

Telegraph reporters (2019) 'Michael Dugher to quit Labour amid concerns over "institutional" anti-semitism', *Telegraph*, 17 February. Available from: www.telegraph.co.uk/politics/2019/02/17/micahel-dugher-quit-labour-amid-concerns-institutional-anti/, accessed 1 July 2019.

Tibi, A., Ganaim, M., Jabarren, Y. and Zahalka, J. (2018) 'As Palestinian Arab MPs in Israel, we salute Corbyn as a champion of peace and justice' [Letter to the Editor], *Guardian*, 2 September. Available from: www.theguardian.com/world/2018/sep/02/as-palestinian-arab-mps-in-israel-we-salute-corbyn-as-a-champion-of-peace-and-justice, accessed 1 July 2019.

The Irish Times (2019) 'Anti-Semitism rising sharply across Europe, latest figures show', 15 February. Available from: www.irishtimes.com/news/world/europe/anti-semitism-rising-sharply-across-europe-latest-figures-show-1.3794934, accessed 2 May 2019.

The Scotsman (2019) 'Scottish Jewish leader blasts Labour as racist party', 28 February. Available from: www.scotsman.com/news/politics/

scottish-jewish-leader-blasts-labour-as-racist-party-1-4880778, accessed 18 April 2019.

The Times (2015) 'Illiberal democrat: A chastened party has chosen a maverick leader. Labour must not do the same', [Editorial], 17 July. Available from: www.thetimes.co.uk/article/illiberal-democrat-cb5vt7gm3m7, accessed 1 July 2019.

Thiec, A. (2015) '"Yes Scotland": More than a party political campaign, a national movement fostering a new active citizenship', *French journal of British studies*. Available from: https://journals.openedition.org/rfcb/401, accessed 30 April 2019.

Thrall, N. (2018) 'BDS: How a controversial non-violent movement has transformed the Israeli-Palestinian debate', *Guardian*, 14 August. Available from: www.theguardian.com/news/2018/aug/14/bds-boycott-divestment-sanctions-movement-transformed-israeli-palestinian-debate, accessed 20 April 2019.

Tomlinson (2017) Hugh Tomlinson QC, Counsel's opinion on the IHRA definition: In the matter of the adoption and potential application of the International Holocaust Remembrance Alliance working definition of antisemitism, 8 March. Available from: https://freespeechonisrael.org.uk/ihra-opinion/#sthash.NLpY1Xey.dpbs, accessed 12 May 2019.

Toube, D. (2019) David Toube Twitter, 2 February. Available from: https://twitter.com/ToubeDavid/status/1091744288839557121, accessed 6 June 2019.

Tran, M. (2016) 'Labour opens inquiry into antisemitism allegations at Oxford student club', *Guardian*, 17 February. Available from: www.theguardian.com/politics/2016/feb/17/labour-condemns-anti-semitism-oxford-university-labour-club-claims, accessed 1 July 2019.

Trew, B. (2019) 'Racism against Arab Israelis will reach unprecedented levels by Israel's April elections – and the world won't care', *Independent*, 3 February. Available from: www.independent.co.uk/voices/israel-elections-latest-racism-arab-israelis-palestinian-racism-benjamin-netanyahu-lukid-a8760871.html, accessed 22 April 2019.

Tuchman, G. (1978) *Making News: A Study in the Construction of Reality*, New York: Free Press.

UK IHRA Experts (2018) Statement by Experts of the UK Delegation to the IHRA on the Working Definition of Antisemitism, 7 August. Available from: https://holocaustremembrance.com/news-archive/statement-experts-uk-delegation-ihra-working-definition-anti-semitism, accessed 12 May 2019.

Valadares, H. (2019) 'Why is France facing an upsurge in anti-Semitic attacks?', France 24, 13 February. Available from: www.france24.com/en/20190213-france-surge-anti-semitism-jews-hate-speech-yellow-vests-far-right, accessed 1 May 2019.

Wagner, A. (2019) 'Labour's antisemitism problem is institutional. It needs investigation', 7 March. Available from: www.theguardian.com/commentisfree/2019/mar/07/labour-antisemitism-investigation, accessed 12 May 2019.

Walker, P. (2018) 'Chuka Umunna says Labour is institutionally racist', *Guardian*, 9 September. Available from: www.theguardian.com/politics/2018/sep/09/chuka-umunna-labour-is-institutionally-racist, accessed 1 July 2019.

Walker, P. and Elgot, J. (2018) 'Jewish leaders dismiss Corbyn meeting on antisemitism as "missed opportunity"', *Guardian*, 24 April. Available from: www.theguardian.com/politics/2018/apr/24/jewish-leaders-dismiss-corbyn-meeting-on-antisemitism-as-missed-opportunity, accessed 1 July 2019.

Walker, P. and Mason, R. (2019) 'Nearly 500 Corbyn allies sign letter of apology over antisemitism', 28 February. Available from: www.theguardian.com/politics/2019/feb/28/labour-worst-day-shame-tom-watson-luciana-berger-resignation, accessed 1 July 2019.

Watts, J. (2018) 'Antisemitism: Two-thirds of Britons think Jeremy Corbyn's Labour has problem with prejudice, poll reveals', *Independent*, 17 April. Available from: www.independent.co.uk/news/uk/politics/jeremy-corbyn-labour-party-racism-anti-semitism-religion-jewish-ukip-israel-palestine-a8305706.html, accessed 1 July 2019.

Waugh, P. (2018) 'Jeremy Corbyn told by veteran Jewish MP "You're A f***ing anti-Semite and a racist"', *Huffington Post*, 17 July. Available from: www.huffingtonpost.co.uk/entry/jeremy-corbyn-told-by-veteran-jewish-mp-youre-a-fucking-racist-and-anti-semite-margaret-hodge_uk_5b4e34cbe4b0fd5c73bfe020, accessed 1 July 2019.

White, B. (2018) *Cracks in the Wall: Beyond Apartheid in Palestine/Israel*, London: Pluto Press.

Winstanly, A. (2019) 'Fake Labour accounts fueling "anti-Semitism crisis"', *The Electronic Intifada*, 17 January. Available from: https://electronicintifada.net/content/fake-labour-accounts-fueling-anti-semitism-crisis/26441, accessed 8 April 2019.

Wintour, P. (2015) 'Jeremy Corbyn: I would never use nuclear weapons if I were PM', *Guardian*, 30 September. Available from: www.

theguardian.com/politics/2015/sep/30/corbyn-i-would-never-use-nuclear-weapons-if-i-was-pm, accessed 1 July 2019.

Wintour, P. and Perraudin, F. (2015) 'Labour leadership: Yvette Cooper rejects poll predicting Jeremy Corbyn victory', *Guardian*, 22 July, Available from: www.theguardian.com/politics/2015/jul/22/yvette-cooper-rejects-leadership-poll-predicting-victory-jeremy-corbyn, accessed 1 July 2019.

Wintour, P. and Watt, N. (2015) 'The Corbyn earthquake – how Labour was shaken to its foundations', *Guardian*, 25 September. Available from: www.theguardian.com/politics/2015/sep/25/jeremy-corbyn-earthquake-labour-party, accessed 1 July 2019.

Withnall, A. (2015) 'Jeremy Corbyn calls Osama bin Laden's killing a "tragedy" – but was it taken out of context?' *Independent*, 31 August. Available from: www.independent.co.uk/news/uk/politics/jeremy-corbyn-calls-osama-bin-ladens-death-a-tragedy-but-was-it-taken-out-of-context-10479396.html, accessed 1 July 2019.

Withnall, A. (2016) 'Watch the moment Ken Livingstone is accused of being "Nazi apologist" by Labour MP John Mann', *Independent*, 28 April. Available from: www.independent.co.uk/news/uk/politics/watch-the-moment-fellow-labour-mp-john-mann-calls-ken-livingstone-a-nazi-apologist-a7005011.html, accessed 1 July 2019.

Wyatt, T. (2018) 'Criminal investigation launched into "antisemitic hate crimes"' within Labour Party', *Independent*, 2 November. Available from: www.independent.co.uk/news/uk/politics/labour-party-anti-semitism-latest-criminal-investigation-met-police-jeremy-corbyn-hate-crime-a8613851.html, accessed 1 July 2019.

Zeffman, H. (2018) 'Corbyn accused of comparing Israel to Nazis', *The Times*, 11 August.

Zoch, L.M. and Turk, J.V. (1998) 'Women making news: Gender as a variable in source selection and use', *Journalism & Mass Communication Quarterly*, 75(4), 762–75.

Index